W9-AQD-967

POWER AND CONFLICT IN THE UNIVERSITY

POWER AND CONFLICT IN THE UNIVERSITY

Research in the Sociology of Complex Organizations

J. Victor Baldridge

Stanford University
Stanford, California

John Wiley & Sons, Inc.
New York · London · Sydney · Toronto

Library of Congress Catalog Card Number: 70-140548
ISBN 0-471-04574-8

Printed in the United States of America

10 9 8 7 6 5 4 3 2 1

TO RITA

PREFACE

The activities of the academic community are now at center stage among the concerns of the society. University-based science continues to score important and visible successes; intellectuals join the government at high places; big military and big business buy academic knowledge in ever-growing amounts; the influx of students into the universities continues to bring changes in the occupational and social structure of the society. The universities and colleges have become the dominant cultural institutions of contemporary society.

At this critical moment in the life of the academic community there is a deep-rooted crisis of confidence about the university's ability to govern itself and to manage its affairs. On one hand, radical students, faculty, and others are charging that the university is too entangled with the failures of the society, that its knowledge is being prostituted away for evil ends, that the university's intellectual concerns are often insensitive to human needs, and that many people who are most affected by the university's activities are systematically excluded from its decision-making councils. On the other hand, many other groups in the society insist that the university is allowing its achievements to be undermined by a radical minority and that the academic community has grown lax in protecting the very values that have made it strong. In short, there is a welling sense of frustration over the university's role in spite of its many successes.

At such a time of crisis it becomes important to know how decisions are made, how policies are constructed, and how university "governance" processes operate. Governance is the process by which the university's destiny is shaped; it is the complex of structures and processes that determines the critical decisions and sets the long-range policies. Wise governance is at the heart of the success—or failure—of any organized human effort, and this is particularly true of the contemporary university.

This book deals with decision making and policy formulation in the changing modern university. It draws heavily on the insights offered by the sociological analysis of complex organizations and bureaucracies and on political science studies of decision making. The basic argument of the book is that to understand the events on the modern campus the decision making activities must be seen as a *political* process, not as a simple bureaucratic mechanism. For this reason it is a study of university "governance" rather than university "management." The research reported here is an attempt to develop a new theory of academic governance and to apply that framework to empirical events that occurred during an eighteen-month case study at New York University. Hopefully the political image of decision making that developed out of that research will give us a more adequate intellectual tool for understanding the conflict and rapid change that is sweeping the contemporary campus.

J. VICTOR BALDRIDGE

Stanford, California
October, 1970

Acknowledgments

In the course of a project such as this there are countless debts incurred that can never be adequately repaid. To render an expression of simple thanks seems at once inadequate, yet the most appropriate thing to do. First, my thanks must go to the "Thursday Night Beer Drinkers and Poker Players," Dan Gilbertson, Jerry Gaston, Phil Person, and Mike Farrell. Their critical comments, warm friendship, and sustained interest provided both intellectual stimulation and emotional support as my ideas developed.

The guidance and encouragement of many former professors should be noted. A special note of appreciation goes to Emily Clark who taught me to love sociology, to Burton R. Clark who opened up the world of academic governance for me, and to Stanley Udy, Jr., who sharpened my knowledge of complex organizations. The ideas and attitudes of these people have so permeated my thinking that it is difficult to separate my own from theirs. My intellectual and personal debt to them is enormous.

The cheerful and sustained cooperation of New York University—its administration, faculty, and students—must certainly be acknowledged. Without their wholehearted cooperation the study would have died an early death. A special vote of thanks goes to Chancellor Allan M. Cartter whose personal interest in the research opened many doors, to President James M. Hester who cooperated so fully, to Assistant Chancellor Harold Whiteman who provided the initial contact and continued support, to Erwing Smigel whose sociology department lent a constant helping hand, and to Stan Crazier whose lunchtime discussions provoked scores of ideas. Not to be overlooked are the hundreds of people—faculty, administrators, and students—who granted interviews, answered questionnaires, and gave access to their institutional lives.

Many people offered advice and encouragement during the analysis and writing stages. Burton R. Clark, Stanley Udy, Jr., Kai Erikson, W. Richard Scott, Sanford Dornbusch, and James G. March all gave valuable criticisms of the preliminary manuscripts. In addition, my thanks go to the Danforth Foundation, which gave some financial support during the project, and to the Stanford Center for Research and Development in Teaching which gave some financial support during the writing stage. In addition, excellent editorial help came from Ernest Havemann, John Richardson, and Wayne Price. Helen Kay went far beyond the call of duty in cheerfully and efficiently typing the manuscript.

Finally, honoring tradition by saving the most important until last, my wife Rita gave the love and support that made the project at all possible. Moreover, her endless editorial and typing assistance always spelled the difference between chaos and a similance of sanity. To her goes my biggest vote of appreciation and to her this book is dedicated.

J. V. B.

CONTENTS

POWER AND CONFLICT IN THE UNIVERSITY

Chapter I

INTRODUCTION

The modern university is in turmoil and the changes that are overwhelming it are outrunning our ability to understand them. The small college of yesteryear has become the contemporary multicampus giant, and academic decision-making structures, once relatively simple, have mushroomed into complex bureaucracies. In the process the academic community has become a complex political tangle, with forces inside and out struggling to gain control over its destiny.

Internally the campus is often torn by dissent. Many previously apathetic student bodies have embarked on ever more violent revolutions to transform the university. Meanwhile, faculty activism is generating new patterns of faculty influence and new forms of collective bargaining. The burdened bureaucracies of the educational establishment have grown more and more difficult to manage, in spite of the new managerial techniques being developed. Many internal forces are on the move to change the shape of the university's governance and decision-making procedures.

In addition to these internal changes, new pressures are building up in the outside world. The larger society has turned its attention to the university for many reasons: campus radicalism, the recognition of the critical importance of the university's knowledge, and the success of university-based science in dealing with physical and social problems. Once the university could retreat behind its ivy-covered walls and be relatively secure and isolated, but that has all ended now. As turmoil engulfs the campus, the university's decision-making structures are increasingly cross-examined and scruitinized by an aroused public. While the strife increases on the inside, the public on the outside peers into the academic halls with intense concern.

There are many manifest symbols of the changing scene: the placard of the student picket, the union card of the faculty activist, the subpoena of the congressional investigating committee, the new antidisruption laws of the legislatures. Other signs of an overtaxed organizational structure are less obvious as it struggles to adapt to the new situation: the student member of the faculty committee, the computer that processes data for administrative decisions, the organization chart that tries to capture on paper the essence of the complex bureaucracy, and the ever-present IBM card that defines a student's paper identity. All are the symbols of change, and change is the essence of the modern university.

All of this turmoil leaves social-science observers with an overwhelming sense of frustration, for the pace of change has far outrun our ability to understand and conceptualize the processes. We are confronted with a new situation, but there has been lag in developing the new intellectual tools for clarifying the action. For the most part ideas about academic governance and decision making are still plodding along under old assumptions and worn-out orientations.

Where can we look for interpretations of the contemporary university and its changing organizational nature? The traditional sources of knowledge in organizational dynamics are sociologists, psychologists, and management experts who have studied "bureaucracies" and "complex organizations."[1] However, when we look to these organizational experts for knowledge of the changing university, the information is slim, for compared with other types of organization little systematic research has been done on the academic system.[2] The irony of the situation is that these university-based scholars

[1]Most sociologists use the terms "complex organization," "bureaucracy," and "formal organization" almost interchangeably and this procedure is followed throughout this research. In particular, it should be noted that "bureaucracy" is an entirely neutral term and does *not* necessarily imply the red tape and inefficiency so frequently pictured in the popular derogatory use of the word.

[2]There are four good bibliographies on university governance that do a fairly good job of reviewing the field: Karl W. Biglow, *Selected Books for College and University Administrators*. New York: Bureau of Publications of Teachers College, 1958; John Corson, *The Governance of Colleges and Universities*. New York: McGraw-Hill, 1960; Terry Lunsford (Ed.), *The Study of Academic Administration*. Boulder, Colorado: Western Interstate Commission for Higher Education, 1963; and Betsy Ann Olive, "The Administration of Higher Education: A Bibliographical Survey," *Administrative Science Quarterly*, Vol. II, No. 4, 617–677 (March 1967).

have rarely turned their inspection glasses on their own home base. It is hoped that this book will provide more information about universities and their policy-forming decision networks.

There are three basic thrusts to this research. First, we shall study *policy formulation*, the dynamics involved in setting long-range goals and arranging basic decision structures. This is somewhat different from decision making in general, for the term "policy formulation" refers only to that subset of decisions which has long-range import, the "critical" decisions rather than the "routine" decisions.[3]

The second emphasis is the study of *conflict* processes in the university. Of course, campus conflict is a major concern today and many interpretations are being offered to explain the dynamics of the situation. One of the critical goals of this research is to develop some perspectives that draw not only from sociology but also from political science and community-power studies. Of special concern is the type of conflict that develops when interest groups try to influence policy decisions. Thus the study of conflict processes is at the heart of this book.

The third concern is the study of *change* dynamics in the university. Sociologists have long complained that studies of organizations usually focus on static structures but seldom study the organization as it changes. Presently no one can fail to note the transformations that are sweeping the campus. What are the forces that are shaking the campus and how are they changing the policy formulation procedures of the academic community? Understanding these issues is one of the chief goals of this book.

Let us turn now from the special emphases of the research and examine the organization of the book. It has been divided into several parts, each with a different goal. The basic concern of Part One is to introduce a different type of organizational "model" than has previously been used to explain policy making and change. Other explanations have relied on images or models of university governance that are inadequate to grapple with the changing situation. Moreover, most research on university decision making up to this time has failed to integrate isolated findings into an over-all theoretical framework. This is not difficult to understand, for the available theoretical interpretations fall short of handling the university's complexity. Part One, therefore, reviews two previous explanations of university governance and offers a brief overview of a new "political" model, a bare framework that will later be filled in with empirical research.

Part Two reports on a field study of New York University. The political interpretation of policy formulation and conflict grew out of this study, and

[3]Terms adopted from, Philip Selznick, *Leadership in Administration*. Evanston, Illinois: Row, Peterson Company, 1957.

the major part of the book shows how the birth of this interpretation went hand in hand with the field study.

Part Three goes back to the theoretical framework that was only sketched in Part One and elaborates on its elements, drawing on the material from the New York University research. Finally, Part Four is a single chapter conclusion that tries to show some of the theoretical and practical consequences of using a political framework for interpreting policy formulation, conflict, and change. Hopefully the results can be used not only for studying university governance but for studying policy formulation in other types of complex organizations as well.

PART ONE

Outline of a Political Model

Chapter II: BUILDING A POLITICAL MODEL

Chapter II

BUILDING A POLITICAL MODEL

One of the most urgent needs is a theoretical framework that can unify isolated ideas and findings about academic governance. Without a unifying model facts about the university are fragmented and contribute little to an over-all understanding. Copernicus once commented that astronomy was in a similar condition under the old Ptolemaic theory of the solar system:

> . . . it is as though an artist were to gather the hands, feet, head, and other members for his images from diverse models, each part excellently drawn, but not related to a single body, and since they in no way match each other, the result would be a monster rather than a man.[1]

The study of academic governance is in the same condition, and indeed some say it is a monster! The task of this chapter is to begin building a framework that may offer some unity in certain areas. There are four steps in the argument. First, the concept of scientific "paradigm" is introduced; second some previously used paradigms of university governance are discussed and evaluated; third, theoretical inputs to a new framework are reviewed; and fourth, the outline of a political model is sketched.

[1]Thomas S. Kuhn, *The Copernican Revolution.* Cambridge: Harvard University Press 1957, p. 138.

THE ROLE OF PARADIGMS IN SCIENCE

Although the idea of scientific models, or paradigms, is certainly not new, Thomas Kuhn's book entitled *The Structure of Scientific Revolutions* has been a benchmark in the thinking of historians of science as they approach the problems of scientific advancement.[2] Kuhn suggests that scientific enterprises occur within the bounds of certain conceptual frameworks, which he calls "paradigms." According to Kuhn's argument, science does not advance by piecemeal accumulation of facts, but instead major advances are related to conceptual revolutions, to critical shifts in intellectual frameworks, and to changes in the scientific paradigms.

The scientific paradigm governs the thinking of a particular segment of the scientific community and serves as a conceptual framework within which the group's investigations occur. The paradigm becomes the governing framework that defines and legitimizes the efforts of scientists working within this area. First, it defines the *problems* that are critical. The scientific community does not address all problems at once but instead selectively confronts certain issues as critical for the moment; the paradigm becomes the determining factor in their selection. Other problems are considered outside the range of legitimate concern for these scientists in the paradigm's community. Second, the paradigm provides a *theoretical framework* for addressing the critical problems. It defines those empirical phenomena that are considered significant and theoretically describes the behavioral interrelations among them. Third, the paradigm selects certain types of *instrumentation* as valid and appropriate for tackling its given problems, thus providing the methodological arms for studying the conceptual and theoretical problems. Fourth, the paradigm defines *"legitimate proof"*; that is, it specifies the type of experience and empirical phenomenon that will be accepted as empirical evidence in studying the paradigm's significant problems. Not all the "facts" are relevant—only those facts that are judged legitimate by the paradigm's conceptual framework. Finally, the paradigm always involves *ideological components*, that is, emotional attachments and world views. The scientist working within a given framework adopts a consistent "weltanschauung" that defines his problems, his instrumentation, his conceptual framework, and his theoretical propositions. Scientists working within a given world view have more than mere scientific allegiance, for their very life-styles and emotional commitments are tied to this particular interpretation of the world.

[2]Thomas S. Kuhn, *The Structure of Scientific Revolution*. Chicago: University of Chicago Press, 1962.

Organization theory, as a subdiscipline of sociology, has its miniature paradigms that guide thought and provide a framework for research. Unfortunately, most of these have proved inadequate when applied to the university. It is important to examine some of the weaknesses of the previously used models before we go on to build a new one.

ORGANIZATIONAL PARADIGMS APPLIED TO THE UNIVERSITY

The study of universities as organizations has typically relied on one of two organizational paradigms. The famous "bureaucratic" model derived from the work of Max Weber and his followers has frequently been used to provide the theoretical framework. Many contemporary observers, however, maintain that the Weberian model, although well suited to the analysis of business and governmental organizations, does not adequately account for what they believe to be the unique nature of universities as organizations. Some of these writers turn therefore to the so-called "collegial" paradigm as a theoretical foundation for examining the universities. In the following sections both paradigms are examined and evaluated, and another paradigm which may offer some new insights is suggested.

The University as a Bureaucracy

There can be little question that the most influential description of complex organizations ever developed was Max Weber's monumental work on bureaucracies.[3] Weber tried to describe the characteristics of bureaucracies that separated them from other, less formal, types of work organizations. In skeleton form, he suggested that bureaucracies are organized for maximum efficiency and are based on the principle of "legal rationality." The structure is hierarchial and is tied together by formal chains of command and systems of communication. Weber's description involves such characteristics as tenure, appointment to office, salaries as a rational form of payment, and competency as the basis of promotion. Most of his ideas are well known and need little elaboration.

Several authors claim that university governance may be most fruitfully understood by applying the bureaucratic paradigm. For example, in *Bureau-*

[3] See Hans Gerth and C. Wright Mills, *From Max Weber*. New York: Oxford University Press, 1958, Chapter VIII; Max Weber, *The Theory of Social and Economic Organization*. New York: Free Press, 1947, Part III; Reinhard Bendix, *Max Weber: An Intellectual Portrait*. Garden City, New York: Doubleday Anchor Books, 1962, Part III.

cracy in Higher Education Herbert H. Stroup points out some characteristics of colleges and universities that fit Weber's original discussion of the nature of bureaucracy. Those characteristics are the following:[4]

1. Competence is the criterion used for appointment.
2. Officials are appointed, not elected.
3. Salaries are fixed and paid directly by the organization rather than determined in "free-fee" style.
4. Rank is recognized and respected.
5. The career is exclusive; no other work is done.
6. The style of life is centered around the organization.
7. Security is present in a tenure system.
8. Personal and organizational property are separated.

Stroup is undoubtedly correct that the university fulfills these criteria, and most observers are well aware of the bureaucratic factors involved in university administration.[5] In fact, the evidence is so strong that G. Lester Anderson, Vice President of the State University of New York at Buffalo, concludes "Our assumption continues to be, then, that the prevailing basic organizational pattern of institutions of higher education is bureaucratic."[6]

To what extent is the bureaucratic paradigm valuable when applied to the universities, and how does it miss the point? Certainly there are many bureaucratic elements in the university and they cannot be ignored. The university is a complex organization chartered by the state and in this respect is like most other bureaucracies. This seemingly innocent fact has major consequences, for the university is thus a corporate "person" with public responsibilities. Second, the university has a formal hierarchy, with offices and a set of bylaws that specify the relations between those offices. "Professors," "instructors," and "research assistants" are bureaucratic officers in the same sense as "deans," "chancellors," and "presidents." Third, there are formal channels of communication that must be respected—as many a student or young professor finds out to his dismay. Fourth, there are definite bureaucratic authority relations in which some officials exercise authority over others. In a university the authority relations are often blurred, ambiguous, and shifting, but no one would deny that they exist. Fifth, there are

[4]Herbert H. Stroup, *Bureaucracy in Higher Education*. New York: Free Press, 1966. Extracted, not quoted, from Chapter Four.

[5]For example, see Algo Henderson, *Policies and Practices in Higher Education*. New York: Harper, 1960, Chapter 15.

[6]G. Lester Anderson, "The Organizational Character of American Colleges and Universities," from Terry Lunsford (Ed.), *The Study of Academic Administration*. Boulder, Colorado: Western Interstate Commission for Higher Education, 1963, p. 17.

formal policies and rules that govern much of the institution's work. The library regulations, budgetary guidelines and the procedures of the university senate are all part of the system of regulations and procedures that hold the university together and control its work. Finally, the bureaucratic elements are most vividly apparent to students in the "people-processing" aspects of record keeping, registration, graduation requirements, and a thousand other routine, day-to-day activities that enable the modern university to handle efficiently its masses of students. Of course, students often cry that this results in impersonality and callousness, but it makes the operation of the university possible as it struggles with an overwhelming influx of students. The list of bureaucratic elements could be expanded, but it seems unnecessary, since they are fairly obvious and apparent to most observers.

On the other hand, in many ways the bureaucratic paradigm falls short of explaining the university's policy formulation systems. First, it tells us much about "authority," that is, legitimate, formalized power, but not much about the other types of power—power based on nonlegitimate threats, power based on the force of mass movements, power based on expertise, and power based on appeals to emotion and sentiment. The Weberian paradigm is weak when it attempts to deal with these nonformal forms of power and influence. Second, the bureaucratic paradigm tells us much about the formal *structure* but very little about the *processes* that give it dynamism. A description of the static institutional arrangements may be helpful but it does little to explain the institution in action. Third, the bureaucratic paradigm deals with the formal structure at any one point in time but does not explain how the organization changes over time. Finally, the bureaucratic model does not deal with the crucial task of policy formulation. The paradigm explains how policies may be carried out in the most efficient fashion *after* they are set, but it says little about the process by which policy is established in the first place. It does not deal with political issues, such as the struggles of groups within the university who want to force policy decisions toward their special interests. In these ways, then, the bureaucratic paradigm falls far short of explaining decision making in the university.

The University as a Collegium

Many writers have consciously rejected the bureaucratic image of the university and instead have declared that the university is a "collegium," or a "community of scholars." This is a rather ambiguous concept when closely examined. In fact, there seem to be at least three different threads of argument running through this type of literature: (a) a description of a collegial university's management, (b) a discussion of the faculty's "professional" authority, and (c) a utopian prescription of how the educational process should operate.

First, there is the description of the practical management of a university, based on a collegial plan. The supporters of this approach argue that a university should not be organized like other bureaucracies, but that instead there should be full participation of the members of the academic community—especially the faculty—in its management. There are few actual examples of such "round table" democratic institutions outside a few small liberal arts colleges but the image persists. Under this concept the "community of scholars" would administer its own affairs, and the bureaucratic officials would have little influence. The image of the college and university as a collegium has been the subject of several essays on academic organization. John Millet, one of the foremost proponents of this model, has stated his views quite succinctly:

> I have already expressed my own point of view in so far as the organization of a college or university is concerned. I do not believe that the concept of hierarchy is a realistic representation of the interpersonal relationships which exist within a college or university. Nor do I believe that a structure of hierarchy is a desirable prescription for the organization of a college or university. . . .
>
> I would argue that there is another concept of organization just as valuable as a tool of analysis and even more useful as a generalized observation of group and interpersonal behavior. This is the concept of *community*. . . .
>
> The concept of community presupposes an organization in which functions are differientiated and in which specialization must be brought together, or coordination if you will, is achieved not through a structure of superordination and subordination of persons and groups but through a *dynamic of consensus*.[7]

The *second* thread running through the collegial argument relates to the "professionalization" of the academic community. Talcott Parsons was one of the first to call attention to the difference between "official competence" derived from one's official office in the bureaucracy and "technical competence" derived from one's ability to perform a given task.[8] Parsons devoted most of his attention to the technical competence of the physician, but others have extended this logic to other professionals who hold authority on the basis of what they *know* and can *do* rather than on the basis of their official positions. The scientist in industry, the military advisor, the expert in gov-

[7]John Millett, *The Academic Community*. New York: McGraw-Hill, 1962, pp. 234–235. (Emphasis added.)

[8]Talcott Parsons, "Introduction," from Max Weber, *The Theory of Social and Economic Organization*. New York: Free Press, 1947, p. 59.

ernment, the physician in the hospital, and the professor in the university are all examples of professionals whose influence depends on their knowledge rather than on their formal positions.

The argument for collegial organization is given strong support by this literature on professionalism, for its emphasizes the professional's ability to make his own decisions and his need for freedom from organizational restraints. Consequently, the argument is that a collegium is the most reasonable method of organizing the university. Parsons, for example, notes that, when professionals are organized in a bureaucracy,

> . . . there are strong tendencies for them to develop a different sort of structure from that characteristic of the administrative hierarchy . . . of bureaucracy. Instead of a rigid hierarchy of status and authority there tends to be what is roughly, in formal status, a company of equals. . . .[9]

The *third* collegial argument has more to do with the educational process than with the administration aspects of the university. There is a growing discontent in contemporary society with the impersonalization of life, as exemplified in the massive university, with its thousands of students and its huge bureaucracy. There is growing concern about the "alienation" of students in the midst of this tangled educational jungle. The dozens of student revolts have been symptoms of a deeply felt chasm between the average student and the massive educational establishment. The discontent and the anxiety are well summed up in the now-famous sign worn by a Berkeley student: "I am a human being—do not fold, spindle, or mutilate."

In the midst of this impersonal bureaucratized educational system many critics are calling for a return to the "academic community," with all the accompanying images of personal attention, humane education, and "relevant confrontation with life." In recent years the student revolutionaries often lifted this banner as they sought to reform the university. Paul Goodman's work in the *Community of Scholars* appeals to many of these same images and cites the need for more personal interaction between faculty and students, for more "relevant" courses, and for more educational innovation to bring the student into existential dialogue with the subject matter of his discipline.[10] Most observers can appreciate the call being raised by sensitive social critics. Indeed, this view of the collegial academic community is now widespread as one answer to the impersonality and meaninglessness of today's large multiversity. Thus conceived, the idea of the collegium and the academic community is more of a revolutionary ideology and a utopian projection than a description of the real shape of governance at any universty.

[9] *Ibid.*, p. 60.

[10] Paul Goodman, *The Community of Scholars.* New York: Random House, 1962.

How can we evaluate these three strands of ideas that are tied into the collegial model? To begin, there are many appealing and persuasive aspects to this approach. The emphasis on the professor's professional freedom, the need for consensus and democratic consultation, and the call for more humane education are all legitimate and worthy goals. Few would deny that our universities would be more truly centers of learning if we could somehow implement these objectives. However, there is a misleading simplicity about the argument that glosses over many of the realities of a complex university. Several of the weaknesses of the collegial model should be mentioned.

First, there is often a confusion between the *descriptive* and *normative* enterprises in the collegial literature. Are the writers saying that the university *is* a collegium or that it *ought* to be? Frequently it is obvious that the discussions of collegium are more a lament for paradise lost than a description of present reality.

Second, the collegial discussion of a round-table type of decision making is not an accurate description of the processes at many levels in the university. To be sure, at the department level there are many examples of collegial decision making, but at higher levels this usually does not hold true except in some aspects of the committee system. Of course, the proponents of the collegial model may be proposing this only as a desirable goal rather than a present reality. This may be a good strategy of reform, but it does not help much if our aim is to understand and describe the actual workings of universities.

Finally, the collegial model fails to deal adequately with the problem of *conflict*. When Millett emphasizes the "dynamic of consensus," he fails to see that much consensus occurs only after prolonged battle and that many decisions are not consensus but the prevalance of one group over another. The collegial proponents are correct in declaring that simple bureaucratic rule making is not the essence of decision making, but in making this point they take the equally indefensible position that major decisions are reached primarily by consensus. Neither extreme is correct, for decisions usually are neither bureaucratic fiat nor simple consensus. What is needed is a model that can include consensus factors and bureaucratic processes, but can also grapple with power plays, conflict, and the rough-and-tumble politics of a large university.

Both the bureaucratic and collegial models offer some helpful suggestions about the organizational nature of the university, but at the same time each misses many important features. Certainly it would not be fair to judge them as completely bankrupt models, for their sensitivity to certain critical issues is quite helpful. By themselves, however, they gloss over many essential aspects of the university's structures and processes. Without abandoning their insights we shall try to develop another approach that incorporates and expands their ideas.

THEORETICAL SOURCES OF THE POLITICAL MODEL

In this book three theoretical sources have been used for building a new political interpretation of university governance. First, the sociological tradition of "conflict theory" seemed ripe for application to organizations and especially to the power struggles that were taking place at NYU. Second, it became more and more apparent that the political dynamics of the university were similar to those studied by "community power" theorists in political science. Third, the so-called "informal groups" approach in organization theory was a good framework for analyzing the activities of interest groups as they fought for influence. Each of these theoretical positions has greatly influenced the political model, and it seems worthwhile to examine them briefly.

Conflict Theory

In recent years a body of theoretical thought characterized as "conflict theory," has been growing in sociology. Conflict theory has actually been a major part of sociological analysis at least since Marx, but there has been a revival of interest in this approach to social behavior in recent decades. Marx's analysis, of course, centered on the social conflicts in industrializing England, while Ralf Dahrendorf, Lewis Coser and others have extended the same conflict analysis to the modern society.[11] Many conflict ideas proposed for the larger society can be applied to the smaller social system of an organization. Several points of anlysis are critical to this orientation. First, conflict theorists emphasize the fragmentation of social systems into interest groups, each with its own particular goals. Second, conflict theorists study the interaction of these different interest groups and especially the conflict

[11] Ralf Dahrendorf, *Class and Class Conflict in Industrial Society*. Stanford: Stanford University Press 1959; Lewis Coser, *The Functions of Social Conflict*. Glencoe: Free Press, 1956; Lewis Coser, "Social Conflict and the Theory of Social Change," *British Journal of Sociology*, Vol. 8, 197–209 (September 1957); William A. Gamson, *Power and Discontent*. Homewood, Ill.: The Dorsey Press 1968; Dorwin Cartwright, "Influence, Leadership, Control," in James G. March (Ed.), *Handbook of Organizations*. Chicago: Rand, McNally, 1956, pp. 1–47; William A. Gamson, "Rancorous Conflict—Community Politics," *American Sociological Review*, Vol. 31, pp. 71–81 (February 1966).

processes by which one group tries to gain advantages over another. Third, interest groups cluster around divergent values, and the study of the conflicting interests is a key part of the analysis. Finally, the study of change is a central feature of the conflict approach, for change is to be expected if the social system is fragmented by divergent values and conflicting interest groups.

The research in this book concentrates on applying conflict theory to the university setting. Instead of looking at stability, we shall examine change; instead of looking for common values, we shall examine divergent values held by various groups; instead of emphasizing concensus, we shall examine the dynamics of conflict; instead of focusing on the integration of the whole system, we shall stress the role of interest groups as they disturb the system. Taken together, these conflict emphases provide one set of undergirding principles for building a new model.

The Community Power Studies

A second scholarly tradition useful for understanding the "political" university is the literature on community power. For several decades sociologists and political scientists have studied power articulation in American communities. Again and again these scholars have charted the complex processes by which various groups in the community influence governmental policy. The students of community power tried to map the distribution of power in the community and in the process they showed how the fragmented, complicated political scene is welded together by a multitude of political processes. Floyd Hunter's *Community Power Structure* and Robert Dahl's *Who Governs?* are classic studies in this field.[12]

Several of the community power emphases are useful for organizational analysis. First, one of the prime objectives of the community power theorists was a study of the *nature of power* in the political system. What kinds of power are available and how are they articulated? A second emphasis was on the role of *interest groups* in the political arena.[13] The theoretical and

[12]Floyd Hunter, *Community Power Structure*, Garden City. New York: Anchor, 1963; Robert Dahl, *Who Governs?* New Haven: Yale University Press, 1961. For extensive reviews of the community power literature see Nelson Polsby, *Community Power and Political Theory*. New Haven: Yale University Press, 1963; and John Walton, "Discipline, Method and Community Power: A Note on the Sociology of Knowledge." *American Sociological Review*, Vol. 31, No. 5. 684–89 (October 1966).

[13]For example, see David B. Truman, *The Governmental Process*. New York: Alfred Knopf, 1951, Robert Dahl, *Who Governs?*, New Haven: Yale University Press, 1961. See also Earl Latham, *The Group Basis of Politics*. Ithaca: Cornell University Press, 1952; V. O. Key, Jr., *Politics, Parties and Pressure Groups*, New York: Crowell, 1958, and Arthur Bently, *The Process of Government*, Chicago: University of Chicago Press, 1908.

empirical research by political scientists is a vast reservoir of knowledge that can be tapped for studying interest groups in universities.

A third emphasis adopted from the community power theorists is a stress on *goal-setting activities*. In the past many organization theorists have concentrated on "efficiency," that is, on improving the technical *means* by which the organization carries out its goals. In fact, in the popular mind the "efficiency expert" was the predominant image of the organization theorists. This is not difficult to understand, since most of the previous research was done in industrial organizations where the goals were clearly set. The real problem was determining how best to accomplish those predetermined goals. The most commonly studied organizations—business, industry, and governmental agencies—were similar in their high degree of "goal-specificity." The role of organization theory for these organizations was to improve efficiency and cut costs but rarely to confront the problem of goal selection.

The community power theorists can help us break out of this kind of provincialism, for they deal with political communities with very diffuse, differentiated goal-systems. For them it is senseless to deal only with efficiency in technical means, for the goals themselves are ambiguous, contested and changing. The political system is clearly a situation in which goal-setting activities are paramount. Since the university is similar to the goal-diffuse local community, we can fruitfully adopt the community power theorists' emphasis on goal-setting activities, as well as their stress on interest groups and the conflict between such groups.

Interest Groups in Organizations

A political interpretation of the university must deal with organizational interest groups, and among the best studies of this type is research done on prisons. There are strong pressures in a prison that promote the formation of militant interest groups. On the inside the sharp cleavages between the prisoners and their captors make conflict the normal state of affairs. Powerful groups form on every side to fight for privileges and favors. On the outside there are strong sentiments about the prison and numerous community groups try to influence its operation. Interest groups may take a variety of forms, some calling for stricter punishment, others demanding more rehabilitation, and still others investigating alleged mismanagement. The prison studies, then, are an excellent source for the study of organizational interest groups.[14]

[14] Some of the prison studies most directly involved with this issue are the following: D. R. Cressey and W. Krassowski "Inmate Organization and Anomie in American Prisons and Soviet Labor Camps," *Social Problems*, Vol. 5, 217–230 (1957); F. E. Hartung and M. Floch, "A Social-Psychological Analysis of Prison Riots: An Hy-

A second body of organizational interest group studies has come largely from industrial settings. By and large these studies have focused on the man-to-man interaction patterns that develop within a peer group, and thus they are not particularly helpful for developing the interest group theme. However, a few have focused on the influence that the peer group exercises on the larger organization. The classic work by Roethlisberger and Dickson sometimes shifted attention away from the operation of the peer group itself to the influence that the group might have on the organization by restriction of work and violation of work rules. Most of the writing in this "human relations" tradition devoted some attention to the group's influence on the total organization, but this was seldom their prime concern.[15] More recently Melville Dalton applied this orientation quite successfully to industrial settings by emphasizing the informal group cleavages and their effects on the whole organization.[16]

A third source of insights into organizational interest groups is the excellent work of Phillip Selznick in *TVA and the Grass Roots*.[17] Selznick provides a vivid interpretation of the pressures that impinged on TVA both from the community at large and from powerful groups within. The outcome of the struggle among interest groups largely determined the fate of this great New Deal social experiment.

All the bodies of material listed above deal extensively with interest groups and the importance of group processes in the determination of the goals of the entire organization. When interest group theory, conflict theory, and community power theory are linked together they form the theoretical background to a political interpretation of university governance. Some of the major emphases of each strand are shown in Figure 2-1.

---

pothesis," *Journal of Criminal Law and Criminology*, Vol. 47, 51–57 (1956); R. H. McCleery, "The Governmental Process and Informal Social Control," in D. R. Cressey (Ed.), *The Prison Studies in Institutional Organization and Change*, New York: Holt, Rinehart and Winston, 1961, pp. 149–188; L. R. Ephron, "Group Conflicts in Organization: A Critical Appraisal of Recent Theories," *Berkeley Journal of Sociology*, Vol. 6, 56–72 (1961); G. M. Sykes, "The Corruption of Authority and Rehabilitation," *Social Forces*, Vol. 34, 257–262 (1956); and H. P. Gouldner, "Dimensions of Organization Commitment," *Administrative Science Quarterly*, Vol. 4, 469–490 (1960).

[15] Fritz J. Roethlisberger and William J. Nickson, *Management and the Worker*. Cambridge: Harvard University Press, 1939. For a more extensive review see Peter Blau and Richard Scott, *Formal Organizations*. San Francisco: Chandler, 1962, Chapter 4.

[16] Melville Dalton, *Men Who Manage*. New York: Wiley, 1959; "Conflicts Between Staff and Line Managerial Officers," *American Sociological Review*, 15, p. 342–351 (1950); "Unofficial Union-Management Relations," *American Sociological Review*, 15, p. 611–619 (1950).

[17] Phillip Selznick, *TVA and the Grass Roots*. Berkeley: University of California Press, 1949.

Figure 2-1. Theoretical Background of the Political Model

Conflict Theory	Community Power Theory	Interest Group Theory
1. Conflict and competition	1. Forms of power and influence	1. Influence of internal groups
2. Emphasis on change processes	2. Multiple centers of influence	2. Influence of external groups
3. Role of "classes" and interest groups in promoting conflict and change	3. Interest groups and veto groups	3. Conflict and competition
4. Role of conflict in "political" decision making	4. Goal setting as a prime object of study	4. Divergent values as source of conflict
	5. "Spheres of influence" and study of specific issues	5. Goal-setting activities
	6. Interaction of multiple types of influence	

AN OUTLINE OF THE POLITICAL MODEL[18]

Up to this point we have done three things in this chapter: discussed the importance of paradigms, reviewed the bureaucratic and collegial paradigms, and suggested several theoretical strands that might be useful for building a political model. Now this section outlines some of the features of the new model we are proposing.

When we look at the complex and dynamic processes that explode on the modern campus today, we see neither the rigid, formal aspects of bureau-

[18] The term "model" is problematic, for it has recently come to have a rather restricted meaning in sociology and usually implies a set of empirically testable propositions interrelated in a logical and perhaps mathematical system. This formal understanding of the term coexists with a looser traditional terminology. By "model" I mean only a framework for analysis, a set of heuristic questions that can aid in the study of a particular phenomenon by calling attention to some of its more important features. Other terms might have been used, such as "framework for analysis" or "paradigm," but unfortunately they are also cumbersome and ambiguous. So with apologies to the proponents of formal model construction I shall continue to use the term "model" in this looser, less formal manner with the hope that readers will understand that it is not intended to be a formal model or an elegant theory.

cracy nor the calm, consensus-directed elements of an academic collegium. On the contrary, if student riots cripple the campus, if professors form unions and strike, if administrators defend their traditional positions, and if external interest groups and irate governors invade the academic halls, all these acts must be seen as political. They emerge from the complex fragmented social structure of the university and its "publics," drawing on the divergent concerns and life styles of hundreds of miniature subcultures. These groups articulate their interests in many different ways, bringing pressure on the decision-making process from any number of angles and using power and force whenever it is available and necessary. Power and influence, once articulated, go through a complex process until policies are shaped, reshaped, and forged out of the competing claims of multiple groups. All this is a dynamic process, a process clearly indicating that the university is best understood as a "politicized" institution—above all else the Political University.

To get some of the flavor of the political nature of the university let us turn to one of the first interviews at NYU, which was with a dean who was undoubtedly one of its strongest men. Toward the end of the interview he made the following comments:

DEAN: Do you have an organization chart? O.K. Well you can just throw it away. Forget it, those little boxes are practically useless. Look, if you really want to find out how this university is run you're going to have to understand the tensions, the strains, and the fights that go on between the people. You see, this is a political problem of jockeying between various schools, colleges, departments, and individuals for their place in the sun. Each school, group, and individual pressures for his own goals, and it's a tough counterplay of groups struggling for control. You've really got to understand the "politics" if you want to know how the place works.

INTERVIEWER: Do you realize how often you've used the term "political" or "politics" in the last few minutes? Is that a deliberate choice of words?

DEAN: I'll say it is—most deliberate. I think the imagery of politics is very helpful in understanding the operation of this place. Of course, this doesn't necessarily imply "dirty" politics. I simply mean that you've got to understand the political forces—both inside and outside—that are trying to control this place. There are pressures impinging on the officials of the university from all directions, and in a real sense the management of this university is a balancing process. It's a task of balancing the demands of various groups against each other and against the university's resources. People often call the university administrators "bureau-

> crats," implying that they are red-tape specialists, but that is a childishly naive understanding of our role. Sure, there are indeed some lower level administrators who are paper-pushers and bureaucrats in the old sense of the word, but the men in the critical roles are not bureaucrats, they are *politicians* struggling to make dreams come true and fighting to balance interest groups off against each other. This place is more like a political jungle, alive and screaming, than a rigid, quiet bureaucracy.[19]

This comment and dozens of similar observations suggested that a study of the political dynamics surrounding decision making would help unravel some of the difficulties in studying academic administration. However, there simply was no available model in organization theory that could analyze these activities. Instead it was necessary to build a primitive sort of "political model," a framework for study that would provoke some insights into the nature of the political processes in organizations. This was no sophisticated model but instead a set of questions that could be used to get a hold on complex processes. Figure 2-2 illustrates the whole model as it was finally developed. It might be helpful to examine the parts of the model and the processes that hold it together. At this point we only outline it, but in Part Three each of the parts is analyzed extensively, fitting in the data on NYU which is reported in Part Two.

A glance at Figure 2-1 shows that the political model has several stages, all of which center around the policy-forming processes. We selected policy formation as the central focal point, for major policies commit the organization to definite goals, set the strategies for reaching those goals, and in general determine the long-range destiny of the organization. Policy decisions are not just any decisions, but instead are those that have major impact, those that mold the organization's future. In short, policies are the "critical" decisions, not merely the "routine" ones. Of course, in any practical situation it is often difficult to separate major policies from routine decisions, for issues that seem minor at one point may later prove to be decisive or vice versa. In general, however, policies are those decisions that bind the organization to important courses of action. Since policies are so important, people throughout the organization try to influence them in order to see that their special values are implemented. Policy becomes a major point of conflict, a watershed of partisan activity that permeates the life of the university. In light of its importance, policy becomes the center of the political analysis. Just as the political scientist often selects legislative acts in Congress as the focal point of his analysis of the state's political processes, we as or-

[19] Interview No. 14, p. 3.

Figure 2-2. A Simple Political Model

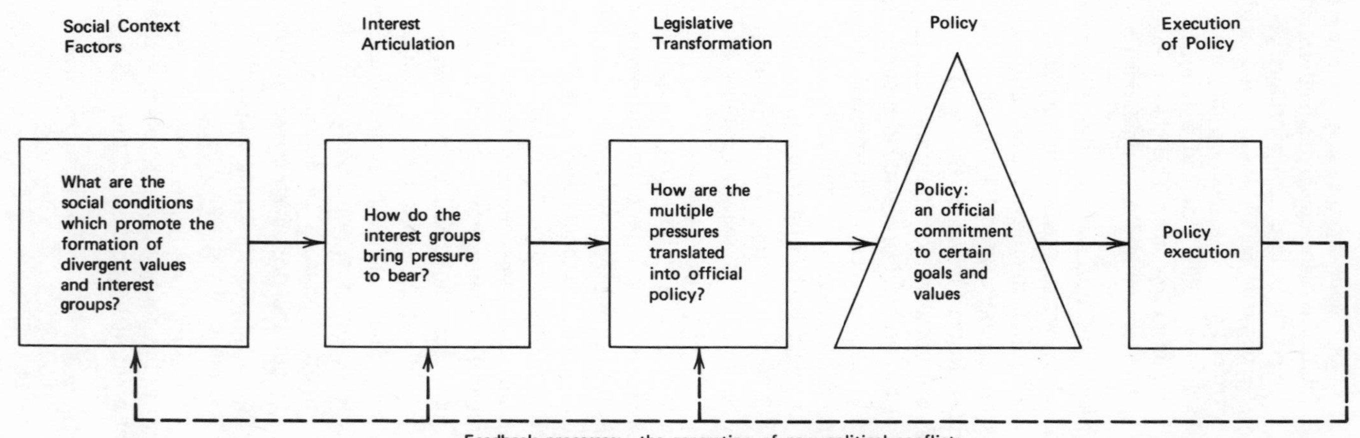

ganization theorists have selected policy decisions as the key to studying organizational conflict and change.

The sociologist wants to know how the social structure of the university influences the decision processes, how political pressures are brought on decision makers, how decisions are forged out of the conflict, and how the policies, once set, are implemented. Thus our political model points to five points of analysis: social structure features, interest articulation processes, legislative phases, policy outcomes, and policy executions.[20] Let us look at each of these stages. Incidentally, it may be helpful for the reader to follow the discussion by continually referring back to Figure 2-1.

First is a *social structure,* that is, a configuration of social groups with basically different life-styles and political interests. The crucial point is that the differences often lead to conflict, for what is in the interest of one group may damage another. It is important, then, to examine the social setting with its fragmented groups, divergent goal aspiration, and conflicting claims on the decision makers. The university has a particularly complex pluralistic social system because many groups inside and outside the organization are pushing in various directions, according to their own special interests. One need only glance at the various outside "publics" of a university to see its external social context, and the same glance turned inward would immediately reveal the internal social structure with its fragmented interest groups. Many of the current conflicts on the campus have their roots in the complexity of the academic social structure and in the complex goals and values held by these divergent groups.

Second is the process of *interest articulation.* Groups with conflicting values and goals must somehow translate them into effective influence if they are to obtain favorable action by legislative bodies. How does a powerful group exert its pressure, what threats or promises can it make, and how does it translate its desires into policial capital? There are many forms of interest articulation at work among the policy makers from every quarter and it assumes a multitude of shapes. Political intervention comes from external groups, from faculty groups demanding authority, from rioting student groups, and from officials who apply their formal authority. In this political tangle the articulation of interests is a fundamental process.

Third is the dynamics by which articulated interests are translated into policies—the *legislative stage.* Legislative bodies respond to pressures, transforming the conflict into politically feasible policy. In the process many claims are played off against one another, negotiations are undertaken, com-

[20]The following discussion depends partly on Gabriel Almond and James Coleman, *The Politics of Developing Areas.* Princeton: Princeton University Press, 1960, Chapter 1. The categories and stages, however, do not directly follow their research.

promises are forged, and rewards are divided. Committees meet, commissions report, negotiators bargain, and powerful people "higgle and haggle" about the eventual policy. Not only must we identify the types of interest groups and the methods they use to bring pressure but we must also clarify the translation process by which all these pressures are negotiated into a formal policy.

Fourth, the *formulation of policy* is the end result. The articulated interests have gone through conflict and compromise stages and the final legislative action is taken. The policy is the official climax to the conflict and represents an authoritative, binding decision to commit the organization to one set of possible alternative actions, to one set of goals and values.

Finally the *execution of policy* occurs. The conflict comes to a climax, the battle is at least officially over, and the resulting policy is turned over to the bureaucrats for routine execution. Of course, this is oversimplified, but it is remarkable that yesterday's vicious battle may indeed become today's boring bureaucratic chore. This may not be the end of the matter, however, for two things are likely to happen. First, the major losers in the conflict may take up their arms again for a new round of interest articulation. Second, the execution of policy inevitably causes *a feedback cycle*, in which the policy generates new tensions, new vested interests, and a new cycle of political conflict.

In summary, the broad outline of the political system look like this: a complex social structure generates multiple pressures, many forms of power and pressure impinge on the decision makers, a legislative stage translates these pressures into policy, and a policy execution phase finally generates feedback in the form of new conflicts.

If we use this basic political model as the framework for studying university governance, we could conceivably devote attention to all the many aspects. However, it seems more reasonable to focus on a few aspects rather than tackle the job of reviewing the whole process. It seems safe to argue that the vast majority of organizational studies up to this time have concentrated on the right-hand side of the chart—that is, on the policy *execution* stages and the question of the most efficient way of carrying out policy. It seems important that a political analysis address itself to problems and issues that have not been well covered before. For that reason our attention is focused primarily on left-hand side of the chart—that is, on the policy *formulation* side of the issue. Thus we stress the political dynamics and processes that lead up to the formulation of policy rather than the more bureaucratic and routine processes by which policy is executed. Incidentally, this is the reason that the term "governance" is used in this research rather than "management" with its overtones of technical efficiency.

This approach brings several factors under close scrutiny. First, it should be evident that we are addressing ourselves primarily to problems of *goal*

Figure 2-3. Comparison of Three Models of University Governance

	Political	Bureaucratic	Collegial
Basic image	Political system	Hierarchical bureaucracy	Professional community
Change processes	Primary concern	Minor concern	Minor concern
Conflict	Viewed as normal: key to analysis of policy influence	Viewed as abnormal: to be controlled by bureaucratic sanctions	Viewed as abnormal; eliminated in a "true community of scholars"
View of social structure	Pluralistic; fractured by subcultures and divergent interest groups	Unitary; integrated by the formal bureaucracy	Unitary; united by the "community of scholars"
Basic theoretical foundations	Conflict theory Interest group theory Open systems theory Community power theory	Weberian bureaucratic model Classical formal systems model	Human relations approach to organizations Literature on professionalism
View of decision making	Negotiation, bargaining and political influence processes	Rationalistic, formal bureaucratic procetdures	Shared, collegial decisions
Goal setting and Policy: formulation or execution?	Emphasis on formulation	Emphasis on execution	Unclear: probably more emphasis on formulation

setting and the conflict over *values* rather than to problems of maximum efficiency in carrying out goals. Second, the analysis of *change processes* and the adaptation of the organization to its changing internal and external environment are naturally a critical part of a political study of university governance. The political dynamics are constantly moving, pressuring the university in many directions and forcing change throughout the academic system. Third, the analysis of *conflict* and *conflict resolution* must be a critical component of a political study. Fourth, the role that *interest groups* play in pressuring decision makers toward the formulation of certain types of policy must be an important element in the analysis. Finally, much attention should be given to the *legislative* and *decision-making* phases, the processes by which pressures and power are translated into policy. Taken together these emphases are the bare outline of a political analysis of university governance. In the coming chapters this outline is used over and over as a framework for analyzing events at New York University.

SUMMARY

This chapter has outlined some of the thinking that went into the construction of a political model of university governance. First, the concept of "model" or "paradigm" was introduced in a discussion of the importance of theoretical models in guiding research. Second, two previously used models of university governance—the bureaucratic and the collegial—were reviewed and criticized. Third, three strands of theoretical literature known as conflict theory, community power theory, and interest group theory were discussed and their contributions to the study of academic policy formulation were outlined. Finally, the new political model was briefily outlined. The model suggests that the organizational analyst should focus on the nature of the organization's social structure, on interest articulation dynamics, on the legislative process, and on the execution of policy. Figure 2-3 compares the new political model with the commonly used bureaucratic and collegial models.

PART TWO

New York University as a Political System

Introduction

Part One was an introduction to the concept of a "political model" for interpreting policy formulation and change processes. Part Two now shows how this new model was used in an empirical case study at New York University. Chapter III outlines briefly the methodology of the research and provides a historical sketch of New York University.

Chapters IV, V, and VI present specific instances of policy formulation and change dynamics. These examples were selected deliberately to cover three different types of action. Of course, there was a strong temptation to focus on a student revolt, for this was the topic of hot news. There was unrest at NYU at that time and its coverage included as one of the chapters, but the temptation to concentrate exclusively on it was avoided. Student unrest is only one part of a larger picture and understanding the nature of the political processes in *all* areas of the university's life will help to place student discontent in a more complete framework. For this reason other issues were included to show the role that political processes played in widely different areas.

Chapter IV focuses on major changes that the university has made to maintain competition with the public universities. These changes had significant impact on the institution and provoked several intense power struggles. Chapter V examines the student revolt at NYU and tries to show how student unrest is part of a larger set of political dynamics and not a unique phenomenon in itself. Chapter VI studies an internal dispute among the various faculties over the organization of departments and the coordination of the liberal arts program. Each chapter uses the political model as a theoretical framework for interpreting change and policy formulation. By throwing these empirical events up against the theoretical insights provided by the model we hopefully can better interpret the concrete events and at the same time refine the theoretical perspectives.

Chapter III

THE METHODOLOGY OF THE NEW YORK UNIVERSITY RESEARCH

The task of this chapter is to explain the framework of the NYU research. First, the methodology of the research is discussed and, second, a brief history of NYU sets the stage for the contemporary research.

THE CASE STUDY AS A METHODOLOGICAL FRAMEWORK

A case study is an intensive investigation of one organization in a field setting. Like an anthropologist in a foreign land, the case-study researcher tries to find out how the local situation ticks. He "lives among the natives," compiling evidence and ideas and acquiring a "feeling" for the dynamics of the situation. He is not bound by one method, but capitalizes on any approach that might help unravel a new puzzle; for example, he might first use interviews with the "natives" to probe his topic, then move on to construct a questionnaire and finally supplement both techniques with participant observation and a study of documents. A case study, then, is basically an exploratory piece of research carried out in one field setting by utilizing a variety of techniques. Hopefully this allows the researcher to assemble a wholistic picture of the institution and some of its dynamics.

This method has two major weaknesses. First, concentration on only one case makes it virtually impossible to make use of contrasting situations. When many organizations are compared, the parallels and differences between them often provoke useful insights. This type of contrast is missing from the case study. The second weakness is the problem of "typicality" or "generalization." Researchers always hope to find results that can be applied (i.e., "generalized") to many situations, not just to the one they are studying. For this reason survey analysts go to great lengths to ensure that their sample is "random" and "representative." Such a random sample is then considered typical of the larger population. In a case study, however, there is no assurance that the organization chosen for study is representative of other similar organizations. In fact, it may be unique. There is really no way to get around this problem beyond reasonable care in the selection of the case, and even then one must live with the insecurity that the results might be empirical freaks; for example, I have no real assurance that NYU is a "typical" university—and in fact I have every reason to believe that in some respects there is not another like it.

The absence of contrasts and the problem of typicality are serious limitations to the case study, but there are several strengths that help outweigh the disadvantages. First, the case study is the classical method of researchers interested in depth of study, for the case study allows many different techniques to be applied in the same situation. Interviews, questionnaires, document studies, and observation techniques are all used and the results integrated and compared.

The second major advantage is that case studies are carried out in the field with the sounds, sights, and smells of the real situation hitting the researcher in the face. The importance of the "feel" of the situation cannot be overestimated, and anyone who has done field work knows that it is a vital part of the intellectual experience. It is difficult to codify the precise factors that make the field situation such an important experience, but there are thousands of intangible, unnoticed, and almost imperceptible experiences that go to make up an over-all impression of the situation. The case study is perhaps unique in this sense.

A third major advantage of case studies is their usefulness in exploring the *processes* of an organization. Unfortunately, many organization studies have concentrated on the formal structures and formal authority networks. The sophisticated social observer knows, however, that official structure and official documents hide a wild, informal, and dynamic set of processes that can be understood only by participation, observation, and depth interviews. The case study, executed in the field in the midst of this on-going process, has distinct advantages to anyone who is concerned with dynamics and change.

In summary, the case study has several disadvantages that make it less than an ideal method, but it also has many strong points that make it useful. It is particularly useful (a) if there are few data assembled on the topic, (b) if the research is basically exploratory, (c) if the objective is research in depth, and (d) if change and dynamic processes are crucial to the investigation. The needs of this project and the special strengths of the case study seem to coincide.

Let us be perfectly clear about one thing: case studies never "prove" anything. In the history of organization theory entirely too many presumptuous claims have been made for theories on the basis of a single case study and it would be wise to avoid that here. Even if there are instances and events at New York University that can be fruitfully studied by using a political interpretation this does not "prove" that the political model is a good tool for analysis. The cases may be chosen wrongly, the events may be atypical, or the facts may be twisted to fit the theory. No, the real value of a case study is to provoke ideas about a new way of viewing the world, to fill in an idea with vivid detail, or to suggest new perspectives. The study is intended to provide food for thought and to make suggestions about pieces of the action that might be fruitful for study, not to prove conclusively that this particular approach has all the answers. Let us turn now from the general logic of a case study and examine the four specific techniques that were used in the research.

Interviews

The first stage of the research was a series of 93 interviews with a variety of university personnel. Primary attention was devoted to faculty members and administrators, but numerous interviews were also conducted with students and other members of the university community. The interviews were "focused;" that is, a definite set of relevant topics was chosen and brought up for consideration in some manner. There was no attempt to force a person to answer the questions in any special sequence or in any special manner. The answers were open-ended, with the respondent making whatever comments he wanted about a topic, taking as long as he wanted, and branching off onto any relevant side issues. Whenever possible, however, the person was encouraged to give his opinion on each of the topics outlined in the interview guide.[1]

[1]Details about the interviews are given as Item 1 in Appendix A. They include the interview guide and characteristics of the persons interviewed.

Participant Observation

The field researcher has unique advantages because of his location within the actual situation, for one of the crucial elements is a simple "feeling" for the environment that is invaluable for understanding what goes on. In addition to this rather vague intuitional feeling, many observational techniques were used more systematically. I regularly attended meetings of faculty committees, university senate sessions, college and school faculty meetings, deans' councils, administrative councils, and many other groups. These observations helped me to understand the processes by which powerful groups and individuals within the university community attempted to shape it in accordance with their interests. The insights obtained at these meetings resulted in an impression of the political and administrative processes that could not otherwise have been gained. These insights are woven into the fabric of the research and provided a backdrop for many of the discussions.

Document Study

Like all bureaucracies, the university records its life in documents of many kinds. NYU allowed access to almost all types of document, and hundreds of pages were studied for this research. Many of the facts found in these documents are reported at various places in the book, and, of course, many were used for background material without being included in specific detail.[2]

Questionnaires

Although interviews are particularly good for exploring a situation, there is no assurance that the people selected for interview will be representative of the larger university community. Moreover, responses to open-ended questionnaires are not easily reducible to quantative data and summaries of the opinion of a whole group cannot be easily given. For this reason "closed choice" questionnaires were developed. As the interview data showed the importance of certain topics, these areas were analyzed so that questions of the short-answer kind could be developed. It was only after seven months of interviewing on the same topics that the questionnaire was constructed. There was an extended period of pretesting to ensure that the questions tapped the areas of research concern and that the wording was simple and concise. In spite of the obvious limitations of any questionnaire, this technique usually provides a reasonably good estimate of the opinions of people on a given topic. The questionnaire went to the entire full-time faculty and

[2] A list of many of the documents studied appears in Item 2 in Appendix A.

administration of NYU. Incidentally, the Faculty Senate of the University conducted a similar study in 1959 and that data was released for comparison. In order to avoid confusion, the Faculty Senate's data are called the "1959 Faculty Senate Survey," whereas the data assembled in this research are called the "1968 NYU Survey."[3]

Thus four different techniques were used in this study: interviews, participant observation, document studies, and a questionnaire. The information from these techniques is woven together throughout the research. We turn now to a brief historical sketch of NYU to set the stage for the analysis.

A BRIEF DESCRIPTION OF NEW YORK UNIVERSITY[4]

New York University is a private, coeducational institution in the City of New York. Although many people are confused by its name, the university is neither supported nor controlled by the State of New York. New York University opened its doors to students on September 26, 1832, and has been a major component of higher education since that time. In the early 1800's before NYU was founded the only college in New York City was Columbia, which at that time was a classical undergraduate college with an enrollment of about a hundred students. New York University was planned as something quite different. The "Considerations upon the Expediency and Means of Establishing a University in the City of New York" stated that the colleges and universities of the day were typically "places of education for a privileged class," directed toward providing "respectability" in a few learned professions. The report stated that New York City needed

> . . . a different kind of institution . . . one so conducted that not only a young man designed to be a lawyer, physician or clergyman may they carry on the preparatory disciplines in language, philosophy, and mathematics . . . but, also, in which young persons designed to be merchants, mechanics, farmers, manufacturers, architects, and civil engineers, may resort with equal privileges and equal advantages, and pursue those studies respectively which will aid them in their future occupations.[5]

[3] Details on the questionnaire, including return rates, the characteristics of the respondents, and the questionnaire itself, appears as Item 3 in Appendix A.

[4] Historical data for this section are taken from T. F. Jones, *New York University, 1832–1932*. New York: New York University Press, 1933; "A Presentation to the Ford Foundation, Part II," New York University, mimeographed, pages 109 to 112, several of which are quoted almost verbatim.

[5] Quoted in "A Presentation to the Ford Foundation, Part Two," mimeographed by New York University, pp. 109–110.

With this new philosophy, radical for its time, the university opened in a rented building in lower Manhattan. Although the school is now the largest private university in the world, during its early years it was a struggling one-building affair with scarcely a dozen faculty members and rarely more than 150 students. One of the most notable facts about the beginning faculty was that a rather awkward, inexperienced young man named Henry Wadsworth Longfellow was refused a post and had to go elsewhere (elsewhere being Harvard).

The history of the university for the first hundred years is studded with one cliff-hanging financial crisis after another. Proposals to close the school were often the order of the day, but always a miracle happened just in time and a few dollars scraped up from somewhere staved off disaster for a few more months.

From its beginning in a small undergraduate unit named University College the university gradually evolved into a huge institution with more than 15 major units. A School of Law was opened in 1835, Medicine in 1841, Engineering in 1854, Education in 1890, and Commerce in 1900. In 1886 the university opened one of the first Graduate Schools of Arts and Sciences in the United States.

When the university was founded in 1831, New York was a city of 200,000 people and the university's site in Greenwich Village was a suburb on its northern edge. Sixty years later there were more than two million people in the city. The population was still growing rapidly, and the area around the old University Building on Washington Square was being commercialized. Thus New York University found itself no longer at the center of a charming suburb but instead crammed into a commercial metropolis. As a result it decided in 1894 to move University College and the School of Applied Science to a suburban campus in Fordham Heights, on the east side of Harlem River. The new University Heights campus became for three decades the center of the university.

Several units of the university, such as the School of Law, the School of Pedagogy, and the Graduate School, remained at Washington Square. Gradually a demand grew among the students for undergraduate courses to supplement their work, and in 1914 a new undergraduate unit called Washington Square College was opened. Today the university supports two major undergraduate units, one in Manhattan and the other in the Bronx. The competition between the two units is intense and figures greatly in many of the present-day tensions within the university which are examined more closely later.

From 1914 to the present many new units were opened: the Graduate School of Business Administration (1916), the School of Retailing (1919), College of Dentistry (1925), Division of General Education (1934), Graduate School of Public Administration (1930), Postgraduate Medical School (1948), and the Graduate School of Social Work (1960). Thus New York University today is a gigantic system with 15 major units, each with a great deal of autonomy, yet each integrated into the total framework of the university.

Today NYU, the nation's largest private university, has more than 40,000 students and about 5500 faculty members. The complexity of the institution is shown by the activities of the students, who work for literally dozens of kinds of degrees in a multitude of academic programs. Numerous institutes and special research centers are integrated into the complex system, offering their own special emphases. Indeed NYU is one of the more complex institutions in America and provides an exciting location for the research.

Chapter IV

THE POLITICS OF CHANGE

SOME SHIFTS IN THE UNIVERSITY'S EDUCATIONAL PHILOSOPHY

The role that a university plays in society is both planned and accidental, both deliberate and a whim of fate. The role that NYU has played as an institution of higher education is a strange mixture of historical events, deliberate planning, and pressure from many sources. In this section we shall examine the critical changes in NYU's role that have been made over the last few years and in the process study the decisions, political pressures, and power struggles that accompanied the changes. This chapter provides the first example of how a political analysis of governance can be carried out in the concrete events at New York University. Using the outline dictated by our political model, we shall first examine some of the changing aspects of the university's social setting, then turn to the political controversy that those changes provoked. Finally, the legislative policy-setting processes will be studied, coupled with an examination of the effect that the new policies are having on the university.

THE SOCIAL SETTING: A CHANGING SOCIAL STRUCTURE PROVOKES NEW GOALS

For many years NYU had a consistent interpretation of its role in New York's higher education. From its founding the university offered educational advantages to all types of people, including underprivileged minority groups. As the founding fathers noted, this was to be "a different kind of institution" from the upper-class colleges that dominated American education in the early nineteenth century. As part of this philosophy NYU accepted students of relatively low academic ability and gave them the opportunity to get an education if they applied themselves. This was all part of a consistent image of the university as a "School of Opportunity," and in this sense NYU was in the best tradition of the great "American Dream." This philosophy was more than idle rhetoric, for it permeated the campus and gave the university a distinct "institutional character." Generations of NYU students and faculty testify to the importance of this philosophy to their lives, and many a Wall Street businessman or New York teacher will give credit to the chance that NYU afforded him. Large groups of the faculty were strongly dedicated to this ideal and were willing to fight for it when the threat came.

Times were changing, however, and this image of NYU came under attack. Not all members of the university community were happy with a philosophy that accepted large numbers of relatively poor students and then failed many of them. As one professor said:

> Sure, we were the great teacher of the masses in New York City. In a sense this was a good thing, and we undoubtedly helped thousands of students who otherwise would never have had a chance. But we were also very cruel. We had almost no admissions standards, and a live body with cash in hand was almost assured of admission. But we *did* have academic standards, and we were brutal about failing people. There were many years in which no more than 25–30% of an entering class would graduate. Sure, we were the great "School of Opportunity" for New York, but the truth of the matter is that we were also the "Great Slop Bucket" that took everybody and later massacred them.[1]

In particular, professors from liberal arts and graduate units objected to standards that lowered the university's student quality. Internal pressure was slowly building up, and external events soon provided an even greater impetus for change.

Organizations are seldom the sole masters of their fate, for external forces of various kinds impinge on them, shaping, remaking, and molding them in

[1] Interview No. 11, p. 3.

many ways. NYU exists in an environment in which other universities are competing for resources, students, and social influence. It was noted earlier that for many years NYU was the major "service university" in New York which took the masses of students. Both the City University of New York and Columbia maintained extremely high standards and did not serve the bulk of the student population. In the early 1960's, however, the picture changed, for the state and city were assuming more responsibility for educating the masses. An extensive network of junior and senior colleges was opened and expanded, and public university enrollments shot up dramatically. Tuition rates at the public schools were low, whereas privately supported NYU was forced to charge extremely high fees—in fact, among the highest in the nation. In short, the competitive position of NYU *vis a vis* student enrollment was severely threatened by the rise in public institutions.

The effects of the public college expansion were rapid and dramatic. In 1956 NYU published the results of its *Self-Study*. This study was a major attempt at long-range planning and foreshadowed many of the changes that were soon to occur. The authors of that far-sighted document were at least aware of the threat that the public institutions held for NYU, but it is doubtful that they understood how close that threat was. In fact, they stated with some confidence,

> Even the enormous expansion of the tuition-free city college system with its excellent physical plan has not as yet substantially affected the character of NYU. . . .[2]

The *Self-Study* went on to predict increasing enrollments for NYU over the decade between 1955 and 1966. By the early 1960's, however, it was obvious that the expected growth patterns were simply not materializing, for thousands of students who previously would have gone to NYU were going to public institutions. Figure 4-1 makes a comparison between the *Self-Study* projections and the actual enrollments for the period 1955 to 1966.[3] By 1966 the actual figures were running a full 20 percent behind the predictions. As one administrator viewed it, "We certainly anticipated pressure from the public universities, but frankly the pinch came ten years ahead of our expectations."

Not only was NYU losing students but the very financial stability of the institution was being undermined by the loss of vitally needed tuition. The question at this point was how to meet the challenge, how to frame policies for a new image of the university that would serve the educational needs of the people and the organizational needs of NYU.

[2]New York University, *The Self-Study*. New York: New York University Press, 1956, p. 11.

[3]Chart source, *ibid.*, p. 20.

Figure 4-1. Comparison of Enrollment Figures, *Self-Study* Projections and Actual Figures

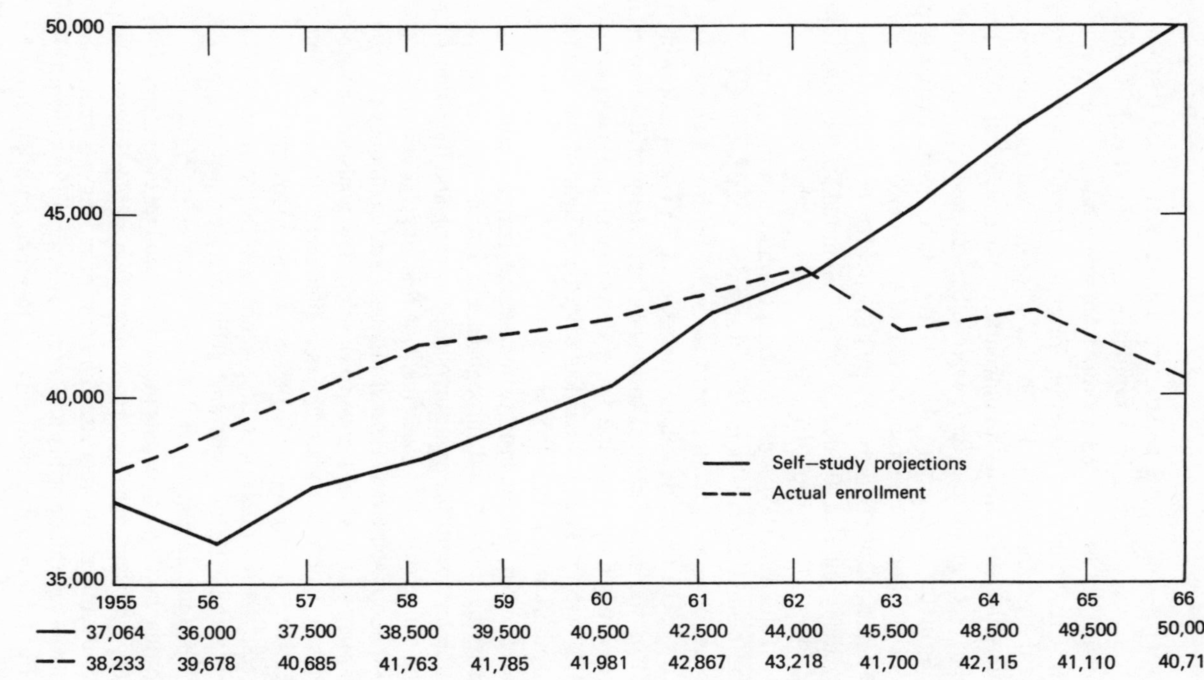

INTEREST ARTICULATION PROCESSES: THE POLITICAL STRUGGLE OVER NYU'S NEW ROLE

From a sociological perspective it is critical to see that the plans for a new role were framed by a political social context and that pressures were impinging on the decision makers from numerous sources. On the one hand, there were the internal pressures for change from the liberal arts groups and from the graduate schools. On the other, the external challenges from the public universities made a confrontation virtually inevitable. The forces for change were great, but there were other groups that had strong vested interests in the *status quo*. At least two major units of the university, the School of Education and the School of Commerce, were strongly committed to the "school of opportunity" philosophy that was being threatened. Moreover, many influencial alumni were committed to the same approach because they had benefited from it.

By the end of 1961 a debate about the future of the university was quietly raging behind closed doors. The discussion went far deeper than the mere question of how to recruit more students, for the essential issue was really about NYU's total educational role. Could NYU continue with business-as-usual or was this a critical turning point? Many of the top administrators felt that the time was ripe for a deep-rooted and sweeping evaluation of NYU's destiny. This was particularly true in light of the financial crisis that the institution was facing.

In terms of the analysis of long-range policy formulation that we have been trying to carry out throughout this reasearch, it is interesting to note that the debate at this point involved the *goals* and long-range commitments of the university. The assessment at this stage was *not* that the university should adopt some new type of management techniques to solve its financial crisis, but that it would have to develop new goals and new orientations to the future if it was to survive as a significant element in American higher education. Confronted with pressures from many sides, the leaders of the university deliberately started to "tinker with the future." NYU was consciously changing its goals and deliberately projecting a new self-image, a new institutional character.

At this time several events pushed the changes even faster. First, James M. Hester who had been the Executive Dean of the Liberal Arts units, was selected as president in 1962. The new president was acutely aware of these problems and made it his first order of business to confront them. Second, the Ford Foundation invited NYU to make an application for a comprehensive development grant. This opportunity was seized as a critical element of financial support for changes that would soon be instituted.

In early 1962 several committees were appointed to formulate plans for the Ford request. At this time it became progressively clearer that most of NYU's critical problems had to be faced if the grant was to be educationally meaningful. The whole issue of NYU's future educational role came under scrutiny. Many faculty bodies were invited to prepare plans that would be included in the Ford requests. How these discussions eventually reached the decision stage is a debatable question. Many faculty members claim that the critical decisions were really made by a small group of administrators without much consideration of the faculty. On the other hand, some administrators claim that the faculty's contribution was limited because of their constant inability to look beyond the needs of their individual departments or schools to the needs of the entire university.

In any event, it is fascinating to note how deliberately and consciously the university began to plan its future. The debate, factfinding, and committee work for the Ford requests went on for more than a year. During this time the university's future was being debated on one of those rare occasions when an organization really maps out its destiny. Rather than responding impulsively to the pressures of the moment, the university was attempting to plot rationally its future course after a careful study of its needs. Of course, this is just exactly what one might expect if textbook-style "rational decision making" were really in control. However, such rationalistic schemes are rarely found in real-life organizations, and NYU's deliberate attempt to chart its future is a remarkable exception to the "muddling-through" policy by which most organizations—and universities in particular—live.

By the fall of 1963 the Ford report had been completed and the implementation of future policies awaited the foundation's decision. Ford responded with one of the largest grants in its history (25 million dollars), thus expressing strong confidence in the plans for reshaping NYU. The university was challenged to raise 75 million dollars from other sources to implement the Ford grant. The financial resources for the changes were now at least possible, although securing the 75 million did not look easy.

No single policy emerged from the Ford report evaluation, but instead there was a complex, interconnected series of changes for promoting NYU's new character. Of course, the planning for the Ford report was not the only factor that provoked these changes, but it was a critical element. The Director of Institutional Research, Lester Brookner, put it this way:

> The Ford report in and of itself did not initiate these changes. Over the years ideas as well as demands for change had been voiced by faculty members, the administration and others. In addition, pressures were increasing from outside the university. We had to act because the public university system would have to assume as one of its roles the availability of inexpen-

sive higher education to all qualified high school graduates. Thus, if New York University were to grow and survive as a private institution, it would have to create a special role for itself. The Ford report simply collected and crystallized these ideas. It gave us a chance to dream about what we wanted to be—and it succeeded in giving us the financial backing to translate that dream into reality.[4]

There were several interlocking goals in the Ford plans. *First*, NYU would significantly upgrade undergraduate admission policies, thus moving itself out of direct competition with the public institutions for the bulk of the medium-ability students. In effect, the "school of opportunity" philosophy that had been a keystone of NYU's general service was being discarded for a more selective approach. Undergraduate admissions in all schools of the university would now have to meet high minimum standards. This had drastic effects on several schools in the university.

Second, most of the key decision makers thought that the multischool system of undergraduate education would have to be abandoned so that duplication of efforts could be avoided. At that time there were several undergraduate units: University College, Washington Square College, and the Schools of Education, Engineering, and Commerce. A plan for partial consolidation gradually evolved amid strong opposition from many quarters. The coordinated Liberal Studies Program, to be discussed later, was the eventual outcome.

Third, an "urban university" theme was adopted as a new institutional character. This new image was carefully articulated around service to the New York community, research in urban problems, and preparation of urban specialists in science, education, public administration, and social science. The university was focusing even more than ever on the problems of urban society and concentrating its limited resources in one area rather than trying to be all things to all men. The urban university theme was not a single specific program but more of an ideal and a philosophy that would help to direct the university. Some critics have suggested that it was more fund-raising rhetoric than concrete fact, but the force of such institutional philosophy in the governance of a university should not be underestimated. It would be naive, of course, to assume that a mere statement of the "urban university" theme would translate it into reality, but it would be equally naive to play the complete cynic and miss the important social consequences of a "tone" or "character" that would guide social action. The urban theme tries to set this kind of tone.

Fourth, the upgrading of quality involved an attempt to get more full-time students instead of the part-time group that NYU had long attracted. More-

[4]Interview No. 52, p. 2.

over, this implied a massive effort by the university to provide student residences, something never done on any significant scale.

Fifth, NYU would concentrate an increasing proportion of its energies toward graduate and advanced professional training. This was in implementation of a 1956 *Self-Study* recommendation:

> It seems clear that the role of NYU in the overall pattern of higher education is gradually changing. The responsibility for collegiate education in the metropolitan area is being shouldered on an increasing scale by the city colleges and the State University of New York. The local community, if we sense the trend correctly, is looking to NYU for educational leadership along specialized lines and at advance, graduate, and professional levels.[5]

Finally, the faculty recruitment would concentrate on obtaining more full-time, advanced-degree people. This would be a shift away from using a very large part-time faculty. It also implied that the university must provide more housing for the faculty in Washington Square.

It is important to note several things about these policy decisions. First, they were really major changes and the old NYU was being significantly transformed. Second, the external social context was particularly critical, for many competing institutions were undermining NYU's traditional role. In large measure these decisions represented a "posture of defense" against those outside forces, but at least this defensive position allowed a realistic confrontation with the future that could well turn potential disaster into a vital new educational role. Once the challenge was acknowledged the opportunity was seized in the midst of potential failure. Thus a posture of defense may have been transformed into a posture of opportunity. Whether NYU can achieve its goals in the long run is still an open question, for finances are a critical issue even at this stage. However, the possibilities for revitalization have been recognized.

THE LEGISLATIVE PHASE: NOTES ON THE DECISION PROCESS

Without doubt it was a small group of top administrators who took the major leadership roles and made the critical decisions. To view it from one side in the conflict, there were strong complaints that the decisions were sometimes arbitrarily made by top officials with little faculty consultation. Many of the persons interviewed felt that these decisions were carried out with a firm hand.

[5] *The Self Study, op. cit.*, p. 12.

To be sure, the University Senate was consulted, but at that time the Senate was relatively weak and many people believe that it had merely rubber-stamped a series of decisions that had already been made. As one Senate member put it:

> We were "informed" about these matters, and we were asked to vote our approval, but I wouldn't say we were actually "consulted" in any meaningful way. It was a one-way street—they told us what they were going to do and we said "OK."[6]

Of course, many faculty committees were working on the Ford report, but many people suggest that the critical decisions did not come from these committees. One rather bitter professor in the School of Commerce commented:

> The School of Commerce was about to have its throat cut and we didn't even know about it until after the blood was flowing! Sure, Hester came over and gave us a little pep talk about how much this was going to improve things, but he didn't really ask our advice on the issue. He didn't exactly say it was going to be his way "or else," but we got the point.

Many other faculty groups were upset by the nature of the decisions that emerged from the Ford report. They felt that these critical decisions had been made by "bureaucrats" without proper consultation with the faculty. Resentment was particularly high in the schools that were adversely affected. The AAUP was the major interest-group spokesman for the entire faculty, but it was paralzed because the faculty was split into opposing factions—some wanting the changes, others bitterly resisting them. This is an excellent example of how a pressure group can be crippled by *cross pressures* within its own ranks. This happens frequently in large interest groups and it usually results in one of two options. Either the group splits into warring factions or the whole issue is avoided in order to preserve internal unity.

In this case the AAUP opted for the second course of action; it never took a stand on the *substance* of the decisions but instead directed its attack against the *method* by which the decisions were made. Since the AAUP could not muster a coherent unified stance on the decision itself, it turned its attention to the decision-making process.

On December 9, 1963, the AAUP adopted a resolution entitled "Faculty Participation in the Determination of University Policies." This resolution stated basic principles about the role of the faculty in the university and then went on to propose changes in the University Senate that would give the faculty a larger voice in major decisions. It is interesting to note that

[6]Interview No. 23, p. 1.

the University Senate never acted in response to this resolution—indeed did not even formally consider it. AAUP resolutions need not be opposed by the administration to be made ineffectual—they can simply be ignored to death; and so it went in this case. Although many people around NYU claim that the AAUP resolution had some influence on the later, more successful, Taggart report on faculty participation, the evidence is very slim indeed. By and large the issue of faculty participation remained a background factor, never quite disappearing, but never in the forefront either. Only after the student revolt of 1966 did the faculty really begin to exert strong pressure for increased participation.

On the other side of the issue the administration clearly saw that something radical had to be done, and done quickly, if NYU was to meet the challenge of the public universities. Several administrators expressed strong disappointment in the faculty's contribution to the Ford report, declaring that most of their ideas were conservative and bound by entrenched loyalties to departments and schools. In effect, many administrators felt—probably correctly—that they had a broader perspective from which to view the problem than most of the faculty and therefore it was their duty to move into the situation as the key "change agents." Facing a major crisis, the administration took the lead, seized the opportunities available, and began to push for needed changes. President James M. Hester explained it in an interview:

> The University was confronted with critical conditions. We had to undertake action that was radical from the standpoint of many people in the University. Some of these changes had to be undertaken over strong opposition and were implemented by administrative directives. In two of the undergraduate schools a number of faculty members had accepted the "school of opportunity" philosophy as a primary purpose of their school. This had been justifiable at one time, but no longer. Many faculty members simply did not recognize that circumstances had changed and did not accept the fact that the service they were accustomed to performing was now being assumed by public institutions at far less cost to the students.
>
> At this point the administration had to be the agent for change. It was incumbent upon us to exercise the initiative that is the key to administrative leadership. In the process, we did interfere with the traditional autonomy of the schools, but we believed this was necessary if they and the University were to continue to function.[7]

It might be helpful to examine some of the factors that enabled the administrators to carry off this change so successfully in spite of the strong resistance that came from many quarters within the university. First, the power of the central administration was greatly enhanced by the fact that

[7] Interview No. 24, p. 4.

centralization had gone on at the university for nearly a decade, starting with the strong leadership of President Henry Heald in the early 1950's. Before Heald's administration NYU had been a loose collection of essentially autonomous schools. During his tenure, however, many changes that brought power to the central administration were implemented. President Hester's success very much depended on President Heald's efforts several years earlier. If the same moves had been made a decade before, they might well have failed.

Second, Hester was a new and popular president who could still rely heavily on the "honeymoon effect" to carry the day for him. The trustees were obviously going to back their new man, even if a substantial part of the faculty opposed the move—which they did not. Moreover, as one Commerce professor noted, "Hester is as close to a popular president as any you'll find, and that makes him a hard man to beat on most issues." The general faculty appeared to agree with this verdict, for in the 1968 Survey, when they were asked to indicate their "General confidence in the central administration of the university," they showed it in high degree. Fortunately we can compare this identical question with the 1959 Faculty Senate Survey. Since 1959 the general faculty's confidence had gone up considerably, as indicated in Figure 4-2.

Figure 4-2. Degree of Confidence in Central Administration. (all faculties combined)

	High	Medium	Low	N
1959	40.3%	17.6%	42.1%	(596)
1968	47.4%	32.0%	20.6%	(693)

The popularity of the central administration and Dr. Hester's newness to the presidency were major assets as the administration struggled to implement its decisions.

A third factor in the success of the changes was the support that came from large segments of the faculty. Cross pressures from interest groups on either side of an issue often allow decision makers more freedom and enable them to press for changes that would be impossible if most groups lined up in opposition. This is exactly what happened in this particular case. Many liberal arts professors were strongly in favor of the rise in admissions standards, especially since the new standard hit the nonliberal arts units hardest. In addition, many graduate-level professors felt that raised standards in the undergraduate levels would indirectly improve the graduate programs and would certainly give them better undergraduates to teach. Thus there were powerful interest groups supporting the change as well as opposing it.

Fourth, the decisions were successful because of the obvious bureaucratic weapons that the central administration controls. Since there is a centralized admissions office at NYU, the central administration could achieve some of its new goals simply by instructing this office to raise standards, thus effectively bypassing the opposition that centered in some schools. In addition, the twin powers of the budget and personnel appointment were often brought to bear in the struggles that followed the decisions.

Finally, there was the external threat that NYU faced from the public institutions. It is one of the most common findings of sociological research that groups threatened by outside forces will tolerate many internal changes that they otherwise would fight to the death. NYU was really threatened. The administration recognized this and was willing to fight to implement changes that would protect the university. Moreover, the trustees were convinced that these changes were imperative, and they stood solidly behind the administration in the struggles that erupted.

POLICY EXECUTION: TRANSLATING POLICY INTO PRACTICE

During the watershed years of 1962–1963 and 1963–1964 the decisions began to be carried out. The effects were dramatic and repercussions were felt throughout the university. For one thing, admissions of undergraduates dropped sharply—20% in the period from 1962 to 1965. This dramatic change can best be shown in Figure 4-3, which compares new entering students (both freshmen and transfers) and the entire enrollment (both full-time, and the full-time equivalent). The sharp dip was due largely to the increased admissions standards. By 1967, however, the new policy appears to have been successful, for enrollment was again rising as the university attracted large numbers of better students.

It is extremely important to remember that the drop in enrollment cut off vitally needed tuition funds when they were desperately needed to carry out various aspects of the quality upgrading. As Chancellor Allan M. Cartter noted, "This struggle for quality was very expensive, and we were trying to do it all and tighten our belts at the same time—a hard process to say the least." Cartter estimates that the shift cost the university an additional 10 million dollars above regular expenses, at the very moment that income was dropping because of lower enrollments. Without the backing of the Ford grant it is doubtful that these problems could have been surmounted. The Scholastic Aptitude Test scores of entering NYU freshmen from 1961 to 1966, shown in Figure 4-4, were another indicator of the rise in student quality. Arnold Goren, the director of admissions, is probably doing more than exercising

Figure 4-3. Undergraduate Enrollment, New York University Fall 1960 through 1967-1968

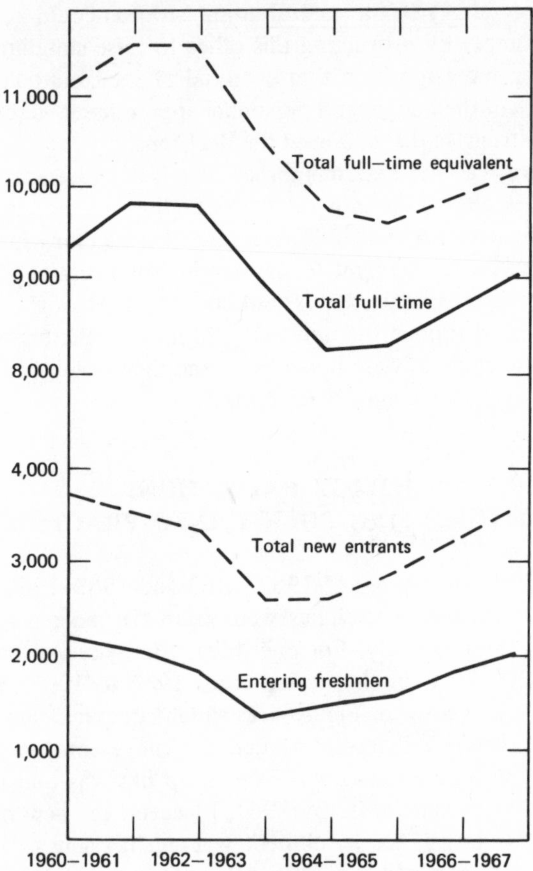

his public relations duties when he calls this increase "fantastic" for this short time.

A third indicator of the changes is related to student housing. As noted above, emphasis was placed on obtaining a wider enrollment from outside New York City and on drawing more full-time resident students. To do so the university was forced to go into student housing on a large scale. Moreover, the recruitment of a full-time faculty also demanded more housing, and the university added faculty housing almost as rapidly as it did student housing. Figure 4-5 shows the increase in students housed directly by the university.

A fourth indicator of the change is the composition of the graduate-student enrollment. There has been a major shift in emphasis toward more full-time

Figure 4-4. Percent of Freshmen with S.A.T. Scores Above 600: 1961-1966

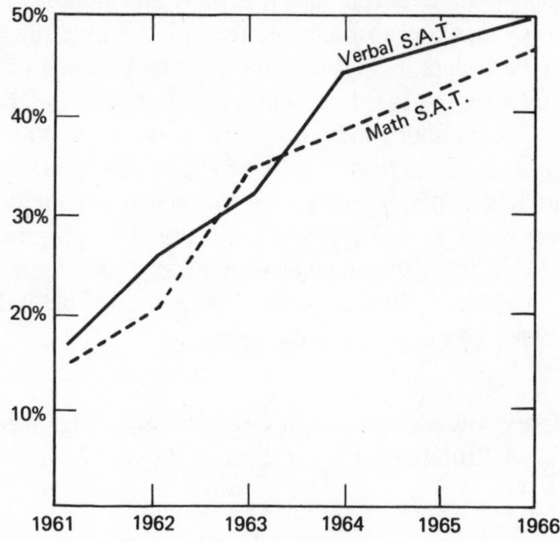

Figure 4-5. Students in University Housing: 1960-67

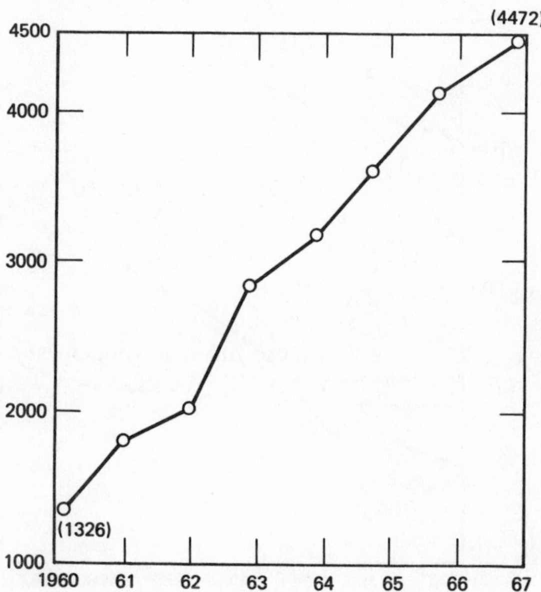

graduate students, whereas the number of professional students has remained relatively constant. Figure 4-6 shows this very clearly. Note that in 1960 only 23% of the graduate enrollment was full-time, whereas by 1967 it was 55%. This means that the absolute number of full-time graduate students *tripled* in only seven years. NYU's commitment to graduate and professional education is shown by the fact that nearly two-thirds of the degrees granted in 1967 (6908) were either graduate or professional (4549).

The four figures indicate that in spite of strong opposition the plans were carried out and had a major impact on the entire university. However, it might be interesting to go more closely into the effect on different units of the university, for in them the changes were most dramatic and strong political opposition developed. In the process we can look behind the raw statistics and see some of the political dynamics.

Figure 4-6. Enrollment in Graduate and Advanced Professional Education: 1960-1967

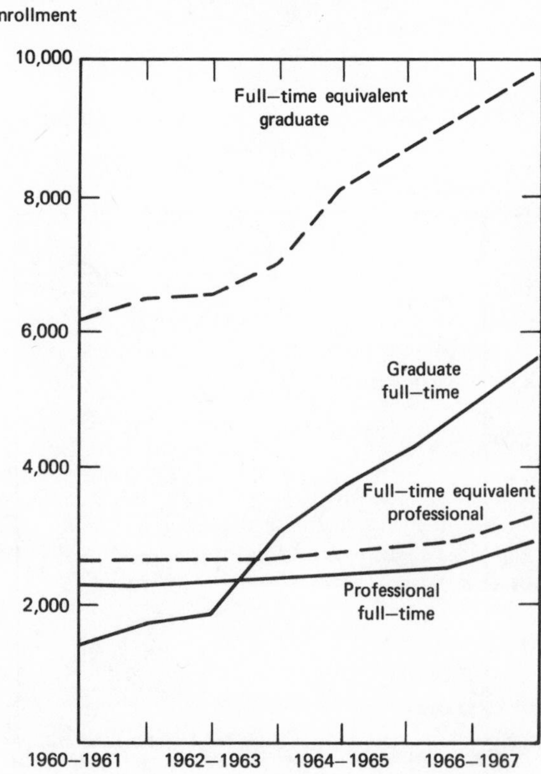

FEEDBACK PROCESSES: THE IMPACT ON THE SCHOOL OF COMMERCE AND THE GENERATION OF NEW CONFLICTS

Increasing admissions standards, emphasis on full-time students and faculty, and a general upgrading in quality changed the School of Commerce dramatically. Commerce was one of the schools most fully dedicated to the "school of opportunity" philosophy and had a large core of professors who fought strongly for this value when it was threatened.

The situation is complicated, however, for not all the faculties of business education in the university were opposed to the changes. To be sure, there was one massive interest group in Commerce that opposed the changes tooth and nail, but it is interesting to note that the Graduate School of Business, a separate unit for graduate and advanced professional degrees, took the opposite side. GSB wanted to establish itself as a major research center and a nationally reputable business education unit. Its professors were much more oriented to scholarly research on industry and business and feared that the undergraduate School of Commerce was severely damaging the reputation of business studies at NYU. Thus the professors of business education formed two distinct interest groups with two different emphases.

This did not make the battle any less difficult, for the Commerce professors rightly believed they might be out of their jobs if all the changes were instituted. They feared reduced enrollments, a loss of the night-school program, decreases in the size of the faculty, and a general lowering of their influence in the university. It is now clear that exactly the things they feared most happened in a short time.

Probably the majority of the Commerce faculty was opposed to major changes in their basic philosophy or to changes in admissions policies. Moreover, the administration's chief representative on the scene, Dean John Prime, was not totally convinced that the changes were desirable. Dean Prime resisted many of the changes, and his faculty was strongly behind him. A real power struggle developed, but in this battle the administration had most of the weapons. As one professor put it:

> I guess now that it's all over these changes were good for us. But we fought it all the way; there was a fantastic battle. Actually, I'd say it was rammed down our throats. Several foundations made reports which suggested we were too "provincial," and we needed to upgrade standards and eliminate the duplication in our undergraduate programs. But remember, this was done by academic types, who really didn't understand a professional school and were prejudiced against us. This would not have happened a few years ago when the whole university lived off Commerce's surplus money. It is only our growing weakness which made this change possible.

> The various schools are always competing and at this moment we are in a bad relative position.[8]

For many months the task of persuading the faculty to cooperate with the new changes went on against strong opposition. Finally two major changes in Commerce leadership were announced. First, in April 1962, Commerce was placed under an "executive dean" who headed both Commerce and the Graduate School of Business. Second, in September 1963, Dean Prime resigned and Dean Abraham Gitlow was appointed as local dean at Commerce. To no one's great surprise both Executive Dean Joseph Taggart and Dean Gitlow favored the administration's plans for upgrading quality in the School of Commerce. About that time the major breakthrough came in faculty cooperation.

By almost any yardstick the School of Commerce is radically different from what it was a few years ago. Figure 4-7 shows how S.A.T. scores went up and how enrollment figures went down.

Figure 4-7. The "X Effect" Changes in the School of Commerce Enrollment and S.A.T. Scores: 1959-67[1]

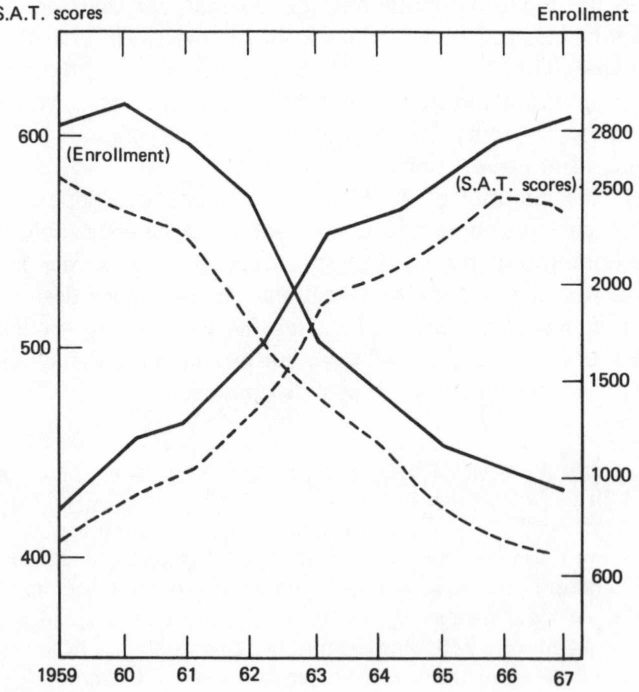

[8]Interview No. 20, p. 2.

Many Commerce professors feared that they might lose their jobs if enrollments were drastically cut—and they were right. From a high of nearly 300 in the late 1950's the faculty dropped to 61 in 1967–1968. Not all those who left were full-time people; but many part-timers were dropped, many nontenured people never were tenured, and even a few senior men were "bought off" to retire early. Few new people were hired. Certainly NYU lived up to all its contractual obligations, but nevertheless the result was that many people had to go elsewhere for work.

From the standpoint of the political battle, one of the faculty's most potent weapons in its fight against the changes—the threat to resign and go elsewhere—was actually playing right into the hands of the administration, since there was a desperate need for decreasing the faculty as enrollment dropped. The decrease in the size of the faculty was also reflected in the decreased number of courses offered in the School of Commerce. From a high in the late 1950's of more than 300 the number of course sections dropped to 179 in 1967. Many courses were transferred to the new Coordinated Liberal Studies Program and taught primarily by the Washington Square College faculty.

Without a doubt the changes hit Commerce very hard. A resisting faculty was cut to the bone; a resisting dean retired; the autonomous School of Commerce was placed under an executive dean who was also in charge of the Graduate School of Business; many courses were wrested away from Commerce and put in the Coordinated Liberal Studies program; the full-time student enrollment decreased from a high of 2800 to a low of 1000. On the other hand, the quality of the students, faculty, and program was vastly improved. Most people at NYU—even present members of the Commerce faculty—now feel that these changes were necessary. Nevertheless, in the political struggle the old School of Commerce died and one of the most powerful organizational interest groups on campus was hobbled. As one Commerce professor put it, "We lost the fight, and now we have less influence on the university than we have had in 50 years."

MORE FEEDBACK: REACTIONS IN OTHER PARTS OF THE UNIVERSITY

The impact of these decisions on the School of Commerce is dramatic but it is by no means the only significant change that occurred. The School of Education, for example, experienced many severe readjustments, although none quite so dramatic as in Commerce. It would be impossible to discuss all the changes in other parts of the university but several deserve mention.

The Coordinated Liberal Studies Program

As has been mentioned, NYU had undergraduate programs in Washington Square College, University College, the School of Engineering, the School of Commerce, and the School of Education. Many of these programs were almost exact duplications, and courses often had the same titles. High administrative overhead, inefficient use of faculty, and the ineffective utilization of space were only a few of the problems that this duplication caused. In addition, segregation of the courses into schools meant that often students were isolated and lacked the intellectual stimulation that comes from diversity in the classroom. A School of Education student, for example, always went to class with Education students, thus limiting his horizons to the confines of the School of Education. In Commerce it was possible for a student to have the most of his classes for several years with the same students.

By the mid-1950's many people believed that the goals of the university could be served best by a consolidation of the undergraduate programs. From a purely rational or purely financial basis there seemed to be little justification for the fragmentation of the undergraduate units, and the so-called "Gallatin College" concept was proposed by Chancellor George Stoddard. This college was to consolidate all the undergraduate units for the first two years, including the professional schools. The plan seemed reasonable and would eliminate much duplication while lowering educational costs and expanding the horizons of the students.

Alas, no change is so simple in a political system, for vested interest groups are sure to fight for what they have and to oppose any plan that undercuts them. The Gallatin College idea seemed eminently wise—except to the faculty, the deans, the department chairmen, the professional schools, and the liberal arts units! The faculties of the various schools felt that their distinctive programs would be undercut and that individual members of the faculty would be hurt by the loss of a favorite course or even a job. The deans were opposed to any decrease in programs for their college, and the department chairmen saw their areas upset by a complete reworking of the course structure. The professional schools feared the loss of their undergraduates, whereas the liberal arts schools feared an influx of professional students who might not be oriented toward liberal arts or who might not measure up to their academic standards. In fact, about the only group actually favoring the Gallatin College idea were some members of the Central Administration of the university. The opposition was so overwhelming that the idea died a quick death. The only action was the creation of a committee to study the problem of duplication. Once again, it was clear that an ostensively "administrative" decision was in fact a complicated "political" battle.

In 1960 James Hester became the Executive Dean of Arts and Sciences at NYU. Coming from outside the university, he was amazed at the administrative duplication in the undergraduate program, but was unable to do anything from his position in the university, especially since the Gallatin College idea was so strongly opposed. However, when he became president of the university in 1962 he renewed the battle for coordination. In February of 1963 a commission was set up to make new plans for some type of compromise coordination system. Eventually plans for the Coordinated Liberal Studies Program were included in the Ford report. In September of 1964 the program was officially launched over the strong opposition of the same groups that had previously been opposed to the Gallatin College idea. This time, however, the plan was less radical, for it involved only the combination of the first two years of study for Washington Square College, Education, and Commerce. Thus the battle was not completely lost by the opponents. The plan has now been in operation for several years and most of the political controversy has died down. What was once a hot political issue is now a routinely administered program that concerns only a few assistant deans. So it usually goes in a large bureaucracy, for today's flaming issue is tomorrow's routine administrative chore. The political scene shifts elsewhere.

The Rise and Expansion of Washington Square College

For years Washington Square College was a stepchild in undergraduate education at NYU. Most of the better students at NYU went to the University College unit at the Bronx Heights campus and it was a symbol of status among the faculty to teach at the Heights. However, the situation had been changing for several years and the decisions of the early 1960's accelerated the change. Two factors were critical. First, an increased emphasis on graduate education began to lend more prestige to graduate teaching and most graduate programs were centered at the downtown campus. Second, the development of the Coordinated Liberal Studies program meant that Washington Square College would be greatly expanded by the courses that were drawing on Commerce and Education students. Both events provided impetus to the aggrandizement of Washington Square College and increased funds and students from the Coordinated Liberal Studies program provided vital stimulation to the college's expansion. In addition, the leadership of a tough, aggressive, and respected dean ensured that Washington Square College would get at least its fair share of the academic pie—if not more. Dean William Buckler did not earn his nickname "Bill the Buccaneer" by being gentle in the competition with other colleges in the university. Once again, personal factors became political factors.

With these advantages and his leadership Washington Square College has claimed an equal partnership with the Heights campus and in many areas claims superiority. The admissions scores of entering students, the number of students going on to graduate school, the number of major scholarships, and other indications of quality all suggest that Washington Square College is now a serious contender for dominance among the undergraduate units of the university.

CONCLUSIONS

The changes in the university's character offer several insights to the exercise of power in the university. A discussion of some conclusions should be helpful.

The Internal Social Structure and Pressure for Change

A complex interwoven set of pressures impinging on the university's decision makers provided both an impetus for change and a drag for the *status quo*. Internally many people favored radical changes but just as many were threatened by such moves. Within the university's pluralistic social structure various subcultures were struggling to implement their values, but often this could be done only at the expense of other groups. The pluralism of the social structure ensured that changes would affect subcultures differently and this provoked the political conflict.

External Pressure for Change

Institutional changes are seldom made in a vacuum, for the social context molds and shapes the options that are available. In fact, it seems safe to say that external factors are often the most important impetus for organizational change. In this case NYU was seriously threatened by the public institutions and radical change was necessary if it was to remain viable. Other external groups were also involved in the transision: The Ford Foundation's massive grant provided the financial undergirding for the change; some alumni pressured for a continuance of the "school of opportunity" philosophy, and various professional accrediting groups entered the debates. External pressures were a major part of this process, and internal decisions were often made in light of external factors.

Role of Central Administration

The central administration took the lead in planning and implementing the changes. Among the reasons for this administrative dominance was the wholistic perspective of the central administration, as contrasted with the provincial viewpoints of the individual school faculties. It appears that innovation in the character of a university will often come from the administration, not from the supposedly *avant garde* faculties. Of course, as the power situation changes—as it is now so radically doing—it may be the students, faculty, or external groups who will act as the change agents in the future. In this particular case, however, the central administration provided the critical leadership for the innovations.

Changes in Authority Relationships

Many of the changes that were instituted in response to an external threat had repercussions on the internal authority and power relationships; for example, in some areas there was increased centralization of authority. It was mentioned earlier that President Heald's administration saw a major shift of power away from the individual schools and toward the central administration. The decisions in the early 1960's proved how far that centralization process had gone and ensured that it would even go farther. Admissions, at least, came to be considered the legitimate—although contested—arena for the central administration. The individual schools had lost an area that they had previously considered entirely their responsibility, and the faculties as individual bodies lost control over what they considered to be vital academic matters. Indeed, most of these critical decisions were executed by the central administration and the net effect was greater control and greater centralization at Vanderbilt Hall.

However, as the quality of the faculty has gone up, and as more and more full-time men have been attracted, there has been increased faculty demand for a voice in the policies of the university. The social context of the university has been subtly altered, for a full-time faculty is much more likely to take an active part in university affairs than a faculty that included many part-timers. Thus an administrative decision concerning the composition of the faculty eventually fed back into the authority system, and the events of a few years later proved that the faculty as well as the students were sometimes interested in power.

Finally, the recruitment of a different type of student body led to increased student activism, a factor that had significant consequences for the authority relations in certain spheres of activity (as reported in Chapter 5). Thus the authority and power relations did not change uniformly in reaction to this set of events. Although there was increased centralization in some areas, there was also an increase in faculty participation in decision making and student activism. In sum, there was a complex interaction effect with many subtle shifts in relationships.

Real Conflict

Again it must be emphasized that this was a real conflict of interests between groups within the university. It was a political battle, not merely a collegial or bureaucratic decision. The image of politics seems more able to explain the events than any other image available. There was a real power play and the proponents of change held most of the cards over the proponents of the *status quo*.

Interest Groups and Their Tactics

A multitude of interest groups was arrayed on every side of the issue and no decisions could be made without political cost to someone. Moreover, these groups used a wide variety of tactics to influence the decisions. The administrators used bureaucratic power of various types, including control over the budgets, appointment of officials, and control of a centralized admissions office. Others used such tactics as pressure on individual officials, resolutions by organizations, and appeals by professional organizations. Moreover, the "charismatic" appeal of popular and impressive individuals must not be underestimated. Again we see that power in the university is not unitary but a hodgepodge of interacting, overlapping, and often conflicting influence.

A SUMMARY CHART

Figure 4-8 places this series of events into the political model's framework and serves as a summary of this chapter. Of course, the chart is obviously oversimplified, for many more factors went into these changes than those that have been discussed. Moreover, the interest groups that were supporting or opposing the changes were not monolithic masses, for there were many shades of opinion within each one. The issues were complex and the groups often subdivided among themselves. The chart, however, serves our purposes, for going into all the subtle complexities would be unnecessary and self-defeating.

Figure 4.8. The Political Model Applied to the Changes.

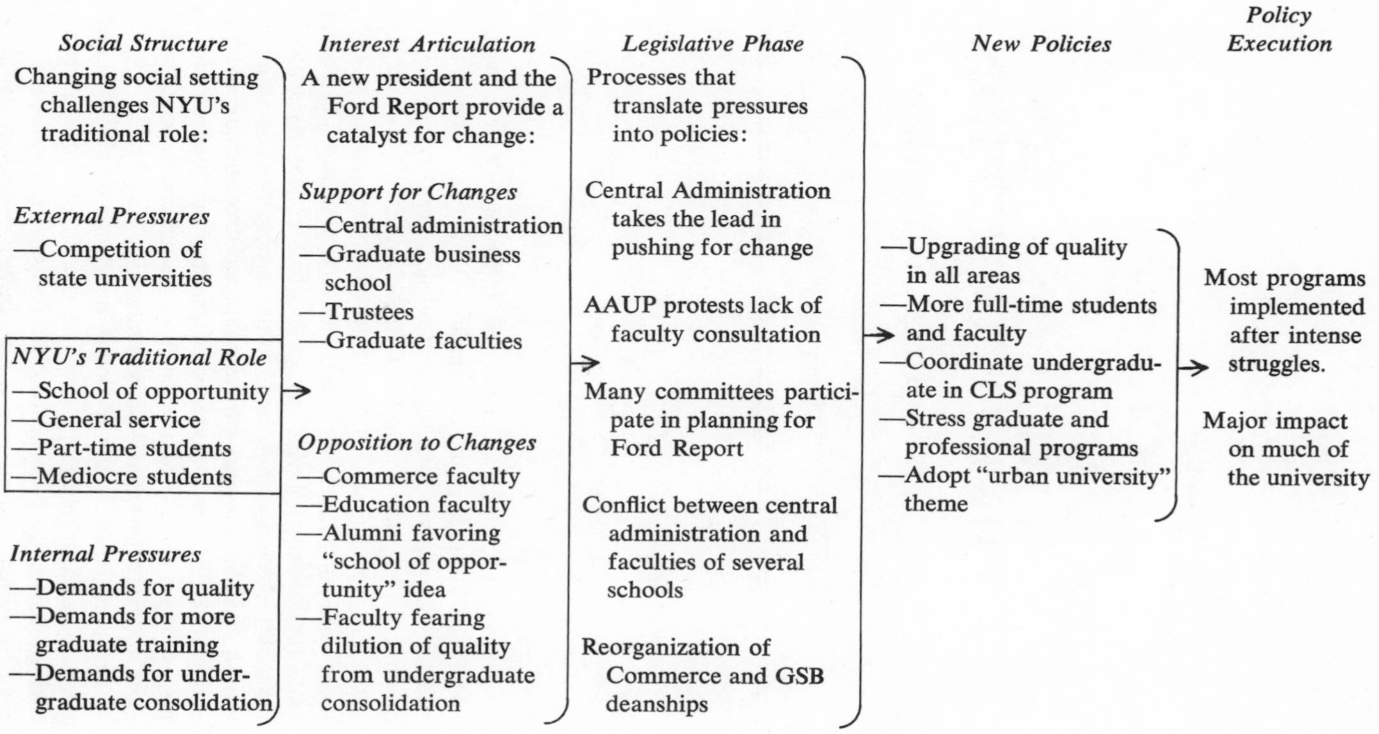

Social Structure

Changing social setting challenges NYU's traditional role:

External Pressures

—Competition of state universities

NYU's Traditional Role

—School of opportunity
—General service
—Part-time students
—Mediocre students

Internal Pressures

—Demands for quality
—Demands for more graduate training
—Demands for undergraduate consolidation

→

Interest Articulation

A new president and the Ford Report provide a catalyst for change:

Support for Changes

—Central administration
—Graduate business school
—Trustees
—Graduate faculties

Opposition to Changes

—Commerce faculty
—Education faculty
—Alumni favoring "school of opportunity" idea
—Faculty fearing dilution of quality from undergraduate consolidation

→

Legislative Phase

Processes that translate pressures into policies:

Central Administration takes the lead in pushing for change

AAUP protests lack of faculty consultation

Many committees participate in planning for Ford Report

Conflict between central administration and faculties of several schools

Reorganization of Commerce and GSB deanships

→

New Policies

—Upgrading of quality in all areas
—More full-time students and faculty
—Coordinate undergraduate in CLS program
—Stress graduate and professional programs
—Adopt "urban university" theme

→

Policy Execution

Most programs implemented after intense struggles.

Major impact on much of the university

Chapter V

THE POLITICS OF REVOLUTION

THE STUDENT REVOLT

The nation has seen a great deal of student unrest over the last few years and literally hundreds of explanations have been offered to interpret the situation. Of course, there simply is no single explanation that can do justice to the complex factors that frame these events. Psychological explanations stress the personal strains placed on youth by modern society; economic interpretations note the contrasts between affluence and poverty that generate resentment; political science evaluations emphasize the blockages in the political system that hinder full participation of youth and minority groups; and sociological explanations note the alienation of youth in the mass university, the importance of small group processes in revolutionary protest movements, and the sense of frustration caused by a "generation gap" and an entrenched "establishment."

Taken together these viewpoints provide a number of clues to student unrest, but no single theory seems adequate. This book offers an interpretation of university governance that focuses on power and influence in a political system and as such it may have some additional insights into the causes and consequences of student unrest, but only as one additional insight into a complex situation.

Concrete examples get old and quickly outdated, and this is particularly true if the study focuses on rapidly changing events such as student unrest. Since the NYU study was completed other student uprisings have been much more dramatic. NYU's campus was not completely shut down for months; the police and National Guard did not encircle the campus for weeks; bombs were not thrown nor deans physically attacked; and the governor of New York did not involve his total political career as some others did.

In most respects, however, the NYU campus revolt had all the features that have characterized the latest, most violent uprisings. There was organized, coordinated effort by students to influence a specific issue and to mobilize student power for political purposes. The confrontations between students, faculty, and administration were similar to the more violent revolts on other campuses but fortunately ended short of total war. Moreover, the student revolt had long-range, major effects on the role of students in the university's governance. Indeed, it was a significant event in the political life of NYU, one from which many other occurrences are dated. However new or old the example, the real test of sociological investigation is the insight that comes from the *interpretation* of the event, for scientific interpretation is the crucial difference between mere journalistic recording of events and sociological charting of regularities in human behavior. For that reason the value of this chapter rests not on the illustrative material from the NYU student revolt, which will certainly be out of date before it is even published, but on its sociological interpretation. If there is insight to be gained it will come from placing it into the larger context of political pressure, influence, and power that forms the theoretical thread running through this entire book.

In essence, this chapter argues that the student revolt is only one type of political influence attempt among many. It is not a unique event that has meaning in itself; instead it is a major element in a complex whirl framed by faculty pressure, administrative authority, outside pressure-group action, and governing boards' activity. It is this larger puzzle of political events that gives meaning to the piece of action known as student revolt.

This chapter generally follows the stages of the political model, beginning with a discussion of the student "social structure" and the many subgroups in it that generate political pressure. Next to be examined is the "interest articulation" stage in which students put pressure on the decision makers by using a number of tactics. Next there is the "legislative" phase in which the students, by gaining favorable action from official bodies, influenced a specific policy (the policy's content) and the right to make such policies (the decision right). Finally, a few comments are offered to interpret these events in light of the political model of academic governance.

THE STUDENT SOCIAL STRUCTURE

NYU is largely a nonresident urban university and the vast majority of its students are commuters who rush to class on dirty, noisy subways. The collegiate image of green campuses on which pretty coeds stroll is by and large a myth at NYU. To be sure, the Heights campus, away from the bustle of Washington Square, has some of this style but it is not available to the average NYU student. Student life is segmentalized, for college is only one part of the day of the busy student who typically lives at home and carries on his precollege activities and friendships. Although the university is rapidly acquiring dormitories, only a minority of NYU students has a strong residential identification.

In addition to the segmentalizing factors of the student's extra-university activities, there are many forces within the university that splinter the student body. One glance at the enrollment figures in Figure 5-1 shows the diversity of the students' educational interest and goals.

This diverse student body is naturally prone to breaking up into smaller subgroups, centered around disciplines, vocational plans, and degree of involvement in the campus. In a word, the student body, like the other elements of the university's social structure, is highly pluralistic. Burton Clark and Martin Trow suggest that large student bodies tend to divide into four subcultures, described as follows[1]:

> The four orientations were tagged with simple names: collegiate, academic, vocational, and nonconformist. The *collegiate* subculture is the classic one of sports and dating and fun, centered in sororities and fraternities, and dominant in this country from the 1880's to after World War II. . . . Today, we still have campuses known as the football capitals of the world and the mass media are still largely wedded to this imagery of the campus.
>
> The *academic* subculture contains the values of serious study, with commitment to classroom and ideas, and with the faculty as important models of behavior. There are at least two major subtypes within this category: one is the little don, the twenty-year-old who is so serious behind his glasses that he already has taken up the rituals of pipe, dandruff, and patches on the elbow of the coat; the other is the grade-grubber, who takes it all down and gives it all back—a posture congenial to girls in American schools and colleges.

[1] Burton R. Clark, "The Subcultures of the American Campus" in *Ventures: Magazine of the Yale Graduate School*, Spring, 74–75 (1968). For one attempt to apply the Clark/Trow typology in an empirical investigation see David Gottlieb and Benjamin Hodgkins, "College Student Subcultures" in Kaoru Yamamoto, *The College Student and His Culture: An Analysis*. Boston: Houghton Mifflin, 1968, pp. 238–255.

The *vocational* subculture fosters the serious pursuit of job preparation. It is a no-nonsense orientation, with little time for leisurely contemplation of ideas or the social round of Joe College. An extreme expression of this set of values and attitudes is the boy from a lower-class or lower-middle-class background (first in his family to attend college), who is majoring in engineering at a state college, has an outside job at which he works twenty hours a week, has a wife, one child and another on the way, and commutes by streetcar or bus or jalopy to the campus for several hours of classes, for the minimum number of days per week that he can schedule. One does not

Figure 5-1. The Diversity of Student Enrollments:
NYU Fall Term 1968 Enrollments by Divisions and Schools[a]

I. Division One: Undergraduates	
[b]University College	2230
School of Education	2524
School of Engineering/Applied Science	1556
School of Commerce	1732
[b]Washington Square College	3874
Continuing Education (degree students)	349
School of the Arts	474
	12,756
II. Division Two: Graduate Students	
School of Engineering/Applied Science	2026
Graduate School of Arts and Sciences	4849
School of Education	7220
Graduate School of Business	3267
Graduate School of Public Administration	480
Graduate School of Social Work	331
School of the Arts	116
	18,289
III. Division Three: Professional Degrees	
Law	2080
Medical Center	715
Dentistry	854
	3,649
IV. Division Four: Nondegree Programs	
Continuing education	11,718
Grand Total	46,412

[a] Source: Registrar's report to the Chancellor: "Statistical Summary of Student Enrollment, Academic Year 1968–69."
[b] These are the only two undergraduate liberal arts units.

learn very much about this style of student life by studying Yale, although minor forms of this orientation undoubtedly exist here.

The *nonconformist* subculture is a commitment to serious pursuit of ideas, as in the academic orientation, but with off-campus groups as main points of reference. The nonconformists are not identified with their professors, except in isolated cases, nor with the campus as a whole. Nonconformity is so much discussed these days that I need not say more.

If we take a simple typology of this kind, we find quite different combinations of the types on various campuses. There are colleges that are nearly all vocational, others that are even a few where nonconformity is the dominant model. On the very large campuses, all four orientations are upheld by impressive numbers of students.

If we turn this subcultural analysis to NYU, it will help to explain some of the distinctive features of the student situation.[2] Most students at NYU fit into the Clark/Trow *vocational* category. NYU was traditionally the school for the working and middle-class student who wanted to get ahead in the world. New Yorkers by the thousands came to NYU searching for better jobs, more pay, and higher social prestige. The proliferation of professional schools at both the graduate and undergraduate levels testifies to the importance of job training for the NYU student. As Figure 5-1 shows, about 75% of NYU's students are directly enrolled in some professional program, and even in the liberal arts programs many students are nevertheless vocationally oriented. Of course, it cannot be assumed that everyone in a professional school would classify himself in the vocational subculture, but undoubtedly the majority would.

The *collegiate* subculture has a small following at NYU, probably because until recently there was no large on-campus student body to promote the growth of the "Joe College" subculture. There are fraternities, but they are not so important as those at many schools, for only a small proportion of the students belongs to them. With the addition of new residence halls, however, a collegiate subculture will probably blossom on campus as never before.

Both *academic* and *nonconformist* groups are present at NYU; they probably form only a small segment of the student body, but even a small segment of 40,000 students can constitute an impressive number. Both Washington Square College and University College have a sizable population of academically oriented students, a large number of whom go on to

[2] Much of the following discussion is frankly speculative, since no data exist on the issue. However, this is definitely the impression I had of NYU's social structure, and several long-time NYU officials concerned with student activities concur in this analysis.

graduate work. The Graduate School of Arts and Sciences, of course, is almost by definition an enclave of the academic subculture. The nonconformist group is much smaller—indeed smaller than it might appear at first glance. Because of NYU's location in Greenwich Village, the university appears to be populated by numerous artists, beatniks, and hippies; but many of them are mere hangers-on, not enrolled as students. At the moment, however, it appears that an authentic nonconformist subculture is beginning to develop at NYU, especially in Washington Square College. The students who make up this growing subculture clearly fit into the Clark/Trow scheme. Although they are intensely intellectual, they find their intellectual stimulation not in the classroom but in the theater, the art film, the marijuana culture, and the antiwar movement.

How does this analysis of the NYU student subcultures tie into the discussion of the student revolt? As long as the vocational subcultures were dominant, NYU recruited a docile, apathetic student body that was much too busy pursuing its particular vocational interests to become involved in student politics. Student organizations were often colorless and weak, and student governments were fragmented among the various colleges and schools. Student elections were generally a farce, with many offices going uncontested year after year and elections being won by 8 or 10 votes—the only votes cast. The All-Square Congress, which was supposed to represent all the students at Washington Square, was really active only on paper and there was little connection between this body and the local college governments. Moreover, until recent years there was little political activism among campus organizations. The social structure of a segmentalized, commuting student body which was vocationally oriented ensured that campus life at NYU was virtually meaningless to the average student.

By the early 1960's, however, this situation began changing because of two related factors: a shift in the internal student culture of NYU itself and a change in the larger student life of the nation. Internally several features combined to promote a different type of student culture. First, the university consciously attempted to build a resident student body. Consequently, nonconformist and academic subcultures that were much more politically active than the vocational subculture had been, began to develop. Second, the university tried to attract more out-of-city and out-of-state students who were unlikely to be the docile vocational types. Third, the undergraduate colleges raised their standards, thus attracting more academic and nonconformists and cutting out many vocationalists. Washington Square College, in particular, attracted students who were politically active. Of course, these changes did not affect everyone and the majority of the students still fit the old pattern, but there were activist pockets developing all through the changing system.

Internal changes by themselves, however, do not explain the whole story, for external developments provided much of the catalyst. Students across the nation were in turmoil and the contagion of mass social movements was a major factor in the growth of student activism at NYU. The student revolts throughout the nation provided models of behavior, strategies of action, and styles of student leadership. In addition, other issues provided the backdrop for student unrest. Without a doubt the Vietnam war, with all its attendant frustrations, crises of national purpose, and threats to the lives of the nation's youth, served as one critical input into the dissatisfaction, hostility, and cynicism of some students. This kind of intense frustration and anger is easily vented on the university. Other external events constantly penetrated the campus: the frustration over the fate of the civil rights movement, the rise of Black Power, the growth of the New Left, the resurgence of the Old Right, the assassinations of political and moral leaders, and the anomie generated by a mass educational network. All of these external factors provided a constant and vivid backdrop that generated a restlessness and loss of purpose that easily became fuel for political fires inside the university.

In combination, the internal and external changes promoted a new spirit of student involvement at NYU; for example, by the early sixties there was a gradual rise in civil rights groups in the university. CORE, NAACP, and the Civil Rights Organizing Committee (CROC) were all active on the campus. Political activism also began to grow, as evidenced by the appearance of the New Student Union (N.S.U.), the Students for a Democratic Society (S.D.S.), and various anti-Vietnam war groups. In sum, there was a growing militancy among small groups of students, a militancy that was framed by changes in the student subcultures, by student revolts throughout the nation, by civil rights activism, and by rising antiwar sentiment. Although a pall of apathy still hung over NYU, there were signs that it was beginning to break up by the time the student revolt began.

INTEREST ARTICULATION: THE TUITION REBELLION

Every student body has its accumulated set of grievances against the university, but it takes a particular combination of events to transform that vague feeling of discontent into political action. Again and again, when the immediate causes of student revolt are examined, we find some action by the university that affected masses of students in a similar manner and thus provided the spark for unifying widely divergent student groups.

John Searle has called this the "Sacred Issue," for usually the militants select some issue that affects large numbers of students and has moral overtones that are appealed to whenever radical action is criticized.[3] What are a few broken windows or even a few crushed heads when the "cause" is the ultimate aim, whether that sacred cause be student power, rights for the black man, or antiwar sentiment? The Sacred Issue is a unifying, legitimating symbol under which all sorts of radical action can be justified. This is not to deny the validity of many such causes, but it is to suggest that their symbolic value is often exploited to justify action that is in a larger sense destructive of the very freedoms they propose to uphold.

At Berkeley in 1964 The Sacred Issue was "free speech" and political freedom; at Columbia in 1968 it was "racism" surrounding the gym in the Morningside Heights Park and the role of the university in national defense planning; at San Francisco State it was the black studies programs; at Berkeley in 1969 it was the "people's park" that the street people built on university property; at Stanford in 1970 it was the role of R.O.T.C. on campus. In each case the Sacred Issue had moral overtones that could legitimate radical action and serve as a unifying force on otherwise divergent student groups.

The NYU revolt shows a similar pattern, for one incident affected the entire student body simultaneously and thus united otherwise divergent groups. The issue was one of the most potent of all: the right of students to decide financial questions. A special edition of the *Washington Square Journal* on Tuesday, December 6, 1966, headlined this story:

> EXTRA, EXTRA: TUITION INCREASE EXPECTED
>
> NYU PRESIDENT HESTER HOLDS CONFERENCE TODAY AT 11 A.M.
> STUDENTS WANT DELAY FOR "DIALOGUE ON TUITION."
>
> NYU President James M. Hester is expected to announce today a raise in tuition, fees and dormitory rates for next year, *Journal* has learned exclusively. The announcement is expected to come at a meeting this morning of high Administration figures and representatives of student governments.
>
> The University's Board of Trustees has already granted the Administration the right to make the tuition and fee changes, NYU Chancellor Allan M. Cartter said. . . .
>
> However, yesterday, when rumors of the impeding tuition hike spread through out the Square, several student leaders said they would protest the move.

The student leaders demanded time for a "dialogue" on the tuition increase, hoping at least to delay the increases until the students were fully informed. Several reactions of student leaders were recorded in the *Journal*:

[3]John Searle, "A Foolproof Scenario for Student Revolts," *The New York Times Magazine*, 4, December 29, 1968.

> New Student Union president Nick Brown said that if tuition is raised NSU "will fight with all means at its disposal to insure that students are consulted as to the timing and the amount of the increase."
>
> Commerce Council president Stephen Sokolovsky said the University "has been expanding too much, too fast."
>
> Sokolovsky, an accounting major, blamed the University's deficit on its holding too many fixed assets.
>
> If tuition is raised he favored "giving them what they deserve and that's a Berkeley on this campus."

That series of annoncements was made on Tuesday, December 6. By Thursday a well-coordinated student reaction had set in. The *Journal* headline for Thursday, December 8, read: "800 March to Protest Tuition Hike; Angry Students State Boycott Today."

> Almost one thousand students last night vocally agreed to boycott classes and picket classroom building this morning to protest a raise in tuition and dormitory fees announced Tuesday. The decision followed the students' rejection of an eleventh hour proposal by NYU President James M. Hester to postpone the raising of dormitory and food service fees. More than 800 angry students had marched to the administration offices immediately after the tuition hike announcement Tuesday morning.
>
> At that time, the students had decided on a simple boycott of classes unless Dr. Hester agreed to a moratorium on the increase, pending discussion of the situation with students. The letter, sent by the New Student Union to Dr. Hester, however, asked for a "rescinding" of the increase rather than the "moratorium" as originally intended.
>
> Dr. Hester refused NSU's demands, but offered to "delay formal action on proposed increases in dormitory rates and food services for next year."
>
> The newly formed *ad hoc* committee on the tuition problem rejected Dr. Hester's proposal and decided to go on with the boycott. . . .
>
> Dr. Hester also promised students that they would be able to meet in the spring with the Board of Trustees, and announced "the creation of a special trustee committee to advise on matters of student services."

At least two events recorded in *Journal's* story had longterm consequences for the shape of power at NYU. First, the formation of the "Ad Hoc Committee on the Tuition Problem" was an act filled with future political consequences. Second, the appointment of the special trustee committee to advise on student services eventually led to a whole series of changes that affected not only the students but the trustees, the University Senate, and the faculty.

On December 8 President Hester met with the students in a stormy session, but little was resolved. The administration refused to rescind the tuition increase but did promise to release financial information to the students so that they could judge for themselves whether the tuition increase was necessary. In addition, the President tried to accommodate the students by offering to postpone the dormitory and board increases. The *Journal* reports that at the end of the turbulent meeting

> . . . a long-haired prophet in sun glasses spoke, "The coming apocalypse!" He smiled. Sweeping his eyes over the crowd of student protestors, he commented, "The greatest thing, it's like Berkeley." Again he smiled, "Berkeley is our ideal."[4]

The Issue Enlarges: A Struggle For Power

In the following week there was a series of major student protests. At first the *Journal* ran editorial headlines such as "Protest Tuition—But Keep it Cool." Later, however, the paper reflected the rising student discontent by gradually becoming more militant. A sit-in began on Friday, December 9, and continued for several days in the main classroom building of Washington Square College. Most classes were disrupted and tempers flared on all sides. However, the police were not called in and no major violence occurred, a fact partly attributable to the restraint of the administration. This was probably a critical factor that prevented the revolt from going violent, as it did on numerous other campuses when police were brought in.

It is crucial to realize that the tuition protest immediately assumed other dimensions. The call for a rollback of the tuition (the policy content) enlarged to become a call for student participation in the decision-making systems of the university (the right to decision). *This expansion from the specific issue to the general question of power and decision making is a pattern that repeated itself in almost every critical event that was observed in the year and a half that the NYU study was under way.* The demand for student power was articulated in a plan advanced by the Ad Hoc Committee. On Thursday, December 15, the *Journal* headline read "Ad Hoc Committee Proposes Powerful 3-Part Commission."

> A three part commission that would take over many of the Board of Trustees' functions was proposed Monday by the Ad Hoc Committee to Oppose the Tuition Increase. . . .
>
> The commission, composed of students, faculty, administration and Board of Trustee members, would "be empowered to initiate, review, abridge and abrogate all policy affecting the University community," a leaflet distributed by the Committee said. Its area of control would include tuition, curriculum and the allocation of funds, said the flyer.

The entire issue of student participation in decision making was now raised, and the rest of the story is more of a fight over this matter than over

[4] *The Washington Square Journal*, Thursday, December 8, 1966, Vol. 12, p. 2.

the tuition increase itself. Symbolic of the shift in issues was a name change: the "Ad Hoc Committee Opposed to Tuition Increases" became the "Ad Hoc Committee for a Democratic University."

Committee leaders demanded an immediate decision on the three-part commission, but President Hester said he could not answer until after the January 15 trustee meeting. The students responded that sit-ins would result if the answer were unfavorable. As a matter of fact, the Ad Hoc Committee made a decision a few days *before* January 15 to hold sit-ins in the campus bookstore, a decision that brought charges of bad faith from the administration. The students responded that the trustee decision on the three-part commission would obviously be against them, so why wait?

In the meantime several noteworthy things happened among the student leaders. Up to this point the various student governments were weak and the All-Square Congress was virtually inactive. On the first day of the tuition protest the student government leaders took surprisingly strong stands, and it seemed for a while that they would lead the revolt, but a second body of student leaders appeared among the political groups and civil rights organizations. Almost immediately a split developed between the student government leaders and the activists, each strongly competing for the allegiance of the students. The government leaders, finding that the militants were outmaneuvering them and gaining the students' support for a more radical stance, tried to reassert their authority by calling for moderation; for example, Stephen Sokolvosky, who had called for "giving them what they deserve and that's a Berkeley on this campus," was urging moderation only a day later. The *Journal* notes the following:

> At a late meeting last night, Stephen Sokolovsky, Commerce Council president, warned that the boycott and possible disruption of classes "would lead to a closing of the dialogue between the administration and the students."
>
> "We're trying to avert a loss of face for the University," he said, "We don't want this thing to blow up."[5]

The split between Ad Hoc Committee's militants and student government leaders became painfully obvious on December 9 when President Hester spoke to a large rally of students. The *Journal* reported:

> After Dr. Hester's address, the students broke off into two groups, one lead by student government members and a much larger one led by (Ad Hoc) Committee members Joe Knock and Bornstein.
>
> After some debate the Committee's followers voted to sit-in at the Main Building.

[5] *The Washington Square Journal*, December 8, 1966, Vol. 12, p. 1.

> The student government meeting, Shapiro [President of the Washington Square College Council] said, "The only people the Administration will listen to are the student leaders."[6]

In the following weeks and months the split between these two groups widened to the point of no return and the shape of student politics at formerly apathetic NYU changed radically, with the new activists wrestling control not only of the revolt but eventually of the entire student government system.

The Response of the University Administration

One might look at the administration's actions from several directions. On the one hand, it could be argued that the administration was shortsighted for not bringing student leaders into the discussion of the tuition increase from the very first. Dr. Harold Whiteman, Chancellor for Student Affairs, notes that with hindsight it is obvious that they might have avoided many problems by having more open discussion with the students at a much earlier stage,[7] but he also notes that there had been no tradition of student involvement, and indeed even identifying the appropriate student leaders in the multitude of fragmented organizations was no easy task. In a sense student apathy was so strongly instituted that no one really gave serious thought to consulting the students.

After the revolt began, however, the administration's reaction was swift. One of the first decisions was that the police would not be called in except under the most unusual circumstances. Instead the administration would try to institute a "dialogue" with the students. On the very first day of the protest President Hester agreed to meet with any interested students in an open session. In the following days several meetings were held between the protesting students and the administration.

During this time it is quite clear that the administration was taking the student revolt seriously and was quickly responding to student calls for action. To be sure, the tuition increase was not stopped, but on the other hand the room and board charges were postponed. (Room charges eventually were left at earlier levels.) Moreover, the administration was clearly negotiating in an attempt to hold the revolt to manageable proportions. One of the most revealing passages in the *Journal* of December 19 was an editorial comment which noted that the administration objected to the use of the word "negotiation."

[6] *The Washington Square Journal*, December 10, 1966, Vol. 12, p. 3.
[7] Dr. Harold Whiteman, Interview No. 51.

The administration, too, is upset because of the use of a word. In this case the word is "negotiating" and it was used by a *Journal* columnist to describe what the University Administration was doing with the student power radicals. Officers of the Administration have bent over backwards to tell us that they are not negotiating with the (Ad Hoc) Committee; rather they are "opening channels of communication" and "discussing" in those meetings in the Board of Trustees' Room in Vanderbilt Hall.

One might add that the administration "protesteth too much," for its actions certainly looked like negotiations from almost every vantage point. As one administrative officer put it, "Hell, there was one point at which we would have done anything within reason to take off some of the heat. Our policy was to talk, to negotiate, and to avoid police interference at all costs."[8]

Expansion of the Conflict: The Faculty Role

Early in the student revolt various faculty members decided to aid the students. Many of the professors who were active in antiwar teach-ins turned their attention to the question of student power. Although they never amounted to more than a handful, they were aggressive and vocal and their influence was all out of proportion to the size of the group. Their involvement usually took the form of encouragement and support, but a few actually joined the sit-ins at the Main Building and the bookstore. One faculty member even suggests in a private letter to me that she was fired because of her role in the student revolt. (However, her department chairman's two-word response when I questioned him about this was emphatically to the contrary—as well as unprintable.)

The faculty activity soon assumed other dimensions, for some militants immediately saw the student revolt as the stimulus for faculty involvement. There was discussion of increasing *both* faculty and student power at the same time. On December 15 the *Journal* reported on a faculty petition:

> A group of faculty members drafted a statement Monday calling for an increase of faculty and student participation in the making of University policy. The statement will be presented to the separate school faculties "as soon as they meet."
>
> Prof. Roscoe Brown, of the School of Education, [later to be elected President of the NYU chapter of AAUP] said that although the group was concerned with the furor caused by the tuition increase its main interest lay in gaining consultations with the faculty and students on major school decisions. . . .

[8] Interview No. 30, p. 1.

> Several faculty members will attend a meeting with NYU President James M. Hester tomorrow, Dr. Brown said.
>
> At the meeting of the 25 ad hoc members, it was mentioned that about three years ago the AAUP suggested that Dr. Hester consult the faculty before reporting to the Board of Trustees. The Elected Faculty Senate never voted on the suggestion.

There is little doubt that the student revolt led to a major reaction among the faculty. One leader of the AAUP phrased it:

> "The student revolt helped wake the faculty up to its own impotence more than anything that has happened here in twenty years. The university was appointing committees to deal with student power and it suddenly hit us in the face that the faculty was powerless."[9]

By the end of January 1967 several faculty resolutions had been passed in various schools of the university and increased pressure was brought on the University Senate to meet student and faculty demands.

THE LEGISLATIVE PHASE: DECISIONS ARE REACHED

After several weeks of protest the revolt finally dissolved, much to the administration's relief. Its effects were only beginning to be felt, however, for a whole series of changes grew out of it. The students' Three-Part Commission was not accepted, but on January 11, 1967, the University Senate established the McKay Commission to study student participation in the university's decision making at all levels. Throughout the spring the McKay Commission, with its eight students and eight faculty members, met to develop plans for student participation. Open forums were held for the expression of student opinion, and numerous student and faculty subcommittees worked on the task.

When the McKay Commission reported back to the University Senate on May 5, 1967, it only outlined general proposals and did not go into the problem of implementation. Many students and faculty members were dissatisfied that the report stopped short of concrete recommendations. Some students responded that it was just what they had expected, "All rhetoric and no action!" Thus the Senate—acting in the time-honored academic tradition—appointed the Griffith's Committee to translate those general recommendations into concrete action. Finally, on November 14, 1967, nearly a year after the student revolt began, the University Senate approved

[9]Interview No. 45, p. 3.

the Griffith's Committee report. The specific recommendations were sent to the various schools and colleges within the university to be implemented in a manner that would best fit their individual needs.

1. That an ombudsman for students be established.
2. That residence halls should be largely self-governing.
3. That student governments be restructured and unified.
4. That students be added to all college or school committees having to do with educational policy, curriculum, and student discipline.
5. That committees on Student Activities with predominant student memberships be established in all schools and colleges.
6. That uniform, written procedural rules should be developed for student discipline.
7. That students should have a large voice in framing these disciplinary rules.
8. That students arrange for evaluation of faculty members and courses.
9. That open forums be instituted in which students could make their views known to the faculty and administration.

The process of actually implementing these recommendations is still going on, and without a doubt it will continue for some time. In spite of all the cumbersome processes, it does seem that the commission report has signaled a genuine milestone in student participation at New York University. The student revolt that appeared to have died was in fact instrumental in provoking numerous innovations in student affairs.

Not only were there policy changes in reference to student activities, but there were also many changes that dealt with the faculty. When the University Senate established the McKay Commission to study student demands, it also set up the Taggart Commission to study faculty-participation issues. The Taggart Commission was active for nearly a year and finally made its report to the University on December 15, 1967. The report contained recommendations about the nature and structure of the Senate itself but did not deal with faculty participation in the individual schools and colleges. The principal suggestions appear to be innocent on the surface but they introduce a significant new role for the faculty.

1. A Senate budget committee to consult with the administration on budgetary policy. Since the university's budget represents the centralized expression of its goals and programs, the Senate felt that it is vital for the faculty to understand the basis of the major decisions, and that opportunity be provided for the faculty and deans to raise questions and concerns.

2. Establishment of committees on educational policy, university development, faculty personnel, and organizational policies.
3. An enlargement of the Senate to include more faculty representatives.
4. Proportional representation by the various schools and colleges, so that small schools would not be overrepresented.
5. More efficient consultation between the administration and the faculty, through the Faculty Council (the faculty members of the Senate), and access to the Board of Trustees.

It was clear from the atmosphere of the meeting that the Senate was pleased with the Taggart Report, indeed its members expressed an enthusiasm that was hardly justified by the actual wording of the formal document. Several suggested that the report represented a genuine change in the opportunities available for the faculty to influence university policy. One long-time member of the faculty said, "This is a revolutionary document for NYU. If we really make it work it represents a new day dawning in the decision-making of this university."

Of course, not all the comments were as positive as this one. Both in private conversations and in his public presentation Commission Chairman Joseph Taggart was highly skeptical of the value of the formal arrangements alone to accomplish the desired changes. "The new plan can only work if the faculty is aggressive and active in its role, but the formal arrangements do little more than provide an *opportunity* for this to happen." Whether the faculty will actually use the new arrangements to become a major voice in the decision-making process is still an unanswered question, but there is no doubt that the Taggart report was viewed as a significant change in the nature of the University Senate.

One other event in the spring of 1967 signaled the increased activism of the faculty. In early March a group of 15 professors met to discuss the possibility of forming a local chapter of the United Federation of College Teachers. As one faculty member discussed it:

> We decided that we needed a more militant group on the NYU campus. We had learned from the student activities and from the activities of faculties at other campuses. We learned that militancy often paid off, and we wanted to cash in on the rich possibilities that a strong group like the UFCT offered. Of course, we already had a chapter of the AAUP, but let's face it, they weren't that active and they certainly were not what you would call militant.[10]

It is interesting to note, however, that many of the more active members

[10] Interview No. 45, p. 3.

of the AAUP were charter members of the local UFCT branch and saw no contradiction in their membership in both groups.

The faculty was more alive and active in the spring of 1967 than it had been within the memory of anyone at NYU. Of course, there was still a great body of professors who could not care less about the politics of the university, but the active minority was probably bigger than it had ever been and its influence on the university was growing. The student revolt, although certainly not the only reason, was one large factor in the faculty's awakening.

SOME SUBSEQUENT EVENTS

Several subsequent events are worth noting. First, the Ad Hoc Committee for a Democratic University eventually split up. The activist members refused to run for positions on the McKay Commission, claiming that they could be better critics outside the formal "system." As a result, there were few strongly activist members on the McKay Commission. Later this split in the Ad Hoc Committee widened to the point that by late spring 1967 it was falling completely apart. The student leadership was splintered into three groups: the student government leaders, the activists of the Ad Hoc Committee who refused to run for student offices for fear of being co-opted into the "system," and a group within the Ad Hoc Committee who wanted to run for office and wrest control from the student government leaders. Finally the Ad Hoc Committee broke up, with the more activist students losing their charismatic control and drifting back to their former obscure roles. The other segment of the Ad Hoc Committee, however, formed the VOICE party and proceeded to sweep the next student government elections in almost all the major schools. By late spring and early fall of 1967 it was clear that the student revolt had been transformed from a rebellion with placards in the street and sit-ins in the buildings to an aggressive political union that was revitalizing student life on the NYU campus.

The other major event has been the continued development of the anti-Vietnam war policy on campus. At first glance this seems like a political movement directed solely against political forces outside the university. On second look, however, it seems that much of the frustration and anger against the war are being turned in against the university. The protests against Dow Chemical recruitment in November 1967 and March 1968 were actually two-pronged attacks, one against Dow, the government, and the war, but the other against the administration of NYU.

In this event, as in others, the student body was divided about the appropriate action to take. The more militant students demanded that Dow not be allowed on the campus, but others argued for an "open recruitment" policy. Several student organizations voted on the issue. The All-Square Congress and the Washington Square College Council voted for a policy of "no recruitment without prior debate," arguing that Dow representatives should debate students on the company's policy. However, the Commerce Student Council, the Graduate Education Student Organization, and the Commission on Student Life all voted for an open recruitment. Thus there were all shades of opinion among the students themselves. The University Senate probably represented the faculty and administrative position when it voted overwhelmingly for open recruitment.

Neverthless, a group of militants actively protested Dow's activity on campus. These students demanded that they be given the right to decide whether Dow or anyone else could come on campus, and a major power struggle developed. On March 6, 1968, the protest against Dow was largely a protest against the university, at least in its vocal expression. Chancellor Cartter met with nearly a thousand jeering students to explain the university's position on open recruitment and the protection of free speech on campus. The protesting students rejected all these arguments and insisted that they—not the administration—be empowered to decide the issues. (Again note the shift from the *content* of the policy to the *decision-right* over that policy.) The administration refused to yield and Dow representatives made a brief appearance. Since that time numerous other issues have surfaced and the struggle for student power that began with the tuition increase is by no means over.

SUMMARY

The object of this chapter was to show that it might be helpful to analyze student revolts by placing them in the context of a larger political framework. If we understand university governance on the grand scale as a political process in which different power blocks—outside pressure groups, trustees, administrators, faculty, and students—struggle for some control over the university's destiny, it is not at all mysterious or shocking that students should be flexing their collective muscles. From this perspective student power is a natural thing alongside many other kinds of power.

This analysis began with a study of the changing student social structure at New York University, where internal and external changes united to produce a more active militant group of students. Next, the interpretation pointed to the tactics used by different groups as they struggled to win their claims in the interest-articulation phase. Then the legislative process was mentioned as the conflict was channeled into committees, student government elections, and negotiating groups. Finally, the new policies, which dealt not only with students but spread to faculty demands as well, emerged. The cycle then started anew with a feedback cycle generating new conflict and the political system continues. Figure 5-2 summarizes some of the major outlines of these events.

Figure [illegible]. The Political Model Applied to the Student Revolt.

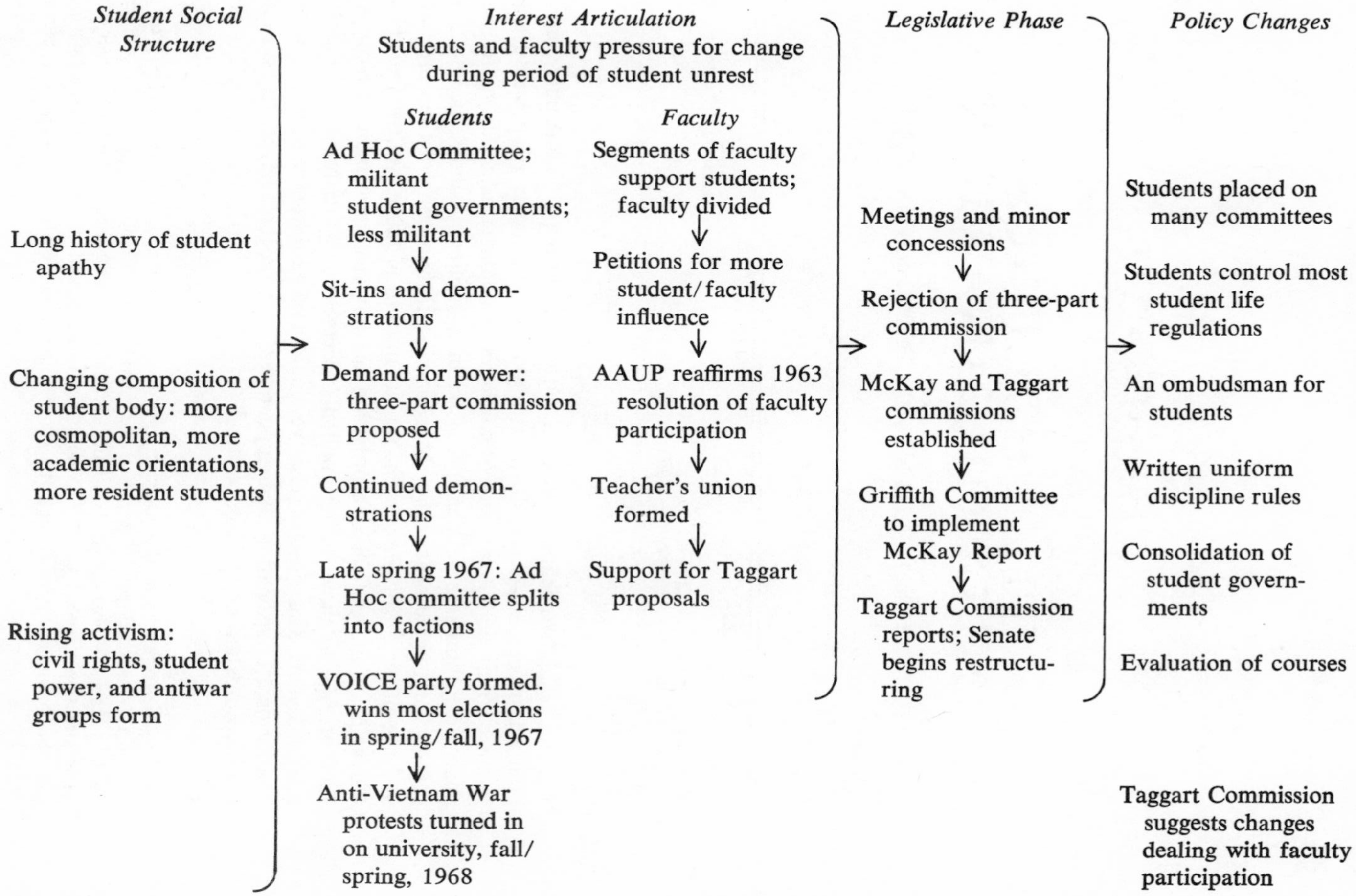

Student Social Structure

- Long history of student apathy
- Changing composition of student body: more cosmopolitan, more academic orientations, more resident students
- Rising activism: civil rights, student power, and antiwar groups form

→

Interest Articulation

Students and faculty pressure for change during period of student unrest

Students

Ad Hoc Committee; militant student governments; less militant

↓

Sit-ins and demonstrations

↓

Demand for power: three-part commission proposed

↓

Continued demonstrations

↓

Late spring 1967: Ad Hoc committee splits into factions

↓

VOICE party formed. wins most elections in spring/fall, 1967

↓

Anti-Vietnam War protests turned in on university, fall/spring, 1968

Faculty

Segments of faculty support students; faculty divided

↓

Petitions for more student/faculty influence

↓

AAUP reaffirms 1963 resolution of faculty participation

↓

Teacher's union formed

↓

Support for Taggart proposals

→

Legislative Phase

Meetings and minor concessions

↓

Rejection of three-part commission

↓

McKay and Taggart commissions established

↓

Griffith Committee to implement McKay Report

↓

Taggart Commission reports; Senate begins restructuring

→

Policy Changes

- Students placed on many committees
- Students control most student life regulations
- An ombudsman for students
- Written uniform discipline rules
- Consolidation of student governments
- Evaluation of courses
- Taggart Commission suggests changes dealing with faculty participation

Chapter VI

THE POLITICS OF COORDINATION

THE DEPARTMENTAL REORGANIZATION

The preceding two chapters provided large-scale examples of the university's political processes—cases filled with obvious examples of power plays, interest-group activities, and organizational conflict. Each example was analyzed to illustrate political processes in two different situations, one concerning large-scale changes in the educational philosophy of the university and the other, a volatile student revolt. In both instances we tried to show the value of a political interpretation of university governance. Now we shall attempt to show similar conflict processes in less dramatic, apparently routine events. For this purpose we shall examine a knotty problem of organizational coordination that appears, at least on the surface, to be thoroughly bureaucratic and nonpolitical.[1]

[1]The events reported in this chapter happened over a period of years and are quite complex. The treatment is simplified considerably and the strict logic of the political model's stages is abandoned to obtain a more interesting presentation. However, the same attention to social structure, interest articulation, and legislative processes permeates the discussion, even though the stages are not so clearly delineated as in earlier chapters.

THE "FEDERAL" IMAGE

It seems helpful to suggest a *federal* understanding of the university. New York University is a bewildering collection of schools, colleges, and institutes, loosely bound together under the university's control but generally going about their own private concerns with little relation to the rest of the institution. Universities vary in the amount of autonomy reserved for various units, but they usually allow great leeway for each school to pursue its own goals within broad university guidelines. The federal university is welded together by numerous ties, some quite weak, others quite strong. At the same time, then, the university is torn apart by centrifugal forces but also bound together by centripetal forces. The exploration of these contradictory processes of centralization and decentralization is a key part of a political image.[2]

Parallels can easily be drawn between university governance and the federal government of the United States. The federal government is composed of a network of states with large areas of autonomy; a university has colleges and schools that go merrily about their own tasks. The United States also has a centralized government that is assuming more and more of the power; the same centralization of power often occurs in the university. Like the nation, the university has its share of "States-righters" and "Federalists." Quarrels over the rights and power of the different units are common to both NYU and the national government.

THE PREVIOUS FRAGMENTATION OF NEW YORK UNIVERSITY

Until recently NYU was highly decentralized and the individual schools and colleges were extremely autonomous. Actually the university was more of a "confederation" than a "*uni*versity." One long-time member of the NYU community described the old system like this:

> Somebody used a feudal analogy to describe our system around here. You know, in the middle ages there were a lot of petty dukes and knights who held power over their estates and only cooperated with the king when they had to. It was the same way around here—we had dozens of minor monarchs located all over this university, and each one pretty well ruled over his domain. The central administration had *some* power, of course, just

[2] One of the best treatments of centralization and decentralization in a large organization is Kaufman's study of the U.S. Forest Service. Herbert Kaufman, *The Forest Ranger*. Baltimore: Johns Hopkins Press, 1960.

> like the medieval king had some influence over his knights. But it was a fragile kind of control, and we sort of hung together in a loose confederation instead of running a tight realm. The administration acted more by persuasion and suggestion than by order and fiat. They just couldn't get away with it otherwise—there were too many people around here with their own base of power. Incidentally, it's a little tighter now, but this picture may still be true.[3]

The various schools at NYU were founded at different times and sometimes demonstrated great independence from the central administration. Each school developed its own educational program, and as long as it was financially stable the central administration did not interfere. In fact, each school was on a pay-as-you-go basis, balancing tuition income and expenses exactly. There was little endowment and each unit was a self-sustaining operation.

There were many unfortunate consequences of this loose confederation. For one thing, the liberal arts schools were usually in poor competitive status. Unlike the professional schools they had no clear connection between the curriculum and a job. Upwardly mobile students were more willing to pay high tuition rates for a professionally oriented curriculum, for they saw immediate cash value in it. Moreover, the professional schools had strong support from professionally successful alumni. The competitive disadvantage of the liberal arts programs was especially apparent in the Graduate School of Arts and Science. All in all, NYU was noted for its excellent professional schools but was seldom cited as a strong liberal arts institution.

Another consequence of the confederation system was a sharp variation among the schools in faculty salary scales, hiring practices, tenure, quality of education, and the nature of the curriculum. Consequently NYU was noted for its spotty development, with some very strong units and some very weak units. At best, NYU had a mixed reputation among the academic institutions of the nation.

A third consequence was that the deans of each college were the prime administrators in the university. It was almost an axiom around NYU that real power lay in the deans' hands, for the central administration was understaffed and generally nonaggressive. The deans were virtually autonomous, for their power was seldom effectively challenged by the central administration.

In the early 1950's the administration of President Henry T. Heald began a concerted effort to overcome this disunity and to impose centralized leadership on the university. In 1953 Heald appointed a Self-Study Commission to chart the future development of the university. One of the key Self-Study

[3]Interview No. 32, p. 1.

recommendations was that NYU should consolidate its administrative system and reorganize the loose confederation of schools. The report called for immediate action to "establish a sense of the organic unity of New York University." The commission declared that although administrative decentralization had its advantage during NYU's period of rapid growth,

> . . . the concept of the university as a loose federation of colleges and schools was carried to an extreme and in recent years has tended to neutralize the advantages. The undesirable consequences are discernible everywhere, but are most apparent in the liberal arts and sciences.
>
> . . . .
>
> For all its size and geographic dispersion, New York University is more than an agglomeration of schools, colleges, and institutes. We have taken the view that it is a single organic entity.[4]

The Self-Study recommendations were implemented in a number of changes including uniform faculty salaries, more aggressive fund raising by the central administration, major shifts in personnel, and the abandonment of the pay-as-you-go budgetary system.

THE ALL-UNIVERSITY DEPARTMENT SYSTEM

One of the Self-Study's additional recommendations concerned the structure of the departments. The Commission observed that each academic discipline had separate departments in University College, Washington Square College, the Graduate School, the School of Education, and the School of Commerce

> . . . each with its independent head or chairman, faculty, and course offering. . . . In consequence, there are inefficient duplications of academic offerings and administrative structure, and too little exchange of experience and opinion across school lines. There is not sufficient University overview in the basic disciplines with respect to appointments, promotions, contract renewals, tenure, and salaries. . . . [Thus] in the interests of unification and integration . . . [the Self-Study recommends that] the faculty members of the present Graduate School of Arts and Science, of Washington Square College, and of University College be organized into University departments, each department to include all the academic levels and to be under the direction of a single head.[5]

[4] New York University, *The Self-Study*. New York: New York University Press, 1956, 1956 pp. 33 and 22.
[5] *Ibid.*, pp. 33–34.

During the academic year 1956-1957 plans for implementing these proposals were discussed by the three deans of the liberal arts units and a committee of faculty members. On May 27, 1957, the University bylaws were revised to establish "all-university departments." All faculty members in the three liberal arts units were placed in one department that cut cross-sectionally across the Graduate School, Washington Square College, and University College. This department was administered by a "head" who was in charge of graduate studies in the department and by two "chairmen" who represented him in the two undergraduate schools.

On the surface this move appears to be a routine bureaucratic reorganization, but behind the scenes several political battles were raging. First, the original discussions concluded that the all-university departments would include *all* undergraduate schools, including Commerce and Education. These two schools reacted violently to the idea, claiming that their special curriculums would be violated and their faculties undercut. Moreover, they feared that many students would be lost if they were exposed to liberal arts courses outside the professional schools. The opposition of Commerce and Education to their inclusion in the all-university departments was so intense that they were eliminated from the proposal, contrary to the expressed wishes of the Self-Study Commission and the central administration.

The second political battle was by far the more heated. The establishment of these all-university departments tended to weaken the autonomy of the individual colleges and the idea was hotly opposed by some of the deans. They feared that their authority would be undermined by heads who would now share control over the local departments. Moreover, the heads were to report directly to the Chancellor's office and to a Committee of Deans, as well as to the local deans. Finally, departmental budgets were removed from the deans' offices and located with the heads. Now there would be 18 budgetary networks, in which the heads rather than the deans would have final authority. The all-university department appeared to be an attempt to break the powerful hold that the deans held on the schools. As one key administrator put it,

> . . . the all-university system was definitely a politically motivated act, for it broke the back of the previously all-powerful deans. The all-university system points to Vanderbilt Hall's desire for more control.[6]

The deans were to act as an advisory cabinet called the Committee of Deans which would try to coordinate the departmental budgets. Further erosion of the deans' authority came in 1960 with the appointment of an Executive Dean (James M. Hester, currently the President) who was placed

[6]Interview No. 73, p. 2.

over all the liberal arts. The heads now bypassed the deans completely by reporting to the Executive Dean instead of to the Committee of Deans.

One additional element in this cycle of centralization was the establishment of the Coordinated Liberal Studies Program. Although earlier the political opposition had exempted Commerce and Education from the all-university department system, Executive Dean Hester never lost the hope that they would eventually be included. When he assumd the presidency, one of his first steps was to renew the pressure for coordination of Commerce and Education. The details of that move were reported in Chapter IV and it is not necessary to repeat them here. It is important, however, to locate the Coordinated Liberal Studies within the general framework of the centralization cycle that occurred in the late 1950's and early 1960's.

THE DEANS REASSERT THEIR INFLUENCE

A complex system never rests, and the resolution of one dilemma generates new conflicts and new political processes. The deans had lost one battle, but the war was not over. In the academic year 1963–1964 the deans renewed their pressure to reclaim some of their lost power. Personal factors played a critical role in many of these events. By this time personnel changes had led to the rise of several strong deans and a new chancellor,[7] Russell Niles, previous dean of the Law School. Niles had been a strong law dean and some people suggested that he was uncomfortable with the weakness of the liberal arts deans. Moreover, the new deans in the liberal arts units were pressing for a revision of the system.

Many other tensions were building up in the system. Bureaucratic mechanisms tend to develop particular types of strain, and in this case a number of critical problems had developed. First, two authority systems were competing, for both the deans and the heads were wrestling for control. In a sense there were 18 little deans who were vying for power against the three liberal arts deans. As one official put it, "Power was falling in the cracks between the deans and the heads. We never were sure who could do what." Moreover, the budgetary procedure was vastly complicated because 18 separate departmental budgets had to be negotiated and then renegotiated in order to fit into the needs of the colleges. The deans constantly complained that although this budgetary system gave much flexibility to the departments it completely undercut the college budgets.

[7] The chancellor, who is in charge of most internal organizational problems, is the second highest university official.

In addition, the deans felt that the interests of the colleges were being sacrificed to the interests of the departments. They argued that the liberal arts program was completely sabotaged by the early specializations that the departments were demanding of their students. With the departments reigning supreme, faculty members began to gravitate toward research interests and graduate teaching rather than toward the development of a well-rounded liberal arts program in the college. The deans suggested that there was entirely too much "vertical" specialization in the disciplines and not enough "horizontal" coordination between the fields. All in all, the deans were extremely dissatisfied and the central administration was beginning to see some of the system's faults.

In the spring of 1964 Chancellor Niles announced that an administrative decision had been made to restore the deans' budgetary authority. At that point the executive deanship was also discontinued and the heads were required to consult with the deans in the preparation of departmental activities. The loss of budgetary control and the elimination of the Executive Dean meant that the department heads were now more dependent on the deans. The balance of power shifted back toward the dean's office.

The decision to restore budgetary authority to the deans was purely an administrative decision by the central administration. The by-laws were not revised and some department chairmen suggested that the whole procedure was illegal. Illegal or not, the decision was made and on October 8, 1964, new guidelines were issued for the interaction of the deans, heads, and chairmen. These new guidelines clearly indicated that the deans had successfully reasserted their power, at least for the moment.

THE POSITION OF THE BRONX HEIGHTS CAMPUS

Another important issue related to the all-university department system was the relation of the Bronx Heights campus to the other units at Washington Square. For many years University College in the Bronx was NYU's prime undergraduate unit and it was a symbol of high status for both faculty and students to be identified with that campus. In the 1930's and 1940's, however, its physical isolation and the growing importance of graduate education at Washington Square began to undermine the Heights' preeminent position. It was increasingly apparent that the Heights was slipping in the status battle, and professors at the uptown campus began complaining about their second-class membership in the university.

The all-university department system was a further blow to University College's status and autonomy. Powerful deans had always been a critical factor in the Heights' struggle for independence. Often a strong dean could carve out a program for the Heights in spite of its physical isolation and lack of graduate programs. When the all-university department system undermined the deans' authority, the Heights' position was further weakened. The vast majority of the department heads were located at Washington Square and were primarily oriented to the Graduate School. The chairmen in both University College and Washington Square College were weak in terms of authority, but the University College chairman was further disadvantaged because of his isolation and lack of contact with the head. In sum, the department heads were constantly accused of favoring the Square over the Heights and this, coupled with the weakening of the dean's power, meant that many of the Heights' faculty felt politically disadvantaged.

The University College faculty became resentful of their status, and complained that their salaries, offices, and general conditions were not so good as those at the Square. This deep discontent shows in both the 1959 Faculty Senate Survey and the 1968 NYU Study. Eight indentical questions for evaluating the university were included in both of the surveys and on these items University College was by far the most dissatisfied of all 15 colleges and schools. In 1959 they rated higher dissatisfaction than the total university average in seven out of eight items! (see Figure 6-1). Even on the eighth item (offices) University College was almost the same as the university total, and the percentage of "dissatisfied" scores was greater than the combined total of "moderates" and "satisfied." They were unhappy about many issues, including salaries, ease of communication with the university administration, their influence on college and university budgets, and their influence on academic policy. On the question of confidence in the university's leadership 72.3% said they were dissatisfied. The over-all picture was one of deep discontent and a pervasive feeling of second-class citizenship.

The cries of discontent finally reached the central administration at Vanderbilt Hall and several steps were taken to alleviate the situation. One step was the decision in 1964 to return more power to the deans which enabled the University College Dean to work for a revitalization of his campus. Another move was the appointment in the fall of 1966 of a provost to oversee the entire Heights complex, which included the Schools of Engineering and Applied Science as well as University College. The provost would be a strong advocate for the Heights' cause in the cental administation. But despite the positive things being done to help the Heights there was a major set-back when the Academic Senate suggested that in the future most graduate work would be concentrated at Washington Square and not expanded at the Heights as the University College faculty had requested.

Thus the faculty's morale at University College was quite ambivalent, with some increases in satisfaction and some decreases. This is evidenced in the sharp lowering in dissatisfaction with the university's administration

Figure 6-1. University College Faculty Reports High Dissatisfaction with the University (1959 and 1968 Data Compared)

Item Evaluated	Comparison: 1959/1968 Total University/University College		% Reporting: Negative Evaluation	% Reporting: Moderates	% Reporting: Positive Evaluation	N
*1. Offices	1959	Total university average	54.0	13.8	32.2	571
		University College	51.0	16.3	32.7	49
	1968	Total university average	28.3	18.3	43.4	662
		University College	31.5	28.8	39.8	73
2. Salary	1959	Total university average	63.8	9.4	26.8	577
		University College	75.0	6.3	18.7	48
	1968	Total university average	41.5	32.4	26.1	660
		University College	61.1	25.0	13.9	72
Faculty influence: **3. Academic policy	1959	Total university average	46.4	26.5	27.1	524
		University College	62.5	16.7	20.8	48
	1968	Total university average	30.2	36.5	33.4	597
		University College	29.3	33.8	36.9	65
Faculty influence: **4. College budget	1959	Total university average	49.3	40.3	10.4	469
		University College	65.9	22.7	11.4	44
	1968	Total university average	76.8	16.8	6.3	536
		University College	75.4	17.5	7.1	57
Faculty influence: **5. University budget[b]	1959	Total university average	49.9	43.4	6.7	459
		University College	66.7	26.7	6.5	45
	1968	Total university average	87.8	9.8	2.4	499
		University College	86.5	11.5	1.9	52

*Item on which university college shows higher satisfaction than total university average in 1959.

**Items on which university college shows higher satisfaction than total university average in 1968.

Table 6-1. (Continued)

Item Evaluated	Comparison: 1959/1968	Total University/University College	% Reporting: Negative Evaluation	Moderates	Positive Evaluation	N
6. Building program						
Faculty influence:	1959	Total university average	51.4	35.8	12.8	486
		University College	52.3	34.1	13.6	44
	1968	Total university average	77.7	16.9	5.3	485
		University College	79.2	13.2	7.5	53
7. University administration						
Communication:	1959	Total university average	45.1	42.2	12.7	515
		University College	59.5	33.3	7.1	47
	1968	Total university average	56.0	29.3	14.7	525
		University College	63.2	28.1	8.8	57
8. University leadership						
Confidence in	1959	Total university average	42.1	17.6	40.3	535
		University College	72.3	12.8	14.9	47
	1968	Total university average	20.6	32.0	47.4	622
		University College	37.8	34.3	26.9	67

between 1959 and 1968 (72.3% dissatisfied in 1959, 37.8% in 1968) and in the fact that dissatisfaction on at least three items was now slightly lower than the university average (items 3, 4, and 5). However, there were also large increases in some dissatisfactions (items 4, 5, 6, and 7). At best the picture was mixed, with general dissatisfaction still predominating. The extent of this continued discontent is vividly shown by the 1968 Survey, in which among all the schools the University College faculty was by far the most willing to leave NYU for jobs elsewhere (see Figure 6-2).

Norton Nelson, appointed the first provost in October 1966, proved to be an aggressive, vocal advocate for the Heights' campus. Pushed by his faculty, he proposed a series of changes designed to advance University College. First, he insisted that the all-university department system be completely eliminated or at least that University College be exempted from it—a move that would revitalize departmental power in the Bronx. Next, he proposed that the Heights expand its meager graduate offerings in order to recruit and hold better faculty and students. In effect, Provost Nelson wanted to establish greater autonomy for the Heights and to develop it into a miniature university in its own right—a "Brown in the Bronx," as he called it.

Figure 6-2. University College Faculty Report Highest Willingness to Leave NYU

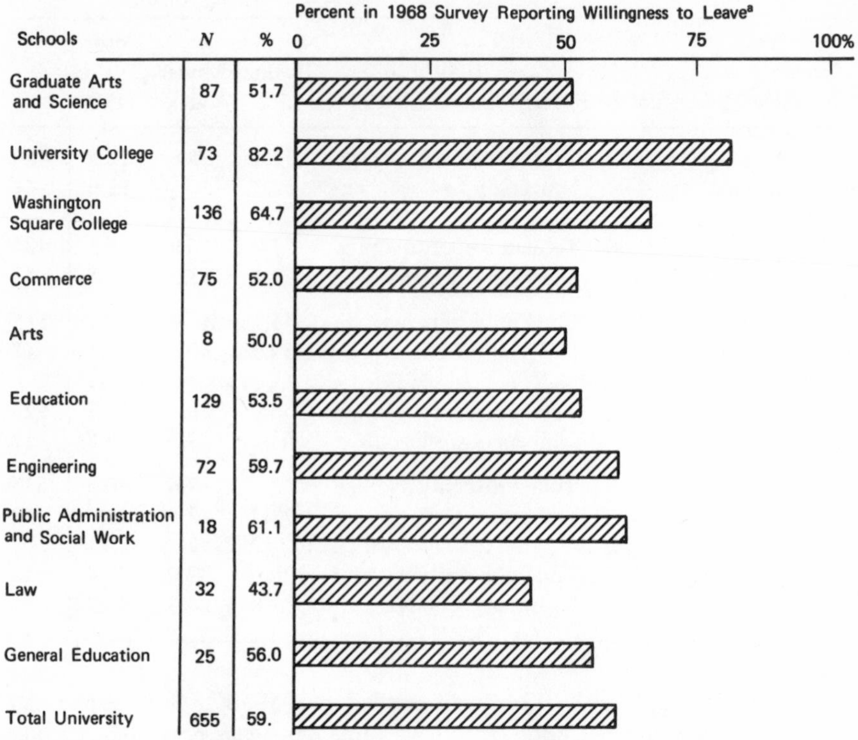

Schools	N	%	Percent in 1968 Survey Reporting Willingness to Leave[a]
Graduate Arts and Science	87	51.7	
University College	73	82.2	
Washington Square College	136	64.7	
Commerce	75	52.0	
Arts	8	50.0	
Education	129	53.5	
Engineering	72	59.7	
Public Administration and Social Work	18	61.1	
Law	32	43.7	
General Education	25	56.0	
Total University	655	59.	

[a]Question 4c of questionnaire

The central administration was somewhat taken back by the aggressiveness of its representative in the Heights. Almost immediately a series of high-level conferences was held in which Nelson advocated his plans. The trustees, the University Senate, and the Executive Group of the central administration were all involved to some extent. Although all sides deny that there were any personal clashes, it is nevertheless clear that sharp differences of policy existed about the future of the Heights. Finally, Provost Nelson concluded that he could not function in the context of the central administration's restrictions on the Heights' development and resigned in the spring of 1967. Meanwhile the University Senate passed a resolution that reaffirmed the university's determination to continue the all-university department system and to restrict the Heights' graduate program. This clash was over, but a continued review of the situation was ensured by the appointment of the 13-member Still Committee to reevaluate the issues.

THE CONFLICT CONTINUES: THE STILL COMMITTEE

The Still Committee reopened the Pandora's box of political struggles related to the all-university department system. The committee noted that tensions were once again building up in the system because of the structural arrangements. Now it was the department heads who were complaining of budgetary inflexibility because the deans controlled the budgets; now it was the department that was being shortchanged at the expense of the college; now it was the authority of the department head that was ambiguous. Continuing through all the conflict, of course, was the Heights' struggle for autonomy and self-identity.

The debates in the committee should not be surprising to anyone who has followed this issue to this point. The deans, happy with the present situation, proposed that it remain the same; the discontented department heads suggested that budgets go back to the departments (as the bylaws indicated); the Heights' representatives demanded more autonomy and a separate "geographic budget"; the central administration's representatives put forth a plan for a new dean of the arts and sciences, a move that might enhance the authority of the central administration. By this time it should not be surprising that these apparently innocent proposals for a bureaucratic restructuring were actually heavily overlaid with political implications.

After a year of deliberation the Still Committee weighed in with its recommendations. First, it suggested that the all-university department system should be extended to all units, including Commerce and Education. Second, it recommended that the deans and the heads should consult together on the budget and that neither should have absolute control. Third, it proposed that "geographic budgets" be set up. For each department nonfaculty budget items would be administered by the head at the Square, but by the chairman at the Heights, thus giving the Heights some measure of autonomy in nonfaculty budget matters. Finally, the committee suggested that a dean of the Arts and Sciences be established to supervise the work of the entire liberal arts system.

The amount of compromise and bargaining reflected in this report is remarkable. Although the committee tried to please all factions, the centralizing tendencies seem once again to be on the upsurge. The pendulum that swung to the deans in the last round of the conflict now seems to be swinging toward the central administration and department heads. The dean of Liberal Arts would be similar to the executive dean, thus superimposing a new central administration official over the deans. The "consultation" on the budget does not represent a clear victory for the heads, but it strengthens their hands considerably in their dealings with the deans. The concession to the Heights in the "geographical budget" for nonsalary items was more than off-balanced by the concessions to the heads centered at Washington Square. In addition, the imposition of the Liberal Arts dean over the University College dean would further limit the Heights' ability to develop a unique program. The centralization processes in this stage wiped out many of the decentralization features of the preceding stage.

Not surprisingly, groups that were disadvantaged by the committee report filed minority dissents. The dean of University College, Brooke Hindle, filed a short memorandum that summarizes most of the political elements that have been noted. It is interesting to examine this eminently political document[8]:

MEMORANDUM ON THE REPORT OF THE COMMITTEE TO REVIEW THE ALL-UNIVERSITY DEPARTMENT CONCEPT AND PROCEDURES

This Committee report represents an extended and very careful effort to come to grips with some of the most serious problems and opportunities in the University. I want here to present my reactions as a minority of one.

I participated in much of the discussion behind this report as a member of the Committee. I agreed to and accepted all of the preliminary guidelines adopted by the Committee which tend primarily to increase the authority of the heads of the departments. This is not the sort of structure I would seek and is counter to the initial proposals made by University College members of the Committee. Nevertheless, I agree that the clarification of roles might counter-balance the disadvantages it has for University College. . . .

My agreement with the guidelines had to be withdrawn when the Committee added the recommendation of a Dean of the Faculties of Arts and Science. I must now oppose the entire report.

The Committee's charge was related to the improvement of the relationships of University College. Indeed, I believe the formation of the Committee followed from certain discontents observed in University College. It is my feeling that the present recommendations prescribe further injury to University College and therefore march in exactly the opposite direction from that intended.

The combination of a tightened All-University Department structure with a Dean of Faculties erects a new umbrella for the Arts and Sciences at New York University. The existing framework of college deans and chairmen will continue to function, but it seems to me that it must fade into a secondary, mechanical, and increasingly irrelevant role.

For the schools at Washington Square this may be all to the good. It will strengthen the entire arts and science complex, improve coordination and relationships, and make standards more uniform. For the quality of arts

[8]Brooke Hindle, "Memorandum on the Report of the Committee To Review the All-University Department Concept and Procedures" (mimeographed April 25, 1968, New York University).

and science throughout the University, this new umbrella may also be beneficial.

For University College the results can only be unfortunate. The changes will increasingly remove the important decision-making machinery from the local scene and transfer it to heads sited at the Square and to a Dean of Faculties sited at the Square. University College must increasingly become an extension school. Academic quality and direction must increasingly be concentrated at the Square.

. . . .

The Committee proposals move toward centralization rather than toward autonomy—their direction is wrong by 180°. University Heights needs artificial defenses—especially University College. University College ought to be developed as a unit within the University, cooperating with the other units of the University, but not absorbed in a centralized structure in the way the Committee now proposes. . . .

Neither the University Senate, the central administration, nor the trustees have had time to act on the Still Committee's recommendations at this writing, but Professor Still offered his own assessment of the chances that they will be approved.[9]

I think the Senate will reject the proposals of the so-called Still Committee. The University College faculty has instructed its senators to oppose them. The provision for a Dean of Faculties, included at President Hester's suggestion, triggered opposition for a variety of reasons. It raised the issue of proliferation of administrative posts, which is something that always has led to protest from this faculty. It also was seen as a threat to local autonomy and to the independence of the local deans, to whom many of the younger faculty have their first loyalty. Once Dean Hindle has asserted that the Dean of Faculties principle threatened University College, local loyalty permitted no other stand but opposition; and of course some used this to express a traditional anti-administration stand. Not unrelated to the attitude toward the proposed Dean of Faculties, both inside and outside the comminttee, was the speculation as to who the Dean of Faculties, if approved, would be. Then, too, the fact that the Senate as a whole is deciding a question of concern only to the liberal arts wing means that the local-autonomy view will have added strength in the Senate decision. Perhaps the members of the Still Committee should have been more sensitive to political realities and should have seen that the Dean of Faculties, however logical and however attractive to the central administration, was not possible of realization at this time, given personal, geographical, and "political" factors in the University.

Regardless of whether the Still Committee's specific recommendations are accepted or rejected, it seems safe to say that the issue is far from

[9]Personal correspondence from Professor Bayrd Still, dated December 18, 1968.

resolved. If history speaks at all and if organization theory has taught us anything about the tensions within bureaucracies, the political conflict over this complicated issue will continue.

COMMENTS ON THE COORDINATION ISSUE

Several comments might be made to summarize the complex series of events surrounding the departmental reorganizations. First, the purpose of this chapter was to show that even behind the apparent routine of bureaucratic systems there is much strife and political action in the formulation of university policies. Student revolts, faculty upheavals, and investigations by government legislative committees may steal the headlines, but political processes occur throughout the campus. In this particular instance the departmental reorganization seems at first glance to have been a purely administrative decision, with few overtones of conflict or political maneuvering. On closer examination, however, it appears that the fortunes of many groups within the university were tied into this issue and there was a great deal of controversy. Many issues that seem "bureaucratic" on the surface have this undercurrent of political activity. Figure 6-3 summarizes the changes in the departmental system.

A second notable feature of this issue is the way many forms of influence were simultaneously interacting. We see bureaucratic decisions tempered by the action of interest groups, and personal influence penetrating both. Bureaucratic officials may appeal to their formal authority, but in the process they protect their interest group stances and they interject personality factors into the struggle. Many examples of that personal influence are at work: Henry Heald's original attempt to centralize, Russell Niles' introduction of the strong-dean concept, Brooks Hindle's plea for autonomy, Norton Nelson's struggle for the Heights ,and James M. Hester's drive for coordination. Each was a bureaucrat working for a given interest group goal while simultaneously infusing personal factors into the process.

Third, a fascinating feature of this issue is the "pendulum effect" that is evident in the long-term processes. Before the early 1950's the university was fragmented and the deans held much of the power. Then there was a centralization process, and the rise of the all-university departments. In 1964 there was a shift back to the deans, and in 1968 the Still Committe recommended more power for the heads and more centralization. The system had a remarkable tendency to solve one set of problems only to generate another; to give advantages to one interest group, but to disadvantage another; to eliminate one structural strain, but to create another. The political processes seem to be self-generating, and there is a constant feedback as the resolution

Figure 6-3. Summary Chart: Coordination of the Departmental Structure

Issue	Phase I Pre-1950's	Phase II NYU Self-Study 1956–1963	Phase III 1964–1968	Phase IV Still Committee's Recommendation 1968–1969
Amount of coordination of undergraduate studies	Extremely low coordination: five separate programs	Moderate: three schools united in coordinated liberal studies program (CLS)-1963	Moderate: CLS continues	Very high coordination: extend CLS to all five undergraduate units
Central administration's influence	Low	Moderately high	High	High (new Dean of Liberal Arts proposed)
Deans' influence	Very high	Lower (Executive Dean 1960)	High	Lower
Unified department head's influence	Heads nonexistent; five separate department chairmen; relatively weak influence	Heads' influence high over three schools	Lower	High: to be extended to all five units
Budget control	Located primarily with deans; pay-as-you-go system for schools	Located with heads; pay-as-you-go system abandoned	Located with deans	Compromise: deans and head "consult" and geographic budgets allow some freedom for schools

Figure 6-3. (Continued)

Issue	Phase I Pre-1950's	Phase II NYU Self-Study 1956–1963	Phase III 1964–1968	Phase IV Still Committee's Recommendation 1968–1969
Height's (University College) position in university	Very strong influence and prestige; high faculty satisfaction	Losing influence and prestige; hurt by department head system and CLS	Somewhat stronger position with strong dean and provost for Heights	Loss of influence; rise of Washington Square College threatens prestige
Strength of this mode of organization	1. Unique programs developed for schools	1. Great flexibility to develop departmental programs 2. More coordination of effort; less fragmentation and duplication	1. Great flexibility to develop school programs 2. More university-wide direction	(Not implemented)
Problems generated at this stage	1. Wide variations among schools in quality and salaries 2. Budget system hurts liberal arts units 3. Waste of resources; unnecessary duplication	1. Too much "vertical specialization of students in departments; no general "horizontal" liberal arts programs 2. Height's campus hurt	1. No flexibility of department budget	(Not implemented)

of old conflicts creates new ones. Centralization rules now, but decentralization takes over tomorrow.

Fourth, the all-university department system is only one facet of a complex centralization and decentralization process. It is important to realize that these centralizing dynamics could be studied relative to other issues and then the political dynamics would be different. In other words, centralization is not one process but many and it is related to specific issues and definite "spheres of influence." For example, the budgetary power and student discipline may be centralizing, with the central administration or the University Senate wresting authority away from the schools. But at the same time the decentralizing forces may be at work in other areas, for admissions policies and curriculum development may be decentralized to the departments. Thus it is no paradox to say that centralization and decentralization may be happening simultaneously, each with respect to a different issue. The departmental faculty may gain control over many new areas while the central administration is making inroads on others. There is no reason to assume that one group's gain is another's loss if the processes are occurring in different areas and if they are not directly competing.

Finally, in this series of events there was the crisscrossing of various authority levels as they struggled for influence. The deans were trapped between the departments and the central administration. The department heads were aligning with the central administration in an attempt to carve out jurisdictions *vis-a-vis* the deans. The central administration was trying to coordinate the far-flung system and in the process had to fight the traditional autonomy of the deans and strengthen the department heads. Cutting across all this was the tricky issue of the Heights' autonomy and its graduate program. What might help the heads at Washington Square might also disadvantage the chairman at the Heights. In effect, the deans and heads at Washington Square were split because they wanted one another's power, but they were united in an effort to held the Square's advantages. A similar process was going on at the Heights. To say the very least it was a complex, knotty issue with literally dozens of strands of political allegiences and conflict woven through it.

PART THREE

Elements in the Political Model

Introduction

To review for a moment, Part One of this book discussed the general problem of using models in the study of organizations, offered a review of several models previously used to analyze policy formultation in the university, and suggested the outline of a political interpretation. Part Two described a series of events on the NYU campus which illustrated three different types of organizational problem, but a common set of political processes cut across all three. Now Part Three draws on these events to expand on the political model. There are many dangling threads and isolated ideas that can be woven together in a more systematic presentation.

In the next three chapters we examine three parts of the political model in detail to show how conflict is handled by the political system. Focusing on the processes that lead up to policy, we look first at the social structure of the university (Chapter Seven), then later at interest articulation processes (Chapter Eight), and finally at the legislative phase (Chapter Nine).

Chapter VII

THE UNIVERSITY'S SOCIAL STRUCTURE

A political interpretation of policy formulation in the university begins with an analysis of the social framework within which the political dynamics occur. At this point the orientations of the political scientist and the sociologist cross once more, for an adequate conceptualization of university "politics" depends on an adequate grasp of the university's "social structure." Figure 7-1 shows how this chapter relates to the discussion of the whole political model.

One of the best words for describing NYU's social structure is "pluralistic." The university is fractured, divided, and complicated by interlaced networks of authority, status, professional outlook, and special interests. There are common values and concerns, of course, that hold the university together as a relatively cohesive enterprise, but this is indeed remarkable in light of the divisions and conflicts of interest that permeate the campus. Power is loose and ambiguous, in large measure because of the complex social framework: there is extreme specialization among the university's participants, extreme fragmentation of its values, and extreme complexity in its structural arrangements. Clark Kerr, former president of the University of California, commented that the university is more like the United Nations than a single unified country and this observation certainly applies to NYU.

Figure 7-1. Chapter VII Focuses on the Social Structure: External and Internal

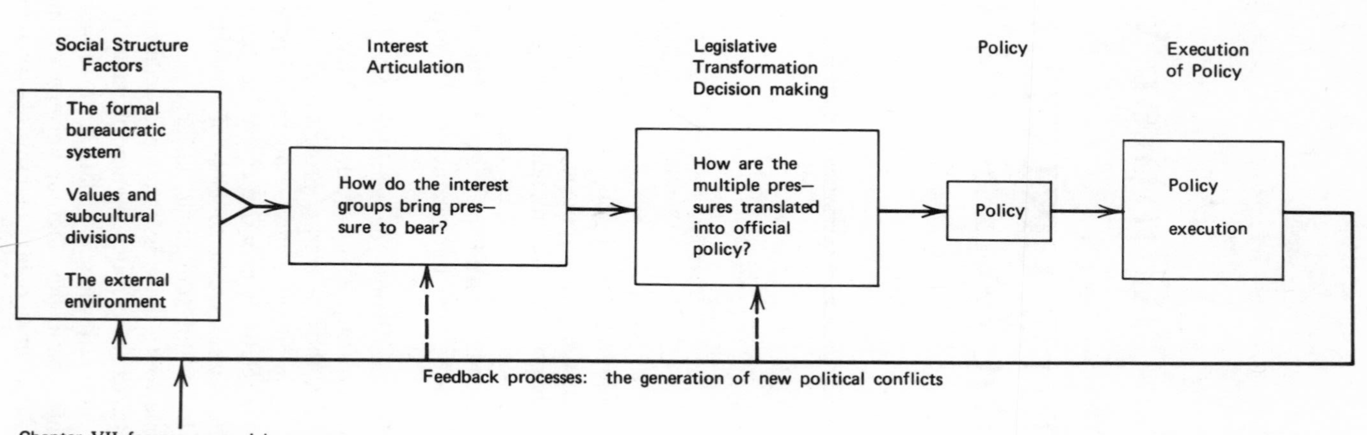

The "Multiversity" has

> . . . several nations of students, of faculty, of alumni, of trustees, of public groups. Each has its territory, its jurisdiction, its form of government. Each can declare war on the others; some have the power to veto. Each can settle its own problems by majority vote, but altogether they form no single constituency. It is a pluralistic society with multiple sub-cultures. Coexistence is more likely than unity. . . .[1]

Rather than a wholistic enterprise, the university is a pluralistic system, often fractured by conflicts along lines of disciplines, faculty subgroups, student subcultures, splits between administrators and faculties, and rifts between professional schools. The academic kingdom is torn apart in many ways, and there are few kings in the system who can enforce cooperation and unity. There is little peace in academia; warfare is common and no less deadly because it is polite. *The critical point is this: because the social structure of the university is loose, ambiguous, shifting, and poorly defined, the power structure of the university is also loose, ambiguous, shifting, and poorly defined.*

There are several ways in which NYU's social structure could be examined, but for convenience this discussion is broken into three parts. First, the complexity of the formal bureaucratic structure is examined. Second, the multiple value systems of the university must be charted, along with the various student, faculty, and administrative subcultures that cluster around those values. Third, the relation of the internal structure to the external environment is discussed.

ELEMENT ONE IN THE UNIVERSITY'S SOCIAL STRUCTURE: THE COMPLEX FORMAL STRUCTURE

The formal bureaucratic structure of New York University is a bewildering collection of colleges, schools, institutes, and departments. There are 15 major schools or colleges, each with some degree of autonomy and independence. Fracturing the university further are dozens of departments and research institutes. To complicate matters even more, the "all-university department system" combines the departments of University College, Washington Square College, and the Graduate School. The heads of these super-departments, in effect, become minor deans in their own rights, further complicating the formal network. Over this complex structure the central

[1]Clark Kerr, *The Uses of the University*. Cambridge: Harvard University Press, 1963, p. 36.

administration tries with varying degrees of success to impose some order and coordination on the whole system. Around the central administration is a cluster of advisory boards, faculty bodies, and even a separate board of trustees for the medical center. At the top of this structure is the university's board of trustees.

One of the easiest ways to get at least a superficial grasp of NYU's formal system is to consult the organization charts. The complexity of the system is readily apparent in the fact that it takes not one but three organization charts to describe it. Even then the charts list only the schools and colleges, omitting completely the array of departments and research institutes. Figure 7-2 shows the academic organization, Figure 7-3 shows the administrative organization, and Figure 7-4 shows the policy determination and communication network.

The Complexity of the Formal Bureaucratic Structure: Some Consequences for the Political Processes

The political processes occur within this complex organizational framework, a network of official structures that provides avenues for channeling conflict, resolving disputes, formulating policy, and executing decisions. The shape of the political dynamics is greatly influenced by the shape of the formal bureaucracy.

First, there is an *insulating and segregating phenomenon*, for the different parts of the system are often protected from direct conflict because they are not concerned with the same issues. To use the sociological jargon, a highly differentiated system may have low degrees of conflict because the various units are highly independent and highly insulated from one another. The department has one set of interactions, the college or school another, the entire university another. It confuses the issue to talk as if all these levels were competing directly for the same types of influence or for control of the same issues. Ordinarily this is simply not so, for each level is charged with different responsibilities and different "spheres of influence." Figure 7-5 is a crude outline of the responsibilities of the various levels within the formal structure. Structural complexity alone is not enough to generate conflict and political competition if there is a high degree of insulation between the concerns of the various units.

The various parts of the system are never completely segregated, however, and a second consequence of the complex system is the generation of conflict when the units compete directly. Sometimes the division of responsibilities causes political fights over competing claims for authority. Often there are power struggles between levels in the system, for each level has its jealous individuals and groups trying to maximize their political influence

Figure 7-2. New York University Academic Organization

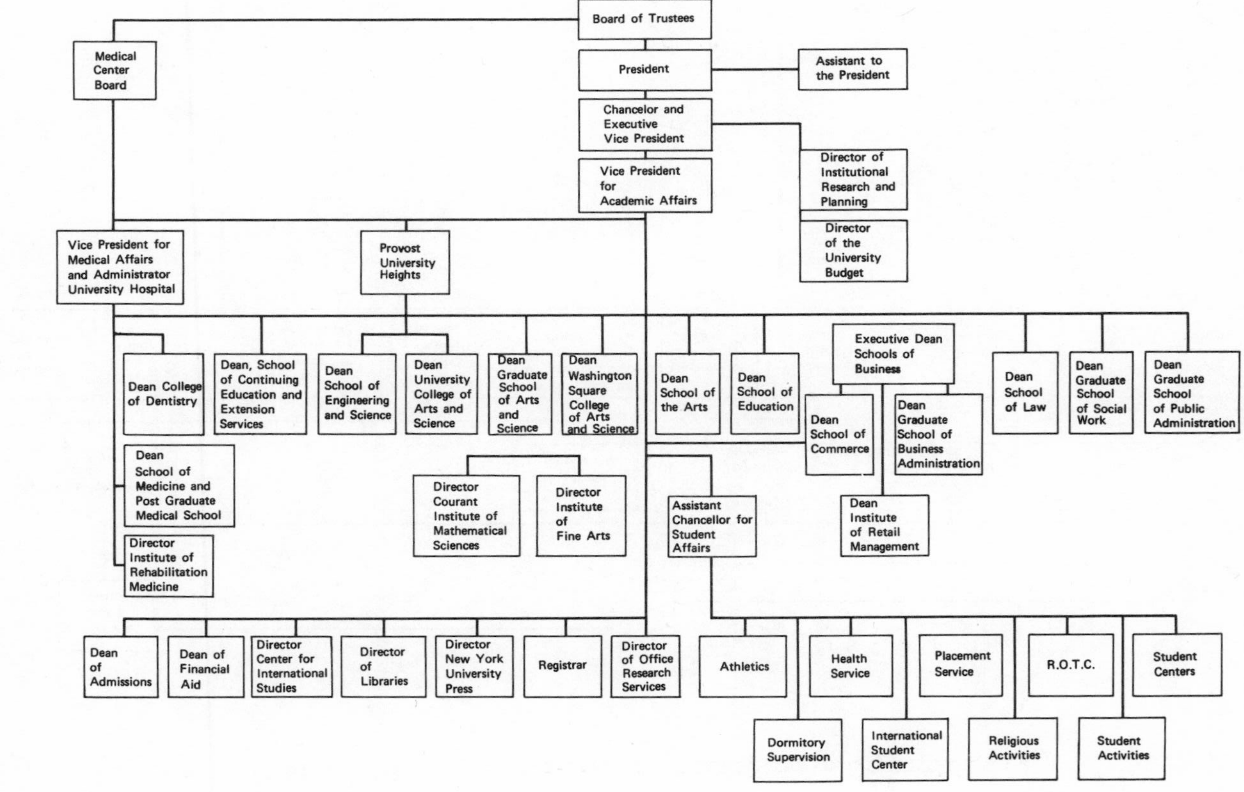

Figure 7-3. New York University Administrative Organization

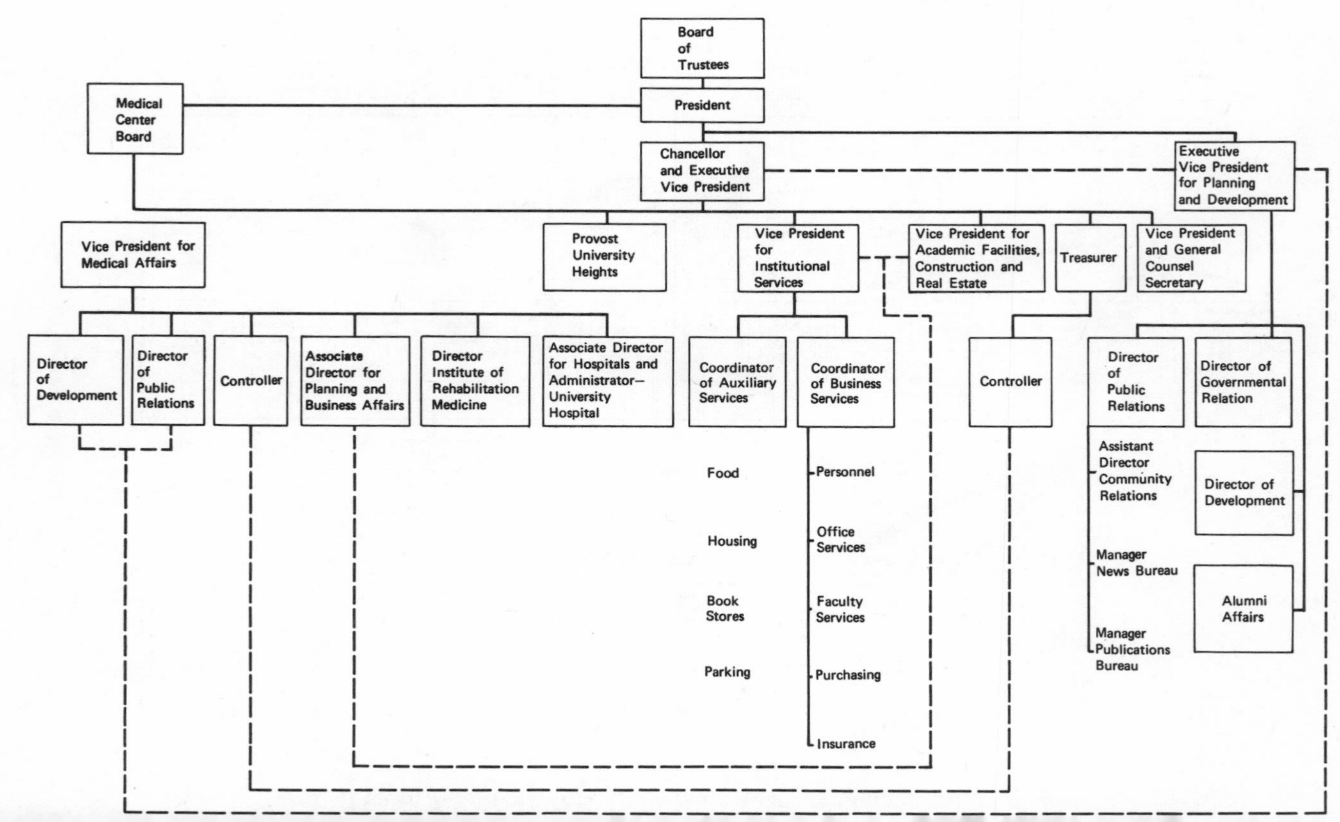

Figure 7-4. New York University Policy Determination and Communication

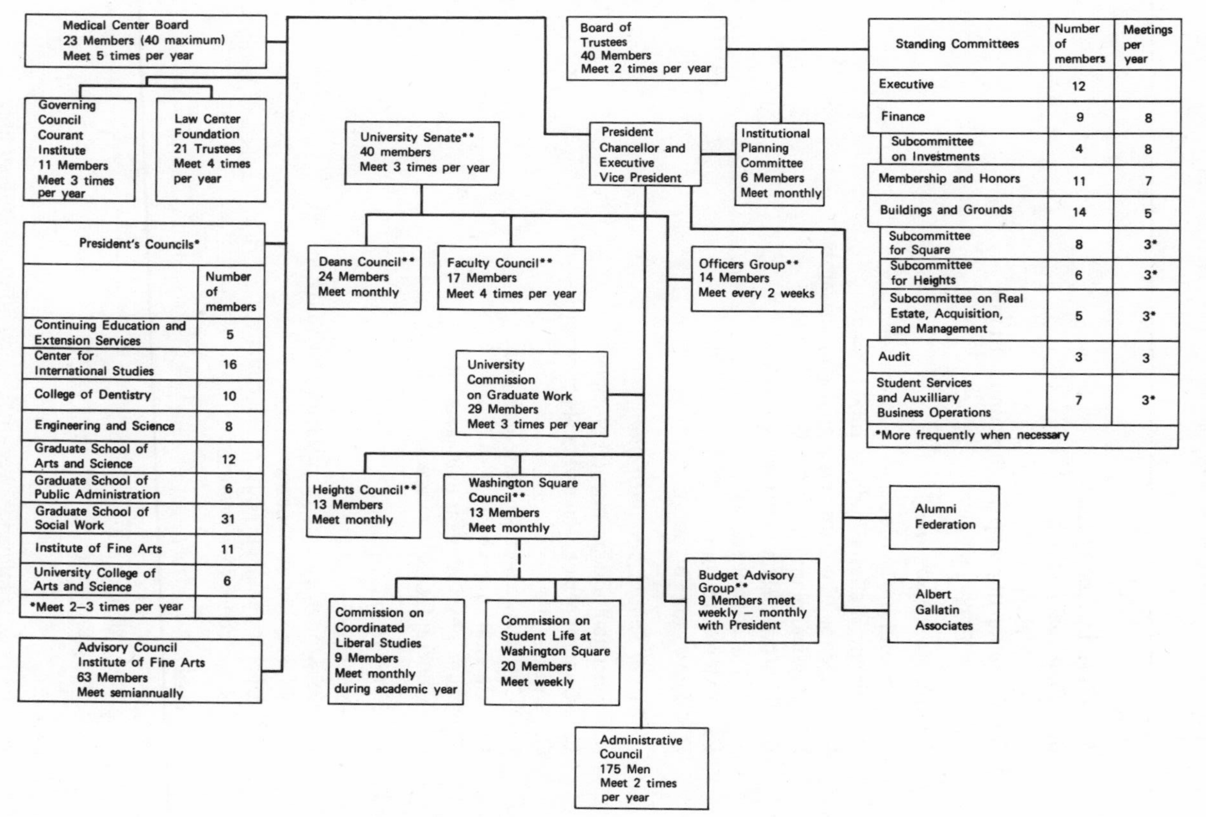

Figure 7-5. Levels of Bureaucratic Authority: Areas of Responsibility for Each Level

I. *Trustees*
   A. General supervision
   B. Financial backing
   C. Physical plant
   D. Selection of president, top administrators
   E. Long-range planning

II. *Central Administration*
   A. General supervision and coordination
   B. Financial affairs, budgets, fund raising
   C. Selection of college and school administrators
   D. Physical plant
   E. Uniform salary systems
   F. Nonacademic services
   G. External relations
   H. Long-range planning

III. *College or School Administration*
   A. Selection of departmental officials
   B. General orientation and goals of college
   C. Admissions
   D. Curriculum and degree requirements
   E. General supervision of students
   F. Some physical plant management
   G. General faculty welfare

IV. *Department and Institutes*
   A. Selection of faculty
   B. Promotion and tenure of faculty (with III above)
   C. Supervision of students
   D. Departmental curriculum and courses
   E. Some control over research

V. *Individual Professors*
   A. Teaching
   B. Research and scholarly work
   C. Student counseling and supervision

VI. *Students*
   A. Increasing influence over student activities and student life
   B. Increasing influence of policy formulation affecting curriculum and instruction.

in relation to others. When one group encroaches on another's traditional area of responsibility, the insulation between units breaks down and direct competition results.

A number of instances in the NYU study indicated how conflict is generated when the insulation between structural units breaks down and they begin challenging one another's traditional domains of influence. For example, the centralization of admissions policies that accompanied the upgrading of student quality provoked a great deal of controversy, for this had traditionally been the responsibility of the individual schools and colleges. In the department reorganization the move to give budgetary power provoked conflict, for this had always been the domain of the deans. In another case, when the students demanded control of disciplinary procedures and recruitment policies, this generated strife, for the administration's authority was challenged. Thus power struggles between levels can play a major part in university governance when the spheres of influence of the various groups are challenged. Then the "bureaucratic" structure becomes more of a "political" system; the cleavages between structural units become battle lines.

A third consequence of the university's multilayered bureaucracy is the development of "role conflicts." There are many sociological descriptions of the problems of persons who are oriented to several different roles at once. Robert Merton called them the "role-set" problems, for every individual stands at the intersection of a whole set of roles that may have contradictory expectations.[2] In industrial organizations the foreman is often singled out for special study, for he stands at the intersection of multiple expectations—he is "labor's man" in his relation to the workers, but he is "management's man" in his relation to management.

In the university we find this same conflict of expectations. The dean is caught between the expectations of the central administration and the local departments; the department head is caught between the dean and professors in the department; the central administration jockeys among the various schools; the individual professor struggles between the expectations of the university on one hand and his students on the other. There is great role strain in the university, for each level exerts strong—and often contradictory—pressures on the role occupants. The dean is often described as the "man in the middle," but it seems more accurate to say that literally dozens of "men in the middle" are scattered throughout the formal system. George Pollach, former vice president of NYU, called this the "sandwich theory" of administration because the behavior of individuals is often related to the levels between which they are sandwiched. The clearest example of role strain in this research was the position of Height's Provost Nelson. He was

[2] Robert Merton, "The Role-Set," *British Journal of Sociology*, Vol. 8, 106–120 (1957).

caught in a bind between his faculty's pressure for more graduate work and the elimination of the all-university departments and the central administration's demand for centralized graduate work at the Square and the continuation of the all-university system. Nelson finally concluded that he could not work effectively in such cross fire.

Parallel Authority and "Representative Government" for the Faculty

The university's bureaucracy is not only multilayered but characterized by complicated parallel authority structures. At least two authority systems seem to be built into the university's formal structure. One is the *bureaucratic* network, with formal chains of command running from the trustees down to individual faculty members and students. Many critical decisions are made by bureaucratic officials who claim and exercise authority over given areas. As long as they go unchallenged they are free to exercise their authority. This is more often true in the relatively "routine" types of administration than in the "critical" areas; for example, a bureaucrat might act on his own authority in routine admissions processing, but in the critical area of changing the admissions standards he would hesitate to act without consulting the faculty.

The other authority system is a *professional* network, for at all levels there are formal mechanisms for bringing the expertise of the faculty into the decision-making process. It is fascinating to note how this parallelism is built right into the formal structure of the university. NYU's organization charts clearly show this; Figure 7-3 outlines the bureaucratic authority structure, whereas Figures 7-2 and 7-4 show some of the parallel faculty influences. The tangled system of committees, faculty meetings, and faculty councils, which is only hinted at in the organization charts, is really not just "bureaucratic madness." On the contrary, if it is madness at all, it is "professional madness." The parallelism between the bureaucratic and professional authority structures ensures that professional goals will have strong advocates in the decision-making councils. Duality of authority and ambiguity of power are the price of ensuring that faculty expertise will have its say.

The parallelism of the authority structure is matched by the growth of "representative government" for the faculty. The "federal university" is simply too big to manage as a pure democracy. In a faculty numbering 5500 the democratic processes tend to break down into indirect representation by committees, councils, and the University Senate. These groups exercise professional wisdom for the entire faculty. The individual faculty member in a huge university such as NYU tends to become apathetic and is quite willing to turn his influence over to representatives who supposedly express his will.

The NYU research often showed the interaction of the parallel authority structures. Probably the best illustration is the restructuring of the University Senate in light of the Taggart Commission's report. The Taggart Commission recommended that the Senate have more power over such matters as budgets and long-range planning. Thus in essence it argued that the faculty half of the parallel system should penetrate the decision-making system more than in the past. The Commission also recommended that the Senate be more "representative," that the faculty have a larger voice, and that school delegations be proportionate to size. Thus the Taggart report was a clear demand for both more representativeness and more interpenetration of the parallel authority networks.

Another factor in the growth of parallel authority structures is the continued development of student influence on policy making. In the past, studies of academic governance have largely ignored the influence of students, but since the early 1960's this obviously is no longer possible. A discussion of the political dynamics of the university without the students as major political actors is simply not an adequate description. We have already noted how the student revolt at NYU resulted in two major policy reports, the McKay Committee report and the Griffith Committee report. Both committees recommended that students be included as a third party in the parallel influence structures, along with the faculty and administration. Many colleges and departments within NYU acted promptly to include students on admissions, curriculum, and teaching evaluation committees. Without a doubt the future will see students assuming a larger and larger role in the policy-forming councils of the university, and the dual parallelism that now exists between administration and faculty will be expanded to include students in significant ways.

Bureaucratic Structure and the Resolution of Conflict

How does an analysis conflict and political processes tie in with the formal bureaucratic system? Much of the university's conflict is channeled through formal structures which provide a mechanism for the adjudication and resolution of conflicts. We have already noted that many conflicts arise out of the competition between structural levels and officials charged with different tasks. In this sense the bureaucratic system is the *generator* of conflict. In another sense, however, the structural arrangements and legitimate procedures provide the paths for conflict *resolution.* Bureaucratic systems are usually thought of merely as coordination mechanisms and their political, conflict-resolving functions are ordinarily overlooked. If we adopt a political approach, we can immediately see that one of the prime functions of the formal system is the resolution of conflict—the transformation of hot political fights into cool bureaucratic routines.

Some concrete examples from the NYU research may help to clarify this point. In Chapter IV it was noted that the Coordinated Liberal Studies Program consolidated the first two years of undergraduate work at Washington Square College, Commerce, and Education. At first many people hotly opposed the idea and it became a "political" issue at that point. However, once the political conflict was resolved by formal decision processes and the program finally initiated, the conflict died down and was "routinized." A flaring political issue became a bureaucratic chore.

The same thing happened in connection with the student revolts, with the riots at the bookstore finally resulting in bureaucratic committees' making their recommendations. The all-university department issue was another event that showed how the complexity of the formal structure itself was a critical conflict generator. Moreover, that conflict was channeled, debated, and resolved by the same formal system.

Thus, in addition to the traditional interpretation of bureaucracy as a mechanism of coordination, we must add an interpretation of bureaucracy as a mechanism for generating, channeling, and resolving conflict. Resolved conflict, in turn, becomes routine in the process we call the "bureaucratization of conflict." Behind the apparent monotony of most bureaucratic systems is a story of strife. The "political" issues are transformed into "bureaucratic" issues and vice versa. The relationship between the two is closer than we may have suspected, for the fragmented bureaucracy provides both the tensions that cause conflict and the mechanism that try to cope with it.

Incidentally, an interesting commentary on the relation between conflict and bureaucratic mechanism was made by the Cox Commission which studied the turmoil at Columbia in the spring of 1968. Apparently many people among the student revolutionaries, the press, and the faculty had argued that Columbia's decision-making system was *overbureaucratized* and that this complexity had led to tensions and finally to revolt. The Cox Commission, however, rendered a different verdict.[3] It argued, in essence, that Columbia's troubles resulted in part because there were neither enough bureaucratic mechanisms for coordinating the complex system nor enough established procedures for dealing with contested issues. Instead of established lines of communication and a stable policy-making mechanism, there was a hit-and-miss form of "situational improvisation" that led to confusion.

[3] Cox Commission, *Crisis at Columbia: Report of the Cox Commission*. New York: Columbia University Press, 1968. pp. 193 ff.

Figure 7-6. Element Number One in the Social Structure of the University: The Formal Bureaucratic System

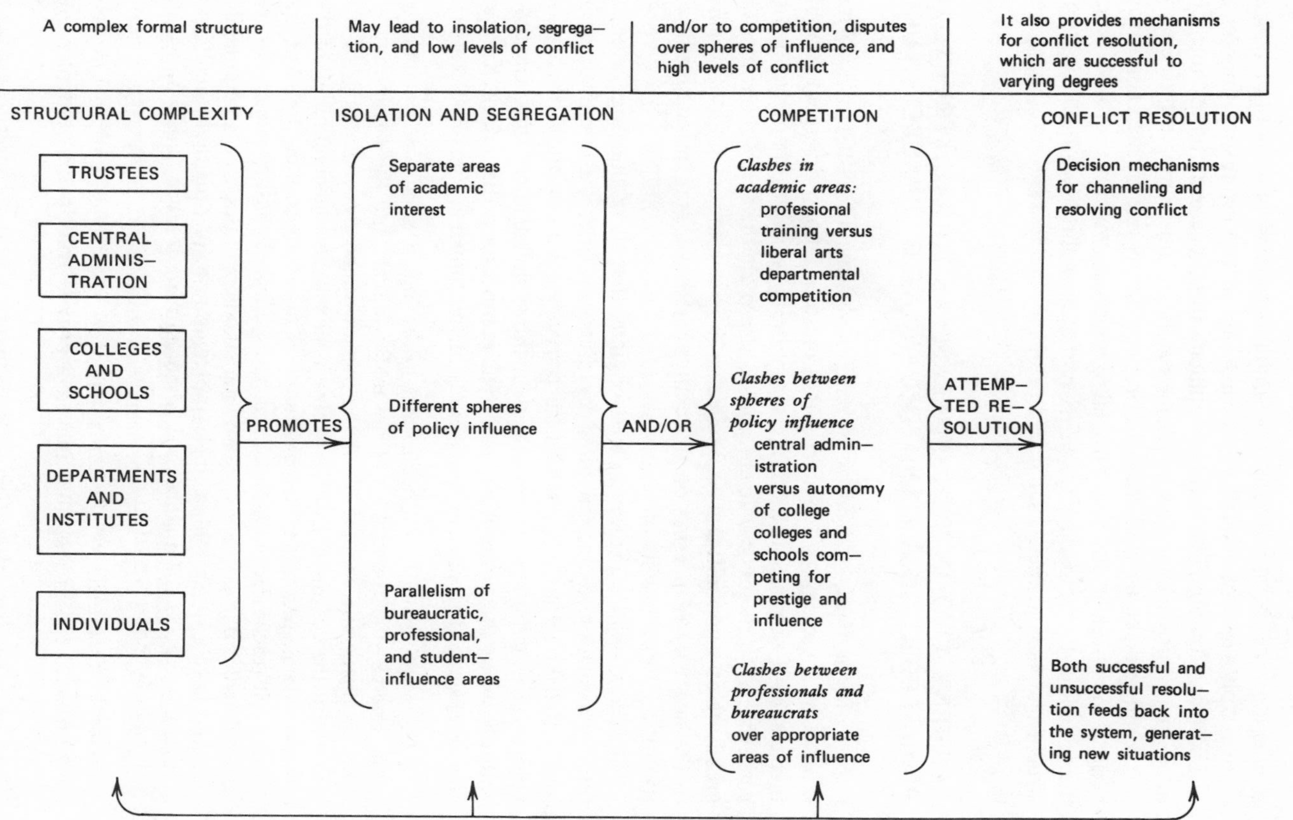

In effect, one of the major causes of conflict was *underbureaucratization*, for there simply was not enough structure to aid in conflict resolution.

The Cox Commission's analysis appears to be perfectly reasonable if we think of the provision of mechanisms for balancing competing claims, for adjudicating disputes, and for resolving conflict as one of the critical functions of the bureaucratic structure, all of which fits well into our understanding of political processes. Figure 7-6 summarizes this section on the formal structure's place in the social structure of the university.

ELEMENT TWO IN THE UNIVERSITY'S SOCIAL STRUCTURE: PLURALISTIC GOALS AND THE GROWTH OF SUBCULTURES

Not only is NYU pluralistic in its formal structure, but it is also fragmented by a system of subcultures that clusters around divergent goals. At first glance it seems that there are many unifying values that bind the university's staff into a wholistic enterprise. These are the academic values on a grand scale: a commitment to intellectual honesty, to the value of research, to the necessity of passing on the cultural heritage, and to humanistic and scientific interpretations of reality.

At second glance, however, it is obvious that these unifying values are often overshadowed and engulfed by divergent interests that fracture the intellectual kingdom into tiny feudal provinces. Values unify when people hold them in common; values fragment the social structure into small subcultures when there are many different competing goals. Clark Kerr succinctly described the many subcultures of the university in these words.

> The Multiversity is an inconsistent institution. It is not one community but several—the community of the undergraduate and the community of the graduate; the community of the humanist, and the community of the scientist; the community of the professional schools; the community of the non-academic personnel; the community of the administration. Its edges are fuzzy—it reaches out to alumni, legislators, farmers, businessmen, who are all related to one or more of these internal communities. . . . A community should have a single soul, a single animating principle; the multiversity has several—some of them quite good, although there is much debate on which should really deserve salvation.[4]

Several subcultures of the university were mentioned earlier. Of special concern were the groups that played a critical role in the student revolt.[5]

[4] Clark Kerr. *The Uses of the University*. Cambridge: Harvard University Press, 1963, p. 19.

[5] See Chapter V.

However, since they were discussed earlier, this section concentrates on faculty subcultures.

Multiple Goals and the Growth of Faculty Subcultures

Faculty subcultures tend to develop around particular values and goals: teaching and research, liberal arts orientations and occupational training, dedication to specialization or to general education, and interest in practical application of knowledge or pure research. Some data from the 1959 Faculty Senate Survey may suggest the complexity of the goals that claim the faculty's allegiance. Figure 7-7 shows how the faculty ranked several goals for the university in terms of their relative importance. The relative rankings are interesting in themselves, but it is also interesting to note that all the goals were ranked fairly high by the faculty, indicating that many different types of goal were seen as legitimate. It might be helpful now to examine some of these diverse goals and the faculty subcultures that grow up around them.

First, it is commonplace to note the spit between *teaching and research*, for the university is committed not only to transmitting the accumulated

Figure 7-7. Faculty's Ranking of Importance of Various University Goals[a] (from 1959 Faculty Senate Survey)

Activities	Mean Average on Nine-Point Scale
1. The teaching of graduate students	8.3
2. The teaching of undergraduates	8.1
3. Advancement of knowledge by research	8.0
4. Maintenance of conditions in this university that are attractive to excellent scholars	8.0
5. Enhancement of the reputation of this university as a center of higher learning	7.8
6. Maintenance of a scholarly atmosphere within this university	7.6
7. Preservation of the cultural heritage	6.8
8. Application of knowledge to life situations	6.0
9. Solution of problems of great national and international concern	5.6
	$N = 569$

[a] The faculty was asked to rate each item *separately*, to indicate on a nine-point scale how important it should be as a goal of the university. They were not asked to rank the nine items against one another. Thus the ranking above is a composite; the average score for each item is combined into a relative ranking for all nine items.

wisdom of the ages but also to the creation of new knowledge. Yet the situation is much more complicated, for within the teaching and research roles there are additional subgoals. Teaching enterprises come in a bewildering array: for undergraduates or graduates, in a professional school or in a liberal arts unit, for full-time students or for noncredit adult education courses. The research goal is no less complex, whether it be research in medieval literature, heart surgery, the psychology of dreams, or the social deprivation of children. Of course, in a major institution like NYU the line between teaching and research is never clear because most faculty members do both, but there are relative differences that persistently influence the outlooks and motivations of people.

Another deep chasm that separates people in the university is the rift between *pure* and *applied* orientations. Much strife and competition occurs along this line, which cuts through both research and teaching. The chemist in his laboratory doing pure research may feel little kinship with the chemist doing air pollution studies. The psychologist teaching graduate students may sharply disagree with the psychologist in the School of Education who is applying the research to socially deprived children. The professor of anatomy may have little interest in the problems of sick patients, whereas the practical M.D. may not care to study the theoretical aspects of his role.

The distinction often breaks along the lines of schools within the university, although this does not always hold true. Some schools are obviously more dedicated to practical application (e.g., Commerce); others are more oriented to pure research (e.g., The Graduate School). Of course, within each school there are variations, but Figure 7-8 lists statistics from both the 1959 Faculty Senate Survey and the 1968 survey that show how sharply the break occurs along school lines.

A third factor that promotes the growth of faculty subcultures is intense *disciplinary specialization*. In the modern university Academic Man is the Expert Man, the Specialized Man. The social scientist is more concretely a sociologist; the sociologist is more realistically a specialist concerned about complex organizations and in particular about academic organizations. Gaul was divided into three parts; the university looks more like a puzzle. Specializations are piled on top of specializations and the lines of connection between them grow ever more tenuous. This is a complex society and the "generalist" who knows a little about everything is increasingly becoming the Obsolete Man. Complex problems require concentrated attention, expensive investments, and detailed study. Only the specialist can tackle these complex issues with anything more than dilettantism. To be the generalist is to be superficial; to be the specialist is to be the expert, the man-in-the-know.

But specialization, necessary as it is, fractures the campus. Only a moment's reflection will reveal a whole cluster of barriers that result from

Figure 7-8. Undergraduate Curriculum: Liberal Arts or Occupational Training?

	Percent Reporting High on Liberal Arts in 1968 Survey (0–80)	Those Reporting Occupation Medium %	Those Reporting Occupation Oriented %	Totals %	Totals *N*
All combined	51.8	38.3	9.9	100	656
Graduate School	58.6	33.3	8.0	100	87
University College	62.1	28.4	9.5	100	74
Washington Square College	70.6	22.8	6.6	100	136
Commerce and GSB	47.4	44.7	7.8	100	76
Education	38.3	54.7	7.1	100	128
Arts	57.1	42.9	0.0	100	7
Engineering Applied Science	8.1	55.4	36.5	100	74
Public Administration and Social Work	66.7	33.3	0.0	100	18
Law	75.0	25.0	0.0	100	32
General Education	66.7	0.0	100	33.3	24

specialization. Language barriers develop because of esoteric use of words. Sources of income are different; some professors are highly dependent on the university, whereas others have independent sources from consultant fees and clinical practice. Styles of research vary from the loner in the laboratory to the research team working on a multimillion dollar project. Career styles differ from the single-minded teacher to the consultant to the clinical worker. Prestige factors vary by fields, with publication as the most salient prestige item for some, consulting for others, teaching for others, and public service for others. Intense specialization, then, is one of the fragmenting forces that is splitting NYU's social structure.

Other factors promote the growth of faculty subcultures. Alvin Gouldner, for example, suggests a sharp cleavage in the faculty between the *cosmopolitans* (who identify with external reference groups in the discipline rather than with local groups in the university, have low institutional loyalty, and are committed to specialized knowledge) and the *locals* (who have opposite orientations.)[6] Burton R. Clark proposes that the faculty can be divided

[6]Alvin Gouldner, "Cosmopolitans and Locals: Toward an Analysis of Latent Social Roles," *Administrative Science Quarterly*, Vol. 2, 281–306, 444–480 (1957–1958).

into four subgroups: the *teachers* (who identify with the college and are committed to pure research), the *scholar-researchers* (who do not identify closely with the college but are committed to pure research), the *demonstrators* (who identify closely with the college and are committed to applied research), and the *consultants* (who do not identify with the college and are committed to applied research).[7] The typologies of both Gouldner and Clark offer additional clues to the nature of academic subcultures. NYU's faculty is certainly fractured by many of these factors.

Subcultures and Political Processes in the University

This discussion of the various subcultures has of necessity been quite superficial, for such a complex topic could easily be a major research project in itself. Moreover, the description of the various subcultures is really not the critical point of the discussion. Instead, the primary concern is with the influence that these divergent groups have on the policy-making processes of the university. The important fact for this particular research is that fragmentation into multiple subcultures makes the governance of the university difficult and complicated. In a sense it is helpful to think of the various subgroups as political "parties," each with its own special orientations, values, and goals. Many of the critical problems of governance are related precisely to the conflicting demands made by these groups. Because of this fragmentation university governance often becomes negotiation; strategy becomes a process of jockeying between pressure groups; "administration" ever more becomes "politics."

Of course, the division of the university into different subcultures is not in itself enough to ensure conflict and political activity. It was noted earlier that the complexity of the formal structure promoted both insolation and segregation (leading to low competition and conflict) and competition between units (leading to high conflict). The same dynamics hold for the subcultural fragmentation, for different subcultures often do not conflict because they simply are not concerned with the same issues. On the other hand, they may clash when they try to redefine areas of concern and influence or when they compete over scarce resources. This was often the case in the three episodes analyzed in Part Two.

Chapter IV, for example, analyzed the conflict generated among the faculty subcultures as they fought over the changes in the university's ad-

[7] Burton R. Clark, "Faculty Culture," in *The Study of Campus Cultures*. Berkeley: Berkeley Center for the Study of Higher Education, 1962.

missions policies and academic standards.[8] Often the professionally oriented faculty demanded autonomy on admissions policies, whereas the liberal arts-oriented people pressed for uniform codes. Meanwhile the discipline-oriented "cosmopolitans" favored increased quality, but the internally oriented "locals" fought for the old "school of opportunity" philosophy. Finally, the research scholars pushed for disciplinary consolidation and the teachers pressured for school autonomy. Cutting across all this conflict was the division between the administration and faculty subcultures.

In Chapter V we saw how the changing student culture contributed to the rise of student activism. At one time the social structure was a vocationally oriented, nonresident student body with "segmentalized" involvement which contributed to the apathy that was so much a part of NYU's scene. However, this social context began to change: dormitories helped to promote an intensely involved resident student body, and higher academic standards tended to cut out many vocational students and encourage more militant nonconformist cultures. Changes in the social configuration of the student body thus played a critical role in the changing political scene.

In Chapter VI we reviewed the influence of various subcultures on departmental coordination problems. Many divisions separated the central administration from the faculty, the Bronx Heights campus from the Washington Square campus, and the deans from the department heads. These cleavages were related not only to the formal bureaucratic system but also to informal differences of life-style and value-orientations. Thus in each political struggle reviewed there was a clear relation between the faculty, student, and administrative subcultures and the political dynamics. These subcultures were one significant element in the social structure, along with the formal bureaucracy and various external factors. The next section moves on to those external factors.

ELEMENT THREE IN THE UNIVERSITY'S SOCIAL STRUCTURE: EXTERNAL SOCIAL PRESSURES AND INTERNAL ADAPTATIONS

Both the bureaucratic system and the subcultural network are elements in the *internal* social structure, but the university also has important relations to the *external* social setting. The university stands as one social insti-

[8] A work of caution: first, there is little "hard" data to support this subcultural alignment on the issues, but this is the impression of most observers at NYU. Second, we must allow for division *within* subcultures—they are not a unified mass and there might be serious splits. However, it does not seem profitable to go into these fine points of detail.

tution among others, and the complex interaction among all of them is a critical factor in academic governance. It is helpful to think in terms of various "publics" that bring pressure to bear on the university, that provide it with services and support, and that indirectly shape its destiny. As the university assumes a critical societal role these external influences encroach more and more into academic halls, always pushing and pulling the university toward some particular image.

Unfortunately, organization theorists have devoted little attention to the relations between organizations and there environments. However, there are several emerging ideas that can help us to understand the context of a university. Beginning within the university itself, we shall examine the various levels in it and how they relate to the environment. Then we shall turn to the "domain" that NYU claims; that is, its unique role among the educational institutions of New York. Finally, we shall discuss the inter-relations between NYU and the other organizations in its "task environment." The logic of presentation is that we begin inside the organization and gradually move out in concentric circles to larger and larger contexts. Figure 7-9 shows the whole picture, and it may be helpful to follow it as the coming sections are read.

Talcott Parson's "Organizational Levels"

Parsons[9] suggests there are three levels in every organization:

1. A "technical" level directly concerned with producing a product or acting on clients.
2. A "managerial" level that coordinates the activities of the technical groups.
3. An "institutional" level that links the organization to its environment by securing needed "inputs" and disposing of "outputs."

The institutional level tends to develop specialized groups of "boundary roles" in which the principal job is to link the university and the outside world. These groups include recruitment personnel, public relations men, alumni officers, managers of fund appeals, and government liaison officials—men who reach out to the world beyond the walls of the university. They are the gatekeepers of the academy. Some of them are particularly powerful, for it is politically significant that the outside world "plugs in" at some points rather than others.

[9]Talcott Parsons "General Theory in Sociology," in R. K. Merton et al. (Eds.), *Society Today*. New York: Basic Books, 1959, pp. 10–16. Also *Structures and Process in Modern Societies*. Glencoe, Illinois: Free Press, 1960, pp. 59–96.

Figure 7-9. Element Three in the University's Social Structure: The External Environment

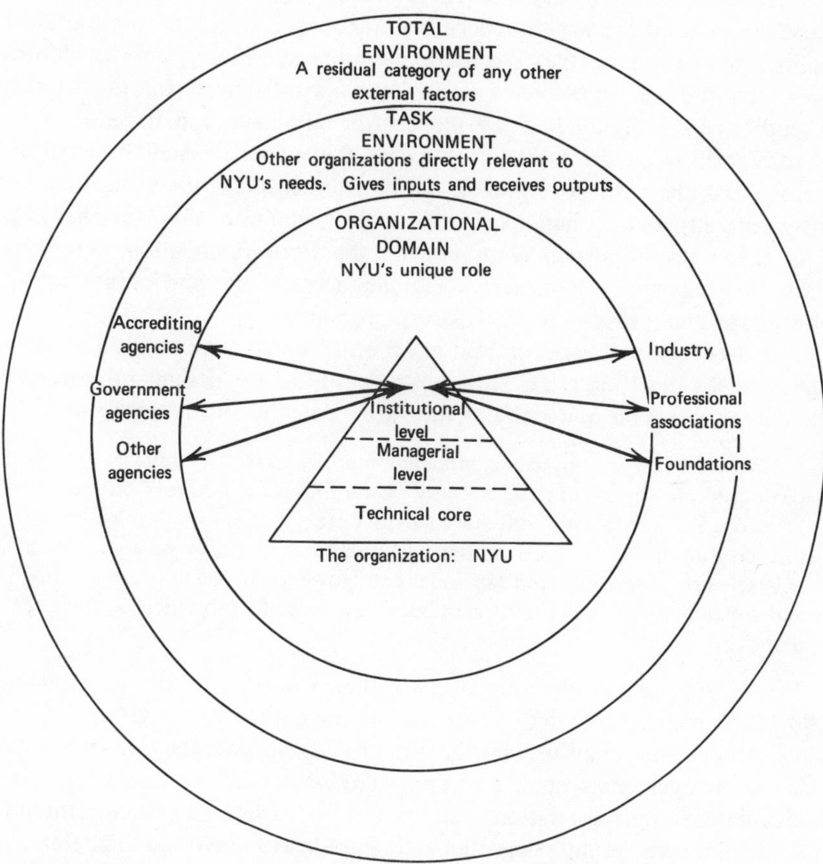

In addition to these clearly designated boundary roles, many other officials have jobs that are orientated heavily to outside factors. They are the key administrators, the men who occupy the "institutional" level positions in Parson's discussion—the trustees, the president, the chancellor, and the deans. These academic decision makers are threatened by literally hundreds of conflicting strains and pressures. The administration must always be like Janus, with one face pointed inward to internal processes but the other pointed outward to the external world. In a real sense the trustees and the administration are gatekeepers. They try to gain support from the outside world but at the same time fend off pressures to give the university enough autonomy to pursue its own destiny. This is a delicate task, and the administrator's nightmare often comes alive as a pressure group gains enough power to threaten the university's very integrity.

The modern university is increasingly dependent on its external environment, and one of the consequences is that the men who hold these critical institutional boundary roles are becoming more and more powerful. Moreover, centralization is encouraged by external influences, for the strands of authority are tightly held by the central administration because of its pivotal position on the boundary between the university and the environment. Relations with government agencies, other than direct negotiations for grants, are usually handled by the central administration; for example, it arranged the important contract with the Ford Foundation. Relations with alumni, potential benefactors, regional accrediting agencies, and a host of other outside groups are also its responsibility.

The exceptional degree of centralization in external relations is vividly illustrated by the 1968 NYU Survey. One question was designed to measure the degree to which university members appealed to outside groups.

> Have you ever attempted to influence internal university policies by appealing to *outside* groups? Check any of the following, and add others you have done. Include only activities which were specifically intended to influence some policy . . . (Example: If you appeared on TV to announce a new scientific discovery, *don't* include that. However, if you appeared on TV and suggested that NYU must raise salaries or lose faculty, then *do* include that.)

Figure 7-10 shows that the overwhelming majority of the respondents (90.1%) reported they had never tried to appeal to outside groups of any kind. Among the minority who did report such appeals the administration was heavily overrepresented. Two things are made clear: there is a high centralization of external-relations activities among a few people, and the administration is the group proportionately most heavily involved. The relation between the university and its environment is a critical factor in the increasing importance of the officials who hold institutional boundary roles.

The Domain of the University[10]

Turning from the internal roles that link the university and its environment, we encounter the "domain," which is the role that the university

[10]Many ideas in this and the next section come from James D. Thompson *Organizations in Action*. New York: McGraw-Hill, 1967. Thompson, in turn, was building on the work of Sol Levine and Paul E. White, "Exchange as a Conceptual Framework for the Study of Interorganization Relationships," *Administrative Science Quarterly*, Vol. 5, 583–601 (1961), and William Dill, "Environment as an Influence on Managerial Autonomy," *Administrative Science Quarterly*, Vol. 2, 409–443 (1958).

Figure 7-10. Relations to the Outside: Comparison of the Whole Sample to Those Who Report External Influence

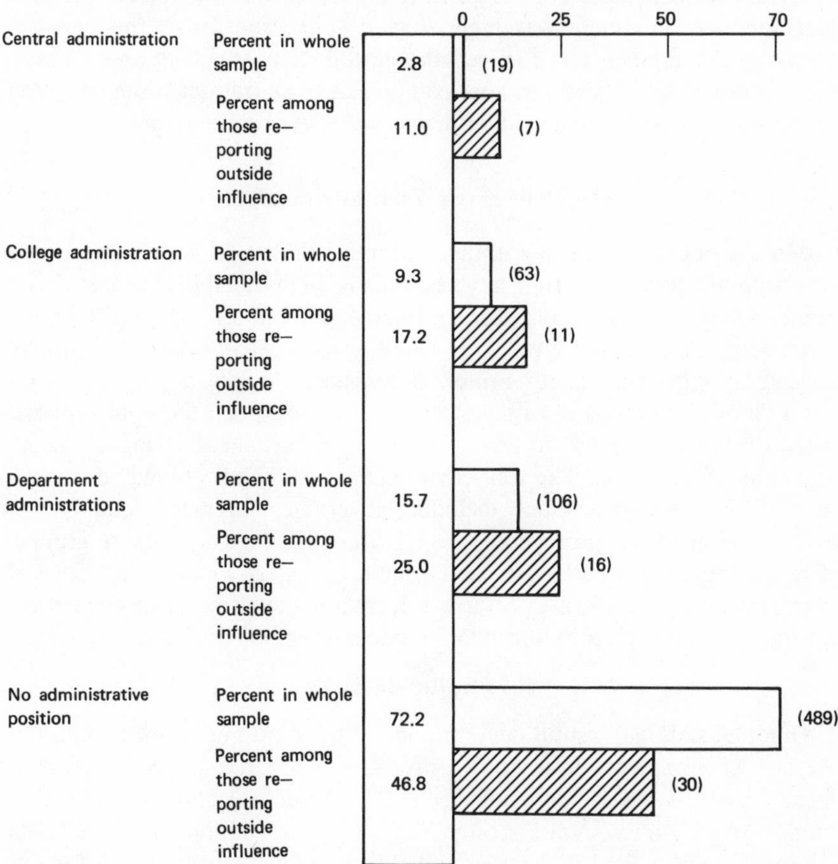

claims as its unique task. The domain includes the kind of student the university tries to serve, the distinctive curriculum it develops, and the kinds of service it renders to the community. In other words, it is an organization's definition of its particular function in contrast with the functions that other organizations play in the same environment. Thus NYU has traditionally defined its domain as service to the masses, based on a "school-of-opportunity" philosophy. This contrasted sharply with the role of, say, Columbia, which defined its domain as service to an elite. Each university claims for itself a peculiar role and interacts with other organizations on the basis of that definition. Other organizations—foundations, city governments, accrediting agencies, other universities—understand the domain claimed by NYU and interact with it on the basis of that shared understanding.

Domains do change, however, as vividly illustrated by the threats posed by NYU's competition with the public universities. For decades other universities had recognized NYU's claim to a particular domain in New York's higher education—there was high *domain consensus*. In the mid-1950's, however, this domain was challenged, and the result was high *domain conflict*. Consequently, there was a redefinition of organizational domains, with major internal adjustments riding in the wake of these external events.

The University's Task Environment

Moving out one more step in the concentric circles, the larger social context beyond a particular university's domain is often called the "task environment." Obviously a university cannot interact with all the elements in its environment; instead it relates to a small group of organizations directly concerned with prime goals. From this task environment the university secures "inputs" in terms of raw materials, technology, and financial support; it then returns "outputs" in terms of completed products, changed clients, and educated students. The task environment of a university may contain a wide variety of organizations, including government agencies, foundations, accrediting agencies, professional associations, ideological pressure groups, state coordinating superboards, and voluntary college associations. Several of the major organizations in NYU's task environment deserve special notice, for they are the key institutions that help to determine NYU's destiny.

OTHER UNIVERSITIES

Other educational institutions form one of the most important elements in the task environment for any university. They cooperate in programs, steal faculty stars, compete for students, and struggle for common sources of funds. An institution's role is often shaped by its relation to others in its reference field, a field that varies greatly for different institutions; for example, NYU has a definite relation to the other institutions in New York City. An interview with one admissions office official drove this point home.

> Let's face it, NYU isn't a free agent, for we live in an educational network that includes most importantly a whole group of other universities. To some extent we cooperate with one another, but to a much larger extent we compete with each other. I guess the most obvious example that we've had lately is our competition with the public universities for quality students. We always had to take what they had left over. Fortunately that's changing now—but don't you ever forget it, our relation to other schools is one of our biggest factors, and we are always thinking in those terms. We fight with them—for students, for faculty, for money, and for community influence. Boy, did the public universities ever fight us when we were trying to get the

new state constitution which would have allowed public aid to private universities. Sure, the other universities of the area—and nation for that matter—have a great effect on NYU[11]

THE PUBLIC SERVICE GOAL

The influence of external groups depends heavily on the university's commitment to the theme of "public service." In a sense, this can be described as a problem of boundaries. Some universities, notably the Ivy League and some elite liberal arts colleges, have rigid boundaries and insulate themselves to a high degree from the public-service role. Other institutions, however, are deeply involved with community service. The land-grant schools and junior colleges are obvious examples, for they respond directly to the particular needs and problems of their constituencies. These public-service institutions have relatively open and flexible boundaries, extending out to meet the demands of multiple groups in the environment. All universities have fuzzy boundaries, but some are fuzzier than others.

New York University has open boundaries, for it caters to the multiple needs of the New York City area. The Institute of Retail Management, the School of Fine Arts, and the Institute of Rehabilitation Medicine are only three examples of NYU's open doors to the community. Of course, there are other obvious connections, such as the School of Education to the educational community of New York, the Graduate School of Business to Wall Street, the School of Public Administration to City Hall, and the Medical School to the medical community. The contact points are many, and the exchange of influence across them is like an electric current. The community shapes the university and the university provides services for the community.

To strengthen the traditional links between NYU and the local community the university deliberately adopted an "urban university" orientation: "Seeking to be to the city, what the land-grant schools were to the rural areas." New York University has always served the city, but the thrust received added impetus in the last few years as the university deliberately set out to develop, support, and enlarge its services to the city. In a recently published statement of purposes the university declared:

> The world needs men and women who combine an appreciation of the best of our cultural heritage and an intimate knowledge of the challenges of urban civilization. . . . New York University is equipped by experience, philosophy, and location to meet this need. In a country where higher education has been inclined to turn its face away from the city, where "academic" still connotes an aloofness from practical affairs, New York University is attuned to the people, the culture, and the realities of urban life. . . . The

[11] Interview No. 62, p. 1.

> case for New York University is intimately related to New York City. As a deliberate, continuing expression of the philosophy of its founders, NYU has created schools and programs to meet the evolving needs of the metropolitan community. As the city has developed, the University has developed.[12]

Even when allowance is made for the typical propaganda Overspeak, which is a major part of such purpose statements, it is still clear that the boundaries of NYU are open, that it reaches far out to the community. In the future deliberate policy will widen the avenues of influence that have always run from the community to New York University.

FEDERAL GRANTS

Federal agencies are another critical element in the modern university's task environment. Government support is becoming increasingly important, for the twin expenses of mass teaching and mass research require huge sums of money. A computer, a new teaching device, or a heart-lung machine all demand enormous sums of cash—usually from outside the halls of the academy. Clark Kerr made several observations on the new "federal grant universities" which are molded by the presence of outside research funds:

> A university's control over its own destiny has been substantially reduced. University funds . . . go through the usual budget-making procedures and their assignment is subject to review in accordance with internal policy. Federal research funds, however, are usually negotiated by the individual scholar with the particular agency, and so bypass the usual review process. Thus 20 to 50 to 80 percent of a university's expenditures may be handled outside the normal channels. These funds in turn commit some of the university's own funds; they influence the assignment of space; they determine the distribution of time between teaching and research; to a large extent they establish the areas in which the university grows the fastest. Almost imperceptibly, a university is changed.[13]

New York University expends more than 40 million dollars a year on research. Most of this money comes from outside sources, and a huge chunk (5.5 million in 1968) is provided directly by the Defense Department.[14] Without a doubt the influence that comes with such huge amounts of money is important, perhaps not in a direct, vulgar manner, but more importantly in subtle, quiet ways.

[12]New York University, *The Mission of New York University* (private printing of NYU; available from the office of the President).

[13]Clark Kerr, *The Uses of the University*. Cambridge: Harvard University Press, 1963, p. 58.

[14]From an article in *The Chronicle of Higher Education*, June 10, 1968 (Vol. II, Number 19), p. 8.

FOUNDATIONS

There are other sources of funds besides the federal government, and private foundations play a sizable role in shaping the future of the institution.[15] One obvious example of foundation influence in NYU's recent history was the Ford Foundation's massive 25-million-dollar grant in 1964. This grant was a challenge that the university had to match with 75 million drawn from other gifts. As reported earlier, this money provided the financial backing and undergirding for a complex series of changes that has wracked NYU for the last several years.

THE STATE GOVERNMENT

Another external factor is the relation between the university and the state government. New York University, in spite of its name, is a private institution and is not currently supported by the State or the City of New York. Traditionally there has been a clear dichotomy between the "public" and "private" sectors of higher education, but recently these boundaries have been breaking down because of increased government aid for private institutions and increased private philanthropy for public institutions. New York University has argued for more interaction between state and private universities, especially in the form of state subsidies.

In the academic year 1966–1967 New York's Governor Nelson Rockefeller appointed the Bundy Committee to study the relationship between the state and private institutions. Of course, NYU was anxious to convince the committee of the need for state aid to private institutions. Chancellor Allan Cartter appeared before the Bundy committee to argue that the state could best serve its citizens by giving modest support to private institutions, instead of establishing public colleges to handle all students. Cartter advanced three propositions about the relations between the state and private institutions[16]:

> 1. The classification of colleges and universities as "public" or "private" is, we believe, an outworn dichotomy. . . . Today's non-secular college or university is a public institution, serving the citizens of the state or region, whether it relies upon fees and philanthropy or tax revenues for primary support. . . . Thus, we believe, that the independent institutions are as much public resources as are the units of the State University. . . .
>
> 2. We believe that the state . . . must be concerned with the development of all its resources. . . . Nothing would be gained for the citizens or industry

[15] The important role of foundations in influencing universities is discussed at length in Jacques Barzun, *The House of Intellect*. New York: Harper, 1959, Chapter 7.

[16] Allan M. Cartter, "An Analysis of New York University for the Governor's and Regents' Select Committee" (mimeographed, July 24, 1967), pp. 19–25.

of New York State if, through great investment of public funds, public institutions of higher education markedly improve coincindentally with a decline in quality of independent institutions within the State. . . . The great advantage to the State of the present mixed system is that it provides much greater diversity than a wholly public system would offer. . . .

3. Perhaps the most pragmatic argument is strictly a utilitarian and economic one. How can the State get the most for its money in training people with the special skills and talents required by modern society? In many areas . . . progress can be accomplished with greater speed, with greater assurance of success, and with greater economy, through a partnership between public and private resources than by reliance on a single type of institution. . . . Perhaps the most cogent economic argument for public support is the multiplying effect of modest supplementary aid to private institutions. . . . A modest cost of education allowance (to private schools) as suggested below, would match fifteen to twenty dollars of spending from other sources with each dollar of State money. . . .

In the fall of 1967 the people of New York voted on a new constitution, one provision of which was the elimination of the Blaine Amendment that prohibited state aid to private schools. If this constitution had passed, one major obstacle to state aid for NYU would have been removed. NYU lobbied hard for the new constitution, and the university's representative at the state capitol had high hopes that it would pass. However, the issue became confused with the matter of aid to parochial schools at the primary and secondary level, and the people of New York rejected the proposed constitution.

Not to be defeated, the private universities of the state, with NYU at the forefront, began an intensive lobbying effort designed to win by legislative action what had been lost at the polls. In the meantime the Bundy Commission made a report which strongly supported the concept of state aid to private universities. Faced with this report and the intense pressure of the private universities, the legislature passed a bill to assist private institutions. The bill provides for state payment of a fixed sum for each degree awarded by a college or university on a sliding scale that starts with 400 dollars for each bachelor's or master's degree and increases up to 2400 for a Ph.D. This bill signals a new era of cooperation between the state and private universities. NYU officials predict that this support will amount to 5% of their operating budget, a modest amount that might nevertheless be the thin margin between quality and mediocrity for many academic programs. Many of NYU's future internal decisions and critical planning now depend on this new relationship with the state.

Other Impacts of the External Environment

We have examined the creation of boundary roles, the concept of domain, and the set of organizations in the task environment. It is important to note a few more environmental effects on the university's operation. Of particular importance are the impacts of research grants.

THE IMPACT OF GOVERNMENT GRANTS

The large amounts of money that NYU receives from the government have many effects on the processes of internal governance. Clark Kerr reviewed some of these influences and suggested that universities are affected by federal grants in several ways.[17] His conclusions certainly apply to NYU.

1. Indirect control by the government is increased, even though direct control is minimal. This is especially true in the recruitment of faculty, who insist that certain kinds of funds be available rather than others.
2. The university's internal priorities are upset as funds are accepted in areas other than those of highest importance.
3. The university's control over its faculty is substantially reduced as they depend more and more on government money. The authority of university officials and of faculty governing bodies is reduced. The faculty member may pay more allegiance to the government agency than to his home university.
4. Campus influence and priorities are increasingly shifted toward the natural sciences and the social sciences, whereas the humanists are cut off without adequate support.
5. There is a definite concentration of wealth among the few universities that obtain most of the government money. Moreover, this wealth has exaggerated the differences between universities and colleges.
6. The teaching of undergraduates suffers because more money flows into research where graduate students do much of the work and benefit most from the specialized instruction.
7. Large staffs of "un-faculties" are established which consist of research assistants, teaching assistants, research professors, and others whose prime work is research or manning the teaching fort while others do the research.
8. Large administrative overheads burden the university with hidden cost and increase the size and complexity of the administrative staff.

[17] Clark Kerr, *The Uses of the University*. Cambridge: Harvard University Press, 1963. This is not a direct quote but is extracted from pp. 57–67.

THE INDIVIDUALIZATION OF FACULTY INFLUENCE

The faculty, in its legislative bodies, is gaining a greater measure of control over many matters, and some forces in the university are pressing for the extension of this control. However, there are other pressures for faculty influence to be fragmented and individualized and thus taken away from the faculty's legislative bodies and placed in the hands of individual professors. Many of the external influences have a tendency to do exactly that.

The most important external factor in the individualization of influence is the phenomenal increase in research money. In his most extreme form the star professor with his massive grant is an independent lord who rules his realm with an iron hand, commanding the allegiance of dozens of graduate students who live off his bounty and even using other young professors as his vassals on the project. The rest of the kingdom may do as it pleases, as long as his particular province is protected and there are few demands on his time. Faculty influence, when tied to outside sources of power, often becomes fragmented and individualized. Decentralization results because research money is channeled directly to individual professors and departments. Although the university attempts to maintain some control over grants, it nevertheless finds that the grant-holding professor is essentially a free agent who makes demands on the university for released time, freedom from undergraduate teaching, research facilities, physical plant space, and fewer university-related responsibilities. One constant danger is that the university will lose its best faculty members if it refuses to give all these special privileges. "Have grant—will travel" is a powerful threat from the star faculty member.

FACULTY INFLUENCE ON GOVERNANCE DIVIDES BETWEEN RESEARCH AND TEACHING

Most observers would probably list teaching and research as the two most important objectives of the university. However, a study of the faculty's principle realm of influence reveals another paradox of academic governance. The faculty's legislative bodies are still pre-eminently powerful in the teaching field, with all its attendant issues of degree requirements and curriculum. On the other hand, the faculty as a body has little control over research. One of the prime academic programs has slipped away from the faculty's legislative authority.

Two things have happened to this authority. First, as noted above, it has been largely individualized. In spite of the role played by institutes and departments, most research is still done by the individual professor and his associates. Second, bureaucratization is constantly encroaching on the research domain. More and more, the administration or the granting agency feels that coordination would help rationalize research. Thus reports and accounting procedures come to play a large role in the administration of research money. Paper work mounts, the bureaucrats reign supreme, and the faculty's legislative councils often watch helplessly from the sidelines.

SUMMARY

The basic argument of this chapter is that the unique configuration of the university's social setting is a major factor in determining the political dynamics. Conflicting demands are generated because the university is splintered by a complex bureaucracy, a fragmented subcultural pattern, and a multifaceted external environment.

The alert reader will notice that the three controversies reported in Part Two are very different in their social structure, each one illustrating one of three elements. Chapter IV discussed the goal changes that were stimulated by *external* competition with other universities. Chapter V analyzed the student unrest that was largely an outgrowth of changes in the student *subcultures*. Finally, the controversy over the departmental reorganization shows how the *formal structure* generates conflict. Thus each type of social structural factor was used as the basis of a separate chapter in Part Two.

The complex social structure generates conflict and struggles over goals; it also leads to the development of many interest groups that use elaborate tactics to influence policy decision. In a word, the social setting creates a complex "demand structure" that impinges on the decision makers. How this demand process works and how these various groups bring pressure to bear is all part of the "interest articulation" phase—and that is the subject of Chapter VIII.

Chapter VIII

INTEREST ARTICULATION PROCESSES

Chapter VII showed how the university's social system is fragmented and divided. This complex structure generates competing claims, divided loyalties, and specialized pressure groups. Each partisan group has different goals for the university and each puts pressure on the authorities to obtain favorable policy decisions.

In fact, William Gamson argues that much of the controversy in social systems develops from this kind of competition between authorities and partisans.[1] *Authorities* are those people in the organization who make binding decisions for the group. There are many different authorities, for the relevant authority will depend on the issue and where it is located in the organization. The organization allows the authorities to commit its resources and to mobilize its energies for the pursuit of particular goals. From the point of view of the authorities the critical problems are the implementation of decisions and the achievement of goals. A necessary part of this activity is the ability to control people in the organization and to direct their work. Thus *social control* is paramount.

[1]William Gamson, *Power and Discontent*. Homewood, Illinois: Dorsey, 1968.

On the other hand, *partisans* are people in the organization who are significantly affected by decisions. They have to live with the decisions the authorities make and must function within the limits set by their policies. By this definition the authorities themselves are a subset of the partisans, for they are certainly affected by their own decisions. However, for all practical purposes we can imagine that the authorities and the partisans are separate groups—those who make the decisions and those affected by them. From the partisans' point of view they must influence the authorities so that their decisions are favorable. Thus, although social control is the critical issue for the authorities, *social influence* is the critical issue for partisans. Consequently there is a complex relationship: the authorities make the decisions and try to control the partisan groups; the partisans try to influence the decisions and perhaps even attempt to overthrow the authorities.

Of course, not all organizational conflict is directly between authorities and partisans, for often the partisans themselves are aligned on various sides of an issue. However, when partisans are fighting other partisans, authorities are still dragged into the conflict, for they have the power to make decisions that will favor one group or the other. In effect, the authorities become third party "referees" who must decide among the competing claims of partisan groups; even the "partisan versus partisan" type of conflict is usually translated into a "partisan versus authorities" issue.

Gamson's discussion of partisans and authorities paves the way for the logic of the coming chapters. This chapter focuses on the "interest-articulation" process; that is, the activities of partisans as they pressure the authorities. Chapter IX takes the opposite position. The focus is then on the "legislative" processes; that is, the action authorities take to transform partisan pressure into policy. Figure 8–1 shows how this chapter's discussion fits into the whole political interpretation.

In order to make sense of the interest-articulation process, we shall try to answer the following questions:

1. What *kinds* of partisan groups develop in the university's social structure and how are those groups organized?
2. What are the *trust orientations* of the partisans; that is, are they alienated from the authorities or have they confidence in them?
3. What are the *goals* of partisans as they try to influence the authorities?
4. What kinds of influence *resources* are available for partisans to use as weapons against the authorities?
5. What are the *responses of authorities* to partisan pressures?
6. How are the actions of partisans and authorities linked together in a *cycle of conflict?*

Figure 8-1. Chapter VIII Focuses on Interest Articulation

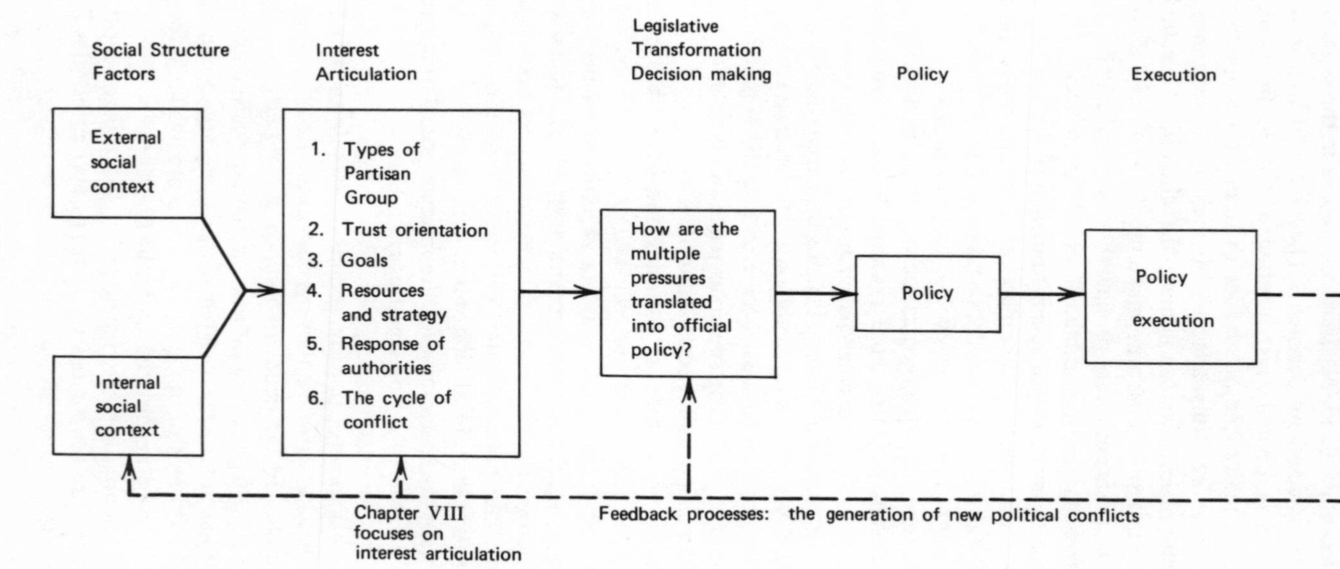

WHAT KINDS OF PARTISAN GROUPS DEVELOP IN THE SOCIAL STRUCTURE?

In a complex organization such as New York University there are literally hundreds of groups that might try to influence decisions. In actual fact, however, there seems to be a continuum of activity, with virtually inactive groups at one end and highly active groups at the other. Those at the least active end of the continuum are called "quasi groups." At the most active end there are full-time formal interest groups called "associations." Between the two extremes are several other types.

Quasi Groups

The least active partisans are quasi groups whose members share common values or common structural positions but are not engaged in influence attempts. They are *potential* partisans; they are not organized, but because they share similar circumstances they might become active if their interests were severely threatened. In spite of their apathy they form an "attentive public" that is an important political force. If the situation changed so that they believed the authoities were making decisions against them, these partisans might become political activists. The authorities must always act with these inactive partisans in mind, and many decisions are couched so they do not offend potential interest groups.

There seem to be two critical factors for promoting the self-consciousness of such groups: "structural" conditions and "ideological" positions. Structural conditions that promote quasi groups usually break along role divisions (student/faculty/administration), along the lines of organizational units (departments/institutes/disciplines/colleges), or along status lines (salary/tenure/age). Ideological factors, however, cluster around value issues and do not necessarily follow the structural divisions. Thus faculty, students, and administrators may find themselves on the same side opposing war or favoring civil rights. Of course, a great deal of overlap often occurs between the objective position and subjective opinion, since any group will usually have both structural and ideological factors that bind the members together. Even though they are not active at a given time, the quasi groups sharing these characteristics form a political pool from which active partisan groups are drawn.

Conditions that Promote the Formation of Active Partisan Groups

Why do some quasi groups become politically active? In an apathetic student body why does a group emerge with "student power" as its motto and the boycott as its weapon? In a politically disinterested faculty why do a few people develop a union or threaten to strike if policy is not changed? These are difficult questions to answer, but at least three sets of factors seem to be critical for transforming inactive quasi groups into active partisans.

The *characteristics of the decision system* are important because apathetic groups are likely to become active if they perceive that legitimate channels for influence are closed to them, if they see that decisions consistently go against their interests, and if they can convince large groups of apathetic people that the negative decisions are affecting them uniformly. This is precisely what happens in almost every student revolt, for the students correctly perceive that many decisions are against their best interests, that they are systematically excluded from legitimate channels, and that they can influence decisions if they work together. Excluded from participating in the formal system, they turn to nonformal forms of partisan influence.

But merely perceiving the injustices (real or imagined) of the decision system is not enough. The *characteristics of the emerging groups* are also critical for transforming apathy into action. In the transition several things happen within the group itself. First, the interaction rate goes up among group members as they discuss, plan, and work to influence decisions. Second, a common set of norms governing the group's behavior gradually develops. Third, symbols are adopted to give identity and emotional expression to the group. Fourth, common "life-styles" are formed as the members of the group adopt similar habits, modes of action, thought patterns, and definitions of the world. More and more the members tend to see other group participants as their significant "reference group." Fifth, the group adopts a "charter" that defines the group's mission, its goals, and its way of doing things. An informally organized group may have a vague and flexible charter, whereas a more formal group may have a written constitution. Finally, the group develops "technical facilities," such as patterns of leadership, strategies for pressuring authorities, and procedures for making decisions, to manage its work.

While these transformations are occurring inside the group, other things are happening outside the group's boundaries. One of the most important factors in developing a group's identity is that *other groups* begin to recognize its existence; that is, a "mirror image" of the group develops, with other people treating the group as a real political force (e.g. when the students were organizing, nothing helped to establish NYU's "Ad Hoc Committee for a Democratic University" so much as the use of that name by the campus newspaper and by administrative officials). In addition to this mirror image, the group also develops a high level of cohesion by confronting the authorities. As the authorities try to control them, the groups draw closer together and fight back. Often confrontation tactics are not intended to influence authorities so much as to develop internal cohesion. Taken together, these interactions between the group and the authorities serve to reenforce the impetus provided by the nature of the decision system and by the group's own internal processes.

All active interest groups go through these processes as they develop, but the most visible examples are the radical student groups of the last few years. At NYU most students were inactive, but small groups became more politically alert, due in part to changes in the student social structure, in part to perceived inequities in the NYU decision system, and in part to influences outside the university. As these small groups developed, they adopted names (Ad Hoc Committee for a Democratic University), developed symbols (the pervasive "peace" sign is an excellent example), structured procedures for making decisions, and developed a clear self-identity. Moreover, people in the surrounding environment began to treat them as formal groups, thus reenforcing their own self-concepts. The transformation from an inactive quasi group to an active interest group had taken place. Faculty groups, administrative cliques, and groups outside the university experience the same processes to a greater or lesser degree.

Four Types of Active Interest Group[2]

Once the quasi groups have changed from apathetic masses into politically active interest groups they tend to act in one of several ways. At one extreme interest groups may act informally, spontaneously, and violently. At the other extreme there are the carefully planned activities of formal associations. In between there are two kinds of semi-organized cliques.

"ANOMIC" INTEREST GROUPS

Political scientists studying national politics often deal with "collective behavior," a type of interest-group activity characterized by spontaneous outbursts of public feeling expressed in riots and panics. This is sometimes called "anomic"-interest-group behavior. Within a large complex organization the same kinds of political activities are frequently apparent; the student revolts are the obvious examples in recent years. The same dynamics are present in prison riots, military mutinies, and mental hospital sit-down strikes.

Several common themes run through this kind of anomic behavior. For one thing, the action is relatively unplanned and unorganized, with few designated leaders. The public usually attributes some kind of "conspiracy"

[2]This section depends partly on Gabriel Almond and James S. Coleman, *The Politics of Developing Areas*. Princeton: Princeton University Press, 1960, Chapter 1.

to these events, but it seems that this is usually not the case in the early stages. In addition, the issue that sparks the uprising usually affects large numbers of people and the members of the anomic group typically feel that they are excluded from the "legitimate" channels of influence on that issue. Faced with political impotency in the normal channels, disturbed groups turn to anomic behavior in order to influence decisions. Their tactics at this stage usually include violence.

The New York University student uprising in late 1967 and early 1968 clearly demonstrated many characteristics of anomic behavior. A tuition increase provoked hostile reaction from large groups of hitherto apathetic students. They were largely unorganized and felt completely excluded from the decision-making processes that were affecting their lives. Their reaction was to turn to relatively violent, unorganized action in the hope of affecting the decisions. In the early stages of almost all student revolts these same characteristics hold.

This activity, however, is inherently unstable. If the issues are persistent and the authorities unyielding to demands, unorganized, spontaneous actions tend to get organized. Leaders emerge to direct the action, careful strategies are developed to influence decisions, and decision-making procedures are set up within the partisan group. When this happens, the group is shifting from anomic behavior to other kinds of activity.

PARTISAN-DOMINATED CLIQUES

Anomic outbursts are fairly infrequent in complex organizations, but there are other relatively stable groups that try to affect policy. When they are enduring and active but still not formally organized into associations, they may be called policy-influencing "cliques." Their distinguishing characteristics are relative stability over time, informal leadership, a low degree of organization, and intermittent activity to influence policies. Thus the cliques are more organized than the anomic groups but much less organized than formal associations.

Like quasi groups, cliques have both "structural" and "ideological" factors that stimulate their action and hold them together. Structural factors that promote cliques are usually some feature of the formal organization, such as department, college, rank, or tenure position. In the local department young professors pressure for a role in departmental committees; in the college the "Young Turks" group tries to wrest control from the "Old Guard." The student group transforms its bull session into an ad hoc committee to complain to the dean about college conditions. The administrator's clique lunches together and shares ideas about protecting the administrative realm from the newest faculty invasion. On a larger scale, whole departments or colleges become structural units defending themselves against intrusions or expanding their domains, as clearly exemplified when both the

School of Commerce and the Heights Campus fought for autonomy from the central administration.

On the other hand, ideological factors are also involved in every group's activities. Not only do cliques hold similar structural conditions but their members also hold similar values. They are unorganized, coffee-break revolutionaries who pressure for a better world; they are friends who share ideas about the importance of liberal arts education and search for ways to protect it from creeping vocationalism; they are students who express their opposition to the war in Vietnam by boycotting Dow; they are the administrators who fight for Dow recruitment because they are committed to free speech and open dialogue. In short, they are the shifting, unorganized, special-interest groups that cluster around value issues. Of course, it is again clear that ideological and structural factors overlap a great deal, for structural positions tend to promote unique values among those who share a similar fate.

It is extremely difficult to get an accurate picture of the activities of cliques. They are neither so publicly visible as anomic riots nor so clearly distinguished as formal associations. In the 1968 NYU Survey the data suggest a few crude facts; for example, the respondents were asked to estimate how many policy-influencing cliques they belonged to and how much influence their groups had on policies at various levels in the university. (See Appendix A for questionnaire: questions 5c and 5d.) The data in Figure 8-2 support four interesting conclusions that emerged from those questions.

1. About half the respondents did not think they belonged to policy-influencing cliques on any level: department, college, or all-university.
2. The policy influence of such groups was seen as moderate. There was a slight tendency for clique members to rank group effectiveness higher than nonmembers.
3. Persons reporting clique membership also reported more "formal authority" (i.e., membership on committees, official positions such as department chairmen or deals, and membership on policy-making councils).
4. Persons reporting clique membership reported more "perceived influence" (i.e., when asked about their personal influence on department, college, and university policy, they believed they were influential).

AUTHORITY-DOMINATED CLIQUES

Up to this point we have argued that interest groups promote a form of partisan activity that is designed to affect the decisions of authorities. However, this ignores the fact that authorities, too, try to influence policies. If

Figure 8-2. Some Characteristics of Clique Members Compared with Nonmembers[a]

1. Members of influence-exerting cliques are a minority:

Percent who report no clique membership at any level	53.1
Percent who belong to cliques in department only	24.7
Percent who belong to cliques in department and college	15.4
Percent who belong to cliques at all levels	6.8
	100.0
	($N = 693$)

2. Clique influence is predominately judged "medium" and clique members rate it higher than nonmembers:

	Degree of influence (%)				
	High	Medium	Low		N
No clique membership	9.4	34.4	56.1	100	212
Department	14.8	50.9	34.3	100	169
Department and college	12.1	57.0	30.8	100	107
At all levels	15.2	52.2	32.6	100	46
	12.2	45.7	42.1	100	534

3. Clique members report more formal influence activities: committees, official positions, meetings

	Amount of Formal Activity (%)						
	None	Department or College	Department and College	University	All		N
No Cliques	28.0	21.7	18.2	7.1	25.0	100	212
Department	17.0	23.4	27.5	4.7	27.5	100	169
Dept. & Col.	6.5	14.0	28.0	2.8	48.6	100	107
At all levels	8.5	4.3	6.4	4.3	76.6	100	46
	20.6	19.8	21.2	5.6	32.8	100	534

Increasing formal influence

[a] Correlation of clique membership with other factors (such as ranking of school affiliation, evaluation of the university, publication, professional memberships, and administrative role) did not show significant differences between those who reported clique membership and those who did not.

Figure 8-2. (Continued)

4. Clique members perceive themselves as having more policy influence than nonmembers—at all levels

	Amount of "Perceived Influence" (%)					
	None	Department	College	University		
No cliques	41.3	28.5	18.8	11.4	100	212
Department	27.5	49.7	14.6	8.2	100	169
Department and College	15.9	27.1	37.5	19.6	100	107
All all levels	10.6	23.4	27.7	38.3	100	46
	31.9	33.2	21.2	13.7	100	534

Increasing perceived influence

an official has unambiguous authority over a given issue, he usually makes the decision without restoring to influence attempts. However, there are many cases in which his word may be questioned: the political opposition may be intense, the issue may be outside his sphere of influence, or it may be contested between two sets of relevant authorities.

Authority over a given issue is often ambiguous and different groups may claim jurisdiction under different circumstances; for example, during the struggle over NYU's new goals the authorities at different levels disagreed violently about the various proposals. In that situation they clearly acted in partisan roles, for they mustered support, formed coalitions, and used many tactics to influence decisions. This was true also in the departmental reorganization, for almost all the relevant participants were authorities who could make some claim over the decisions. Nevertheless, they had to resort to influence attempts against other authorities.

Other than the fact that they are dominated by authorities, this type of interest group displays most of the characteristics of the partisan-dominated cliques. They are informally organized and informally led, act on specific issues, and are intermittently active.

ASSOCIATIONAL INTEREST GROUPS

The three partisan groups mentioned up to this point have varied largely in the nature of their organization; anomic groups are the least organized and the two types of clique, moderately organized. In contrast, an "association" is an interest group that is formally organized and continuously active. Anomic groups and cliques are unstable, for they cluster around momentary issues and break apart with shifts in personnel or issues. Associations are organized, relatively stable, and continue to exist in spite of changing memberships or goals. Cliques often develop into associations, and when they do all sorts of things happen: the group is blessed with a name, officers spring up to provide stable leadership, a few rules of procedure are adopted, and perhaps it even acquires the ultimate organizational symbol—an old hand-cranked mimeograph machine in some dusty corner.

Associational groups also have ideological and structural factors to promote their formation. Although all groups have both factors, some seem to be dominated by either structural or ideological features. Structural associations are formed to protect the interests of persons located in similar life-situations within the formal organizational network. Most common are those that cluster around special roles. The American Association of University Professors is an outstanding example for the faculty; the National Student Association is a student example. In addition, there are many professional associations that promote the interests of specific disciplines, such as the American Chemical Society and the American Sociological Association. The campus is also over-run with associations whose prime concern is with ideological issues; for example, the Faculty Committee on War and Peace, the Students for a Democratic Society, the American Civil Liberties Union, the Veterans for Open Recruitment, and the Young Republicans.

Figure 8-3. "Members" Report More Personal Influence than "Nonmembers"

	Local Association Memberships					
	Members		Nonmembers		Total	
Areas of personal influence	(%)	(*N*)	(%)	(*N*)	(%)	(*N*)
None[a]	18.6	37	37.2	184	31.9	221
Department	34.2	68	32.8	162	33.2	230
College	30.2	60	17.6	87	21.2	147
University	17.1	34	12.3	61	13.7	95
	100.0	199	100.0	494	100.0	693

(gamma = .312)
(chi square: $P < .001$)

[a] Each level of increasing influence includes the lower levels. "University" means that he reported influence in department, college, and university. "College" means both college ind department.

In the 1968 NYU Survey the respondents were asked to list all the *policy-influencing associations* to which they belonged. A number of interesting conclusions emerge from the reports of those who listed membership in at least one association ("Members"). First, association members are a small minority on the campus (28.8%). They report more personal influence at all levels (Figure 8-3); they participate more actively in the formal networks of committees and councils (Figure 8-5); they join more national and regional professional groups (Figure 8-6); they are slightly more loyal to the university than nonmembers (Figure 8-4); and they are generally more dissatisfied with university conditions (Figure 8-7).

In sum, association members seem to be an intensely active minority who become activists to change conditions in the university. The survey data at least suggest this, and a vivid example was given by one respondent. This man belonged to more organizations than anybody else in the survey and wrote one of the few extended comments on the back of his questionnaire:

> A laudable project! It is interesting that you did not ask what my concept of a university and its function was, and whether I thought the administration helped to achieve it. You left few write-ins on most questions (the better to computerize, I am sure). I would like to suggest:
>
> 1. That work-horses like me (92 graduate advisees, 76 doctoral committees, plus classes) take a deep interest in the university which is generally ignored by all administrators. They hire glamor boys.
> 2. It is probably both immoral to claim and impossible to maintain a huge university as an educational institution.
> 3. The more bureaucratic the less human, and the farther from education.

Figure 8-4. "Members" Report Slightly Closer Attachment[a] to the University than "Nonmembers"

	Local Association Memberships					
	Members		Nonmembers		Total	
	(%)	(N)	(%)	(N)	(%)	(N)
High	77.4	154	66.8	330	71.3	484
Low	22.6	45	33.2	164	28.7	209
	100.0	199	100.0	494	100.0	693

(gamma = .259)
(chi square: $P < .01$)

[a] High "attachment" is defined as having few outside interests to detract from primary allegiance to the university.

Figure 8-5. "Members" Report Slightly More Formal Activities than "Nonmembers"

	Local Association Memberships					
	Members		Nonmembers		Total	
Areas of formal activity[a]	(%)	(*N*)	(%)	(*N*)	(%)	(*N*)
None	14.1	28	32.3	115	20.6	143
Department or college	19.6	39	19.8	98	19.8	137
Department or college	22.6	45	20.6	102	21.2	147
University only	3.0	6	6.7	33	5.6	39
All levels	40.7	81	29.6	146	32.8	227
	100.0	199	100.0	494	100.0	693

(gamma = .183)
(chi square: $P < .01$)

[a] Formal activity is defined as membership on committees, attending policy-making councils, and holding official offices. (See Questions 6a, 6b, 6c in Appendix A.) Essentially, moving down the scale indicates increased formal activity.

Figure 8-6. Local Association "Members" Report More Memberships in National and Regional Professional Associations than "Nonmembers"

Number of regional and national associations	Local Association Memberships					
	Members		Nonmembers		Total	
	(%)	(N)	(%)	(N)	(%)	(N)
None	3.5	7	9.2	45	100.0	53
1–2	17.2	34	29.6	144	100.0	178
3–4	37.9	75	32.9	160	100.0	237
5–7	25.3	50	21.8	106	100.0	156
8–10	13.1	26	5.7	28	100.0	55
11–19	3.0	6	0.6	3	100.0	9
20+		0	0.2	1	100.0	1
	100.0	198	100.0	487	100.0	689

(gamma = .298)
(chi square: $P < .001$)
($N = 685$)

Figure 8-7. Association "Members" Are More Dissatisfied than "Non-Members"

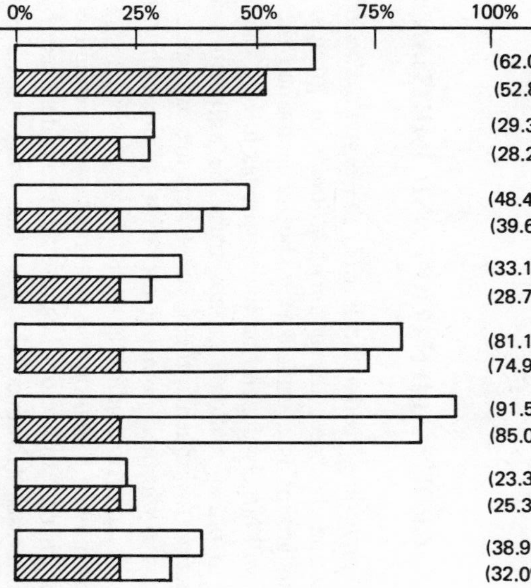

Area Evaluated		Those Reporting "Poor" as Their Rating	"Average"	"Good"	N
7h. Communication with central administration	Members	(62.0%)	25.3%	12.6%	174
	Nonmembers	(52.8%)	30.7	16.6	371
7i. Confidence in university leadership	Members	(29.3%)	35.1	35.7	190
	Nonmembers	(28.2%)	29.5	42.3	451
7o. Value of University Senate meetings	Members	(48.4%)	34.4	17.2	157
	Nonmembers	(39.6%)	36.7	23.7	308
7c. Faculty influence on academic policy	Members	(33.1%)	35.3	31.6	190
	Nonmembers	(28.7%)	37.6	33.6	425
7d. Faculty influence on college budgets	Members	(81.1%)	12.6	6.3	175
	Nonmembers	(74.9%)	19.0	6.1	374
7e. Faculty influence on university budgets	Members	(91.5%)	5.5	3.0	165
	Nonmembers	(85.0%)	12.4	2.6	348
7q. Value of committees for faculty influence	Members	(23.3%)	37.5	39.3	176
	Nonmembers	(25.3%)	36.0	38.7	367
7p. Value of college faculty meetings	Members	(38.9%)	30.0	31.1	180
	Nonmembers	(32.0%)	35.7	32.2	400

What Kinds of Partisan Groups Develop: A Summary

Throughout the campus there are vaguely defined "quasi groups" that share common interests but do not actively influence policy. Under certain conditions small bands of active partisans emerge. They are organized to varying degrees, from loose anomic groups, to semistable cliques, to formal associations. Figure 8-8 summarizes the discussion on the development of interest groups.

GROUP ALIENATION AND PARTISAN GOALS[3]

The preceding section dealt with the *organization* of groups, and now this section discusses the *political attitudes* of groups. The formation of partisan groups is a critical step, but once formed the group's goals and tactics will largely depend on their attitudes toward the authorities they are trying to pressure. Some groups trust the authorities and therefore take mild action to influence them, but others are alienated and will go to any extremes to win their points. Thus "trust" in the authorities becomes a critical focal point of conflict analysis.

Trust may be based on two factors: bias and effectiveness. Partisans may trust or distrust authorities because they consider them biased for or against their interests. However, the partisans will also have feelings about the authorities' effectiveness, for even if the decision makers favor a group's interest it is no help if they are weak, ineffective, and incapable of executing their decisions. Thus to have trust the partisans must not only believe that the authorities are biased for them but also that they are effective enough to carry out favorable decisions.

With trust as the major analytical concept, Gamson outlines three groups. *Confident* groups trust the authorities and believe they are capable of executing favorable decisions. Confident groups are likely to be inactive in most conflicts, for they trust the authorities to act in their behalf. When they do enter the fight, they side with the authorities in order to fight against other partisan groups. If they feel that some influence is necessary to guide the authorities, confident groups will prefer to use *persuasion* as a tactic. They feel that rational appeals will probably obtain the most favorable action,

[3]The next few pages depend heavily on Gamson's discussion. Gamson, *op. cit.*

for the authorities are already biased in their favor. In fact, other tactics, such as payoffs or coersion, would only undermine their favored positions with the authorities.

Neutral groups are partisans who believe the authorities are not necessarily biased either for or against them. Consequently they are more active than the confident groups because they cannot necessarily trust the authorities to favor them. Influence is worth the effort, but usually it is not violent or coersive. Since they are neither favored nor unfavored, they cannot afford to tip the balance against themselves by unnecessary antagonism of the authorities. Instead they are likely to offer *inducements* to the authorities by paying them off in some way to secure favorable decisions.

Figure 8-8. The Development of Partisan Groups

Quasi Groups	Conditions	Active Interest Groups
that share common values and/or positions but are inactive	that transform inactive quasi group into active interest groups:	1. Anomic groups
Structural factors: share common position or role	1. Nature of decision system: • exclusion of partisans • consistent negative decisions	2. Partisan-dominated cliques
Ideological factors: share common value stances	2. Nature of developing group: • high interaction • symbols • leadership • self-identity • charter and goals • technical facilities	3. Authority-dominated cliques
	3. Interaction of developing group with authorities: • promotes cohesion of group • generates "mirror-image" identity	4. Associations
→	→	

Finally, *alienated* partisans feel that the authorities are biased against them or so ineffective that they cannot carry out favorable decisions. Since they are sure that authorities are already opposed to their interests, they are likely to be intensely political and will try to force the authorities to give them acceptable decisions. Moreover, they are likely to use *coersion* as their basic tactic, for they feel that neither persuasion nor inducement would be effective against the intransigent authorities.

Thus the psychological attitudes of partisans greatly affect the course of controversies. Any group, whether loosely anomic or in a formal association, can hold any of these attitudes. The level of disturbance and the degree of restraint exercised will depend largely on the trust that partisans hold for the authorities. Confident groups are likely to go through normal bureaucratic channels to achieve their ends. Neutral groups will be likely to work inside the system but will also try to work through informal channels. Alienated groups, feeling that the authorities and their system are biased against them, will use nonformal, nonlegitimate tactics. The riot, the boycott, and the sit-in are the weapons of alienated partisans who feel that the system must be brought down.

The nature of a partisan group's trust will also influence the kinds of demands they make and the *goals* they try to achieve. In fact, there seems to be a hierarchy of goals in which confident groups try to influence specific issues but other groups escalate until an attempt is made to overthrow the authorities or change the decision structure.

A partisan group's mildest demand will be to influence a *specific policy*. Here the objective is to secure favorable action on some definite issue and to gain advantages in competition with other groups. In Chapter IV the issue for many groups was the specific level of the admissions standards or the specific school in which liberal arts courses would be taught. In Chapter V the students specific goal was a return to lower tuition rates. In Chapter VI the specific issue was the nature of departmental coordination and the location of budgetary authority within the formal system.

Severer demands are made, however, when the group moves from a specific issue to policy on *long-range goals*. In Chapter IV the debate focused on the proposal to abandon the "school of opportunity" philosophy. In Chapter V the long-term goal of the students was to affect the whole area of tuition and student-life decisions, not just to lower a specific increase. In Chapter VI the long-range alignment of departments and schools was at stake, not just the assignment of a particular budget system.

A third goal of partisan groups may be to gain influence over *incumbents in office*. This is usually a severe demand, for the objective is not only to get favorable action on policies and goals but to name the officials who will make the decisions. In Chapter IV much of the struggle was related to the

School of Commerce's opposition to the new admissions policies, and in the end several deans and professors were replaced before the plan could be implemented. In Chapter V we saw that the student leaders were opposed to students' demands. Chapter VI reported that in the controversy over the departmental reorganization one of the critical officials, Provost Nelson at the Heights campus, found that he had to step aside.

Finally, the most radical type of partisan demand is for a *restructuring of the decision-making system*. In this case the partisans not only want favorable action on specific issues and goals, or the removal of opposing officials, but they also demand that the decision structure be revised. In effect, the partisans frequently want to redefine the system so that *they* will be the authorities on a given issue. In Chapter IV we saw that the central administration, acting as an authority-dominated interest group, was successful in restructuring the system so that admissions decisions were taken away from the local schools and lodged with a central admissions office. In Chapter V we saw that the students successfully demanded some participation in the decision making that directly affected them. In Chapter VI many of the struggles centered on a restructuring of the system so that different administrative groups would have control over the departments.

The four types of goal fall along a scale of increasing severity, from influence on a specific issue as the mildest to restructuring of the system as the severest. In the heat of conflict there is usually a "goal-escalation," for groups that originally make mild requests tend to increase the severity of their demands as the conflict cycle advances.

Moreover, the degree of a group's trust influences how far they will try to escalate the issues. Confident groups, trusting the system and the authorities, are inclined to influence only specific issues or long-range plans. Neutral groups are most likely to attempt the same things but may also try to remove an incumbent that they believe will block them. Alienated groups will try to influence all levels of the system, not only to shape specific issues but also to upset the entire decision structure in order to eliminate the built-in biases that they perceive. In effect, this is a truly revolutionary effort, for they believe that the only way to get action is to reshape the whole decision-making enterprise.

To summarize, trust is a critical social-psychological dimension in the conflict between partisans and authorities over organizational policies. Any of the groups we mentioned earlier—anomic groups, cliques, and associations—can hold any orientation toward the authorities. Confident groups trust the authorities, are unlikely to enter the controversies, and if active at all will use mild tactics such as persuasion to influence specific issues. Neutral groups are unsure about the bias or effectiveness of the authorities, so they work hard to influence the decisions. However, they use relatively mild tactics such as inducements and rarely escalate their goals beyond an attack on a given incumbent. Alienated groups, however, are sure that authorities will be against them and tend to adopt radical tactics to achieve radical goals. Coersion is the most likely weapon, and they are likely to escalate all the way up the goal hierarchy to try to upset the decision system itself.

PARTISAN RESOURCES: "POWER BASES" AND THEIR TACTICAL USE

We must now inquire about the resources available to a partisan group—the weapons it can muster to influence policies. This is essentially a question of "power bases" and their tactical employment. Four power bases are critical in university politics: bureaucratic, professional, coercive, and personal.[4]

Bureaucratic Resources

Bureaucratic resources depend on the formal arrangements of the organization. Ordinarily, the formal structures are used by officials as they make policy decisions; they constitute one of the critical resources of the authorities as they resist the influence of partisans. Moreover, when the authorities themselves join authority-dominated cliques in order to influence policies outside their jurisdiction, they also employ bureaucratic resources extensively. In addition, other partisan groups have access to some types of bureaucratic resources, for they are usually linked to decision-making system in one way or another.

The use of bureaucratic resources depends on a variety of "enforcement mechanisms." Often the uses of these resources can influence policies because of the force of *legitimacy*. Members of the university community see

[4]This typology of resource bases is built on a large body of literature that deals with social power. The issue is quite complex and the discussion offered in this section is simplified considerably. For an excellent review of this literature see Dorwin Cartwright, "Influence, Leadership, Control," in James March, (Ed.), *Handbook of Organizations*. New York: Mc-Graw-Hill, 1965, pp. 1–47. For another discussion of the topic see John French, Jr., and Bertram Raven, "The basis of Social Power, in Dorwin Cartwright and Alvin Zander, *Group Dynamics*. New York: Harper and Row, 1953, pp. 606–623. This article has a large bibliography on the concept of power and its refinement. See also Amitai Etzioni, *Comparative Analysis of Complex Organizations*. New York: Free Press, 1961, pp. 5–6; Karl Deutsch, *Nationalism and Social Communication*. New York: Wiley, 1953, pp. 218 ff.; K. E. Boulding, *The Organizational Revolution*. New York: Harper, 1953, pp. xxxi; J. R. Commons, *Legal Foundations of Capitalism*. Madison: University of Wisconsin, 1957, pp. 47–64.

his actions as a legitimate function of his role, one designed to carry out the organization's objectives. Recognizing the legitimacy of his action, the members of the organization usually grant the officer the power to carry out that role. This is the exercise of the control right that we usually call formal "authority."[5]

However strong it might be, the force of legitimacy sometimes fails and a variety of *sanctions* (rewards and punishments) may be applied. First, there is the control of the *budget*. The formal structure invests various officials with financial control and this is one of the most potent sanctions of bureaucratic power. As one NYU dean candidly phrased it, "I feed the horses that run in my direction."

Second, there is the power of *personnel appointment and removal*. This is a powerful bureaucratic weapon, but it is often limited by the attachments and power a man has in the university. An extremely popular dean may be dispensible on paper, but the president may think twice about exercising that paper power. One technique, of course, is the "emasculating promotion" in which a man is promoted up—but out of power. Control of personnel was a critical feature of the conflict between the School of Commerce and the central administration and between the Heights campus and the central administration. In both cases it took a major personnel change to accomplish the administration's goals.

A third bureaucratic resource is the control of *legitimate access*. "Access is power," for the right of access to the decision-making process is a significant advantage for influencing policy. Here, then, is one of the key powers of the authority, for he often controls the access available to individuals and groups. Many political struggles rage around the question of access to decision making. For this reason structural reorganizations are never innocent administrative moves, for in the process of changing the organizational set-up the paths of access are opened to some and closed to others. When NYU tried to rework the departmental organization, this seemingly routine task turned out to be a hot issue, chiefly revolving around the issue of access to decision making.

The fourth bureaucratic resource is the *control of information*. Much of the power of the bureaucrat derives from his access to information; the man of knowledge is almost always more powerful than the man of ignorance. The official has his hand on the information pulse of the organization, for there are formal networks that channel information to decision

[5]One of the best discussions of legitimacy and formal authority is an article by W. Richard Scott, Sanford Dornbusch, Bruce Busching, and James Laing, "Organizational Evaluation and Authority," *Administrative Science Quarterly*, Vol. 12, No. 12, 93–117 (June 1967).

makers. Of course, information is often distorted as it goes through channels, and intricate systems of informal communication supplement the official networks. Nevertheless, legitimate access and the authority to command information are critical weapons for any group or individual.

Although many sanctions are available in the bureaucratic system, there are also many limitations on their use. The other three resource bases—professional, coercive, and personal—exercise a counterbalancing trend against bureaucratic influence and each type has its own sanctions that can be used as defense. Officials in a university, unlike their counterparts in some other organizations, have a ambiguous form of power, for they are dealing with highly trained professionals who seldom take orders and who resent close supervision.

Professional Resources

Partisans who use bureaucratic resources are depending on the legitimate authority of the formal system. By contrast professional influence is based on the authority of expert knowledge. Partisans using professional influence resources are demanding influence because they have knowledge that others lack and other groups allow this influence because they believe that the partisans have information they lack. Bureaucratic influence derives from office; professional influence derives from expertise. If there is to be a new physics building, it is disaster not to consult the physics department; if there is a social service project, sociology and social work had better be included; if there is a new curriculum for business education, the Commerce faculty is the expert body; if there is a need for legal expertise, the Law faculty is the place to go. The university lives on expertise, and the users of professional influence provide that expertise for a price in terms of authority, influence, and political advantage.

The events reported in Chapter IV show how partisan groups apply professional influence on policy questions. Many people were offended because the Ford report, the increased admissions standards, and the abandonment of the "school-of-opportunity" philosophy were instituted with little faculty consultation. In irritation and dismay, the AAUP issued a resolution entitled "Faculty Participation in the Determination of University Policies," a document that appealed to the faculty's professional expertise as the justification for their influence on university policy:[6]

[6]NYU Chapter of the AAUP, "Faculty Participation in the Determination of University Policies," December 9, 1963, p. 2.

> A faculty is made up of men and women appointed for specialized duties in teaching and research. But it is more than a mere collection of such individuals. It is an organized body capable of rendering judgments on educational policies, as a group, and particularly qualified to do so by virtue of the training and continuing interests of its members. The special competence of the faculties in this regard is recognized in the Bylaws of the University which make them responsible for "the educational conduct of each of the several schools". . . A realistic examination of the responsibilities thus delegated to the faculties shows that they encompass, directly or implicitly, nearly everything that is rightly called "educational policy." Responsibility for the educational conduct of the schools must include responsibility for all actions which affect the course of study and methods of implementing. Consequently, policies involving the utilization of the instructional staff, the organization of divisions and departments, research activities, obligations of faculty members to public and private establishments, the University's relations with accrediting boards, and personnel and budgetary policies, are therefore proper subjects for faculty consideration . . . It is also important that there be faculty agencies adequate to deal effectively with this broad responsibility.

There are two important things about this statement. First, there is the claim for faculty jurisdiction—over virtually everything. Second, there is a basis of the claim for influence rights. Although the AAUP does appeal to bureaucratic power (the reference to the bylaws and its specification of the official duty of the faculty), its principal claim is that the faculty is the "organized body capable of rendering judgments on educational policy . . . particularly qualified to do so by virtue of the training and continued interest of its members." This is a clear appeal to professional influence. The professionals know something—they have expertise; *ergo* the demand for power.

The governance processes of the university are particularly complex, due in part to the importance of professional influence patterns that coexist with the bureaucratic patterns. Partisan-dominated cliques in the university are likely to be faculty groups that use professional influence in their attempts to influence policies. Several important consequences follow from the use of professional influence.

TENSIONS BETWEEN BUREAUCRATIC AND PROFESSIONAL ORIENTATIONS

First, there is constant tension between groups that appeal to bureaucratic resources for influence and groups that appeal to professional resources. The tension between bureaucrats and professionals shows up in many ways:

1. The professional relies on expert knowledge, whereas the bureaucrat relies on official position.
2. The bureaucrat relies on supervision by superiors (vertical supervision), whereas the professional trusts peer supervision by other professionals (horizontal supervision).
3. The bureaucrat demands tight organizational control, but the professional demands a great deal of autonomy.
4. The bureaucrat has strong identity with the local organization (the "company man"), whereas the professional has conditional loyalty and is oriented more toward his specialty (the "cosmopolitan").[7]

The conflict between the bureaucrats and the professionals has many consequences for academic governance, for their different orientations give them contradictory perspectives on the problems and needs of the university. The bureaucrats must see that the organization as a whole runs smoothly, is reasonably well coordinated, and can survive in its external environment. Coordination, supervision, holistic viewpoints, relations to the outside world—these are the peculiar and necessary stances of the administrator. On the other hand, the professional is oriented to the peculiar needs and requirements of his specialty. His view is more limited, for it is bounded by his discipline, his subspecialty, his research, and his students. The holistic viewpoints of the bureaucrat are balanced by the particularistic, specialized viewpoints of the professional. The critical point is that these are not necessarily contradictory stances, for both are necessary if the university is to achieve its goals. Warfare between these stances is common, but life would be impossible without both orientations.

The clearest example of the conflict between the bureaucrats' holistic perspectives and the professionals' particularistic orientations is the clash between the Commerce faculty and the central administration. From its viewpoint the Commerce faculty was outraged that the central administration dared to interfere in its traditional realm of competence. Faculty members felt that they were the experts on business education and the specialists in curriculum planning. The central administration, on the other hand, believed that the Commerce faculty was so trapped in its provincialism that it did not understand the needs of NYU as it tried to compete with the public institutions and to upgrade quality. A conflict between the perspectives was virtually inevitable.

[7]For a review of bureaucratic/professional tensions in the organizations, see William Kornhauser, *Scientists in Industry*. Berkeley: University of California Press, 1962; Amitai Etzioni, *Modern Organizations*. Englewood Cliffs: Prentice-Hall, 1964, Chapter VIII; also various sections in Vollmer and Mills, *Professionalization*. Englewood Cliffs: Prentice-Hall, 1966.

THE PARALLEL AUTHORITY STRUCTURE

A second consequence of the overlap between bureaucratic and professional influence patterns is the parallelism that develops between faculty and bureaucratic authority mechanisms. This was mentioned earlier but it bears repeating. From top to bottom the university has strands of bureaucratic and professional organization: the University Senate parallels the central administration, the college faculty committees parallel the dean's staff, the departmental advisory groups parallel the heads and chairmen. One of the most obvious factors in this dual authority system is the layer on layer of academic committees. Although the tangled system of committees is often the subject of sneering humor, it nevertheless constitutes a fundamental method of organizing and regularizing professional influence. The committee system gives the professionals ready access, legitimacy, and points of pressure to penetrate the bureaucratic system.

All these parallel structures overlap and interpenetrate, cooperate and quarrel, claim power and relinquish it. In a given department the faculty committees may be dominant or a department head may be undisputed king. The University Senate is the highest professional body in the university, but it coexists with the bureaucratic organization of the central administration. The lines of influence between these bodies is tenuous, shifting, and often filled with gentlemanly quarrels. In this struggle the partisan groups that use professional influence depend not on official sanctions but on the power of expertise.

SEGMENTALIZATION OF PROFESSIONAL INFLUENCE

A third consequence of professional influence is a remarkable segmentalization of influence patterns. The complexity of the university's social structure, analyzed in Chapter VII, is directly linked to the use of professional influence. Professional influence is based on the tactical use of expert knowledge to influence policy, but in the university this knowledge is specialized, segmented, and fractured. Consequently professional influence patterns often exhibit the same kind of confused picture.

This splintering effect makes academic professionalism different from many other kinds. In the hospital, for instance, there is one dominant professional group which exerts a more or less unified coherent set of professional demands. Burton Clark comments:[8]

> The internal controls of the medical profession are strong and are substituted for those of the organization. But in the college or university this

[8] Burton R. Clark, "Faculty Organization and Authority," from Terry E. Lunsford, (Ed.), *The Study of Academic Administration*. Boulder, Colorado: Western Interstate Commission for Higher Education, 1963, pp. 37–51.

> situation does not obtain; there are 12, 25, or 50 clusters of experts. The experts are prone to identify with their own disciplines, and the "academic profession" over-all comes off a poor second. We have wheels within wheels, many professions within a profession. No one of the disciplines on a campus is likely to dominate the others; . . . The campus is not a closely-knit group of professionals who see the world from one perspective. As a collection of professionals, it is decentralized, loose, and flabby.
>
> The principle is this: where professional influence is high and there is one dominant professional group, the organization will be integrated by the imposition of professional standards. Where professional influence is high and there are a number of professional groups, the organization will be split by professionalism. The university and the large college are fractured by expertness, not unified by it. The sheer variety of experts supports the tendency for authority to diffuse toward quasi-autonomous clusters.

In summary, partisan groups use professional resources, in the form of their expertise, as a basis for claiming influence over policies. This generates constant tension between bureaucratic and professional orientations, promotes the growth of parallel authority structure, and leads to a fragmentation of influence patterns.

Coercive Resources and Tactics

Bureaucratic influence depends on the formal sanctions of organizational authority; professional influence depends on the applications of expert knowledge. If partisans cannot use either of these resources to influence policy, they are likely to turn to nonformal, extralegal action. The sit-in, the appeal to public opinion, the boycott of classes, the faculty strike, the threat of bad publicity—these are some of the coercive weapons that alienated partisans often use. Many an administrator or professor, accustomed by occupational life-style to think in terms of formal bureaucratic power or professional influence, is shocked to find that another kind of power is now so often intruding into the life of the campus.

The students are currently the leading users of extraformal sanctions, but militant faculties across the nation are also resorting to pressure tactics to wring advantages from the university. Strikes, collective bargaining, adverse publicity, and the formation of unions are all coercive strategies employed by them as well. The headlines about student revolts often hide the quieter faculty revolution that is picking up momentum; for example, the American Federation of College Teachers (AFL-CIO) now has a branch on NYU's campus, formed in the immediate aftermath of the student revolt. One AFCT member put it quite frankly:

"The AAUP it not tough enough. They are afraid to play rough—they are more interested in 'professional' status. The AFCT, however, is prepared to get rough, to strike, to bargain—they are ready to fight."[9]

Alienated partisan groups use many different kinds of coercive tactics to protect their interests. First, there is a power of *disruption,* the ability to interrupt the organization's normal routines with sit-ins, boycotts, and strikes. This threat is so commonly used and so often described in the media that it does not seem necessary to discuss it. A similar type of action, closely interwoven with the power of disruption, is the use of *irrationality* as a weapon. Thomas Schelling argues that a strategic advantage comes to the man who can convince others that he is really irrational, that his actions are unpredictable, capricious, erratic, and unreasonable—in short, that he is for all practical purposes "insane."[10] As strange as it may seem, the insane man is often in an excellent bargaining position, for it is impossible to reason with him and he is usually impervious to threats. A screaming child, a man on the ledge of a building, a lunatic with a gun—these are people to whom rationality and negotiation have little meaning. By the same token, alienated partisans who act so unpredictably, who disrupt for no reason, who make irrational demands, who seem impervious to normal sanctions, and who strike out against authority in such capricious ways often have strategic advantages. Many a university administration has caved in under this kind of attack and has granted much more than it would have in a normal bargaining relationship. The power to burn one's bridges, to cut off all retreat, and to make the most outrageous demands may not be irrationality but in fact the most rational kind of interest-group tactic.

A third tactic is the *appeal to public opinion.* Universities are especially sensitive to public opinion, for they depend on the public for students, funds, political support, research money, and faculty recruitment. Bad publicity can undermine all these bases of support. One of the first acts of President Kirk after the 1968 Columbia student revolt was to circulate among alumni, parents, donors, and friends of Columbia a letter that tried to smooth over the public relations ruffle. Partisans are keenly aware that press coverage is a critical factor in the success or failure of a revolution, for appeals to the public bring the spotlight to bear on real or imagined abuses, thus exposing the university to outside pressures for reform. Of course, this tactic is a double-edged sword because public pressure can backfire against a cause as well as support it—as Columbia students well know.

[9] Interview No. 30, p. 1. For a discussion of the increased activities of faculty bargaining groups, see American Association for Higher Education, *Faculty Participation in Academic Governance*, 1201 Sixteenth Street, Washington, D. C., 1967.
[10] Schelling, *op. cit.*, p. 42.

Of course, many other coercive tactics are possible, but disruption, irrational behavior, and the use of propaganda are three good examples. The essential characteristic of coercive tactics is that they attempt to influence policy with nonformal, disruptive strategies instead of through the "legitimate" channels of the formal system.

Personal Influence Resources

All during the struggle at NYU personality factors played a significant part in bureaucratic systems, professional expertise, and coercive pressure tactics. The individuals in these social systems kept making their unique personal marks. The artful administrator who keeps them smiling as he puts the knife in their backs, the star professor who demands his way even if he disrupts a department, the ambitious young man who prods the faculty councils, the imaginative freethinker who generates new ideas—these and many more are the exciting personal elements that go into the political dynamics of the university. One Commerce professor put his belief in personal influence very sharply[11]:

> Personality plays a large role in the running of this university. The little boxes on the organization chart don't mean a thing unless you consider the personal force of the men filling them. For example, business education in this university has been under fire, and we'd be in a hell of a lot worse state if it weren't for the personal power and force of Dean Taggart [Executive Dean of the Graduate School of Business]. He is able to defend us because he is tough and aggressive. A lesser man would let us strangle to death—and many people wouldn't mind if we did!

At NYU one of the most compelling personalities at the dean's level is William Buckler of Washington Square College. Dean Buckler fights for his college and stands behind his faculty. His influence and power derive not so much from simple popularity, for his rough exterior does not always endear him to everyone, but from his strong administrative talents and his aggressive support of his college. One admiring professor noted[12]:

> Buckler is a tough customer—we don't call him "Bill the Buccaneer" for nothing. We don't always love him, but we always respect him—he's sharp as a tack and we know he's usually right. Moreover, he really fights for us in this college. He goes over to Vanderbilt Hall [the central administration] and makes them bleed!

[11] Interview No. 15, p. 2.
[12] Interview No. 44, p. 2.

Others could also be mentioned: Connor O'Brien, the Albert Schweitzer Chair Professor who is active in peace movements; President James M. Hester, who so forcefully pushed through new changes in the image of the university; Chancellor Russel Niles, who played such an important part in the all-university department controversy; Provost Nelson Norton, who fought so hard for the Heights' autonomy; former President Henry Heald, who worked so diligently to coordinate a loose confederation of schools.

Strong individuals are an important resource for a partisan group trying to influence policies. That elusive quality know as "leadership" certainly must be taken into account as a critical element in the success or failure of a group's efforts. Unfortunately, after decades of research on leadership, the literature is confusing and contradictory,[13] and this certainly is not the place to try to settle any arguments. Nevertheless, partisan and authority groups alike are dependent on the personal skills and qualities of their members, and this is one critical resource that must be examined in any conflict.

General Comments on the Tactics of Partisan Groups

The four kinds of tactical resources discussed above constitute the basic features of partisan group actions. Several general comments are necessary, however, to round out the picture of partisans putting these resources into action. First, a partisan group will tend to use its most available resource: for example, authority-dominated cliques are likely to take advantage of the bureaucratic resources to which they have direct access. Students are likely to employ coercive tactics, since they are excluded from bureaucratic and professional channels. Meanwhile, the faculty cliques will appeal to professional expertise as their influence base. In general, then, a group is inclined to use the resources it has most readily available, but this does not prevent them from forming combinations. Faculty groups tend to use professional influence, but do not hesitate to work through the formal bureaucratic channels or to employ personal influence tactics. Authorities sometimes use coercive tactics as well as bureaucratic sanctions, and students are happy to gain access to formal decision systems. Thus there is a tendency for a group to employ a combination of tactics, even if there is a heavy emphasis on one type.

The second general comment concerns the parallelism between the structures of partisan groups and those of the authorities. The influencing groups try to arrange themselves as closely as possible around the "access points"

[13] For a discussion of the literature on leadership see Dorwin Cartwright and Alvin Zander, *Group Dynamics*. New York: Harper and Row, 1953, p. 489 ff.

to the authorities. Moreover, as the decision points change so does the structure of the relevant interest groups; for example, as NYU admissions policies shifted from the local colleges to the central administration, the concerned groups started directing their influence toward the University Senate instead of the college faculties. Thus there is a close relationship between the structure of the decision system and the structures of the partisan groups who are trying to influence it. In general, interest groups show a remarkable tendency to be structured like the authority groups they hope to influence.

Third, it is important to note that partisan groups usually have two somewhat contradictory objectives. Their main purpose is to influence the authorities, but another strong reason is to develop group cohesion. Often a partisan group may seem irrational to an observer; for example, when student groups engage in violence and invite police intervention. However, this may not be so irrational as it seems, for the intention of the group may be to develop a martyr mentality that will pull the group together and make it stronger for future influence attempts. In the March 1968 demonstration against Dow Chemical a group of students was surrounding Chancellor Allan Cartter on the front steps of Vanderbilt Hall, shouting at him and generally abusing him. I asked one student leader if he thought this would convince Chancellor Cartter that he should honor their demands and he replied with shrewd political wisdom, "This has nothing to do with convincing Dr. Cartter of anything. It's an exercise in group-think. It's for *our* benefit, not his. It wouldn't even matter if he weren't here, the real thing is to build up our group spirit for the next round." Another student told me that it was imperative that the administration be goaded into calling the police because "unless the cops bust some heads this group is going to fall apart for lack of a martyr." Irrational behavior may be very rational indeed if the goal is in-group cohesion instead of influence on the authorities.

THE RESPONSE OF AUTHORITIES TO PARTISAN PRESSURE

The effectiveness of partisan groups in influencing organizational policy depends on many factors. First, it depends heavily on the nature of the group itself. If groups are cohesive, disciplined, and well organized, they are more likely to succeed. In the Columbia student unrest in the spring of 1968 it was the consensus that the black students occupying Hamilton Hall were much more successful at achieving their objectives than the white students in other buildings. In general this was attributed to the leadership, cohesiveness, and discipline that the Black Students Union was able to supply in comparison with the relative disorganization and lack of discipline that the white Students for a Democratic Society displayed. The nature of the group and its sophistication in using its resources are critical factors in the success or failure of pressure tactics.

Obviously the other critical factor in the influence equation is the action taken by authorities. On one hand the authorities can *yield* to the pressures and align their decisions with the demands of the partisan groups. This was part of the NYU administration's strategy in the face of student unrest, for some of the tuition increases were revised downward. In the departmental reorganization the central administration yielded first to the needs of the department chairmen, then later reversed itself to favor the deans. The authorities can relieve the tension of the moment by yielding to partisan demands, and if the decision is later vindicated the issue is settled. This is frequently a problem, however, for favoring one group tends to offend other groups and the dissatisfaction is simply relocated rather than alleviated. Of course, authorities often use the tactic of "strategic yielding," a process of partly giving in to calm the situation but then reverting to the original policy when the issue has died down.

On the other hand, instead of yielding to pressure, the authorities can attempt *social control* tactics to stop the partisans. Gamson suggests that authorities try to control partisans with four tactics.[14] "Insulation" is the process of separating the partisans from other groups within the organization, thus holding their effect to a small subgroup. "Persuasion" is an attempt to convince the partisans that their demands are unreasonable and that the authorities are acting fairly. Many types of propaganda tactics are employed in this attempt. "Cooptation" is the technique of picking off partisan leaders and giving them positions within the established bureaucratic structure. This relieves some pressures but also frequently brings new ones into the formal system. Finally, if all else fails, the authorities will apply "sanctions" to stop the partisans. The nature of bureaucratic sanctions was discussed earlier in this chapter.

In addition to these direct actions by authorities, there is the indirect action of acting *before* the partisans begin influencing. This is a process that might be called "anticipatory reaction" to partisans. The authorities try to avoid policies that are likely to generate resistance. Thus interest groups often have power even though they may not even be active on that issue, for the decision makers try to offend as few people as possible. Administrators can often work successfully by maneuvering in "zones of indifference" in which interest groups were inactive. In fact, it seems that administrators often use the "trial balloon" tactic of leaking word about a project in advance to judge the likely response. If the response is favorable, it is an-

[14] William Gamson, *Power and Discontent*. Homewood, Illinois: Dorsey, 1968, pp. 111–144.

nounced that the policy is really planned, but if it is unfavorable it can be denied as a "false rumor." Thus the anticipation of interest-group opposition allows authorities to skirt issues that these groups might oppose, thus saving capital for future big fights and preventing quasi groups from becoming active partisans. As one professor put it, "Why should the administration deliberately fight interest groups on little matters—they don't. Oh no, they might need that capital later in some big battle."

A final general comment about the response of authorities concerns *alliances* and *cross pressures*. Interest groups often depend on alliances with like-minded groups to carry through their sanctions. The students at NYU organized a coalition against the tuition increase that included civil rights activitist, antiwar groups, and student government leaders—not to mention a small group of faculty supporters. None of these groups could have been effective against an entrenched administration, but all of them together gained major concessions. The student groups at the Dow demonstrations were likewise a strange, complex mixture, held together by little more than common antagonism against the administration, frustration against a war they thought unjust, and a hatred of police. Alliances are often effective tools, for they can give power to otherwise impotent, separated groups.

However, the very existence of multiple groups also opens the door to another complex phenomenon, that of *cross pressures*. Not all groups will line up on the same side of any issue, and the competition among them gives a measure of freedom to the authorities. In the 1968 revolt Columbia's administration was faced with a fantastically complex set of overlapping, competing, and cross-pressuring groups. Leftist students held buildings; rightist students tried to throw them out physically; young faculty joined hands to stop police; old faculty threatened to leave if the situation was not cleared up; the city administration cried for soft action to prevent inflammation of neighboring ghettos; the conservative alumni shouted for stern action; university presidents around the nation urged decisive action to stop the spread of student rebellions; and a divided nation sat on the sidelines screaming advice. President Kirk may or may not have done the right things, but who would have traded places with him as he jockeyed among all these groups? Cross pressures can give freedom of action, but they can also produce paralysis, ulcers, and nervous breakdowns.

In summary, the success of partisan influence attempts depends heavily on the characteristics of the group itself and on the responses of the authorities. Authorities often try to anticipate influence attempts in advance and cut them off by appropriate action. Moreover, they work in the cross pressures of many groups and can often gain freedom of action by playing them off against one another. If these actions fail, the authorities have two options: either to change the decisions to match demands or to make social-control attempts to manage the partisans. These control attempts may take the form of insulation, persuasion, cooptation, or sanctions.

THE CYCLE OF CONFLICT

We have now outlined some ideas about the formation and organization of partisan groups, about their attitudes and goals, about the resources groups use in their conflicts, and about the social control devices that authorities employ to control partisans. Now in this last section we have tried to tie some of these ideas together by proposing a "cycle of conflict." Once an interest articulation cycle has begun it goes through a series of episodes, beginning with a provocative issue and ending with new policy legislation.

The Issue

Given the fragmented nature of the university and the conflicting demands that come out of different value stances, it is almost impossible to catalog the different occasions for conflict. The issues can be almost any one of thousands of incidents. It appears, however, that the situations that provoke conflict have several general characteristics. First, there is the *iceberg phenomenon.* Only rarely is the apparent issue really the major factor, for usually other critical matters are hiding just under the surface. Often the cited issue is only a pretense for raising more fundamental issues of participation in decision making, the rights of students or faculty, or the role of interest groups in the political process. Any attempt to settle the issue must go beyond the surface causes to the basic factors, or the conflict will only have been papered over. Second, the issues that cause large-scale conflict will almost always have a *unifying effect* on diverse interest groups; this has been true in almost every student revolt and is also true in less dramatic situations.

Third, the conflict is often the result of *rising expectations* rather than intolerable conditions. Many an administration has been startled to find that major concessions and improved conditions actually provoke new conflict rather than calm. This has been noted many times in political revolutions against governments, and it is not surprising that the same pattern repeats itself on campuses. Feeding a hungry man only a morsel may not stop his appetite—it may stimulate it.

Fourth, John Searle's discussion of the *Sacred Issue* is important, for often the issue in conflict will have moral overtones that justify and legitimate radical action. This is clear in student unrest when rights for the black man, antiwar sentiment, and student power are used as ultimate goals to justify almost any short-range excesses. However, the same tactic is used by faculties when they appeal to "academic freedom" and by administrators pleading for "institutional autonomy" in their battles with legislators. The Sacred Issue factor is a key element in defining the boundaries of academic conflict at all levels.

Intensity Increases: Moderation Gives Way to Radicalism

Once the first demands are made the issue usually develops a momentum of its own, which dramatically increases in intensity. Leadership becomes more radical, and the earlier leaders are cast aside for more aggressive ones. The Martin Luther Kings are supplanted by the Rap Browns; the Provisional government is overturned by the Bolsheviks; the Jacobins replace the monarchists; the NYU student government leaders are ousted by the Ad Hoc Committee. The cost of compromise is raised, and intense *polarization* occurs between the two sides of the issue.

The Issues Expand: From Specific Issues to Generalized Questions of Authority

Although specific issues almost always spark the conflict, the situation rapidly expands to general questions of authority. This is the escalation up the issue hierarchy that we mentioned above. "What will the particular policy be?" gives way to "Who has the right to make this policy?" Again we see the critical nature of the struggle over legitimacy, for each group not only wants the specific issue to be decided in its favor but it also demands the legitimate right to decide that kind of issue in the future. This is illustrated in several places in the NYU research. The students not only demanded that the tuition increase be rolled back but they also demanded a right to sit on the bodies that make such decisions; the students not only wanted Dow off the campus but they also wanted to control the decision processes regulating access to the campus. The AAUP could not decide what position to take on the specific issues in the goal changes, but it called loud and clear for faculty authority over such matters in the future; the Commerce faculty not only wanted the admissions standards left alone but also wanted the central administration to keep its hands off Commerce's autonomy. An axiom could be pronounced: in any major conflict specific issues often expand to questions of legitimate power and authority; the controversy over policy content becomes a battle over the decision right. The conflict moves up the issue hierarchy as the partisans attack incumbents and the decision structure.

Sanctions Are Applied

As the conflict increases and as radicalism takes over, sanctions begin to be applied by all parties. At first there is the threat stage: if you don't do X, then I will do Y—and will you be sorry! Then come the actual sanctions: the AAUP passes a resolution that might give the university a black eye; the students stage a boycott; the administration applies disciplinary rules; the faculty strikes; professors appeal to accrediting agencies. The sanction arsenal contains many weapons, and under different circumstances different ones will be used.

This is the stage of strategic bargaining and negotiation in which each group tries to obtain concessions as cheaply as possible. The cost of sanctions goes up with the severity of the action, and the repercussions can often far outweigh the strategic advantage. The police *can* be used to clear buildings; sit-ins *can* become virtual riots; faculty strikes *can* cripple the campus. In each case, however, raising the severity of the sanction raises the political consequence, alienates the opposition even more drastically, and pushes public opinion even further toward conservative reaction. Thus it is to everyone's advantage to hold sanctions to the lowest possible level. The early stages of the conflict see the price quickly escalating in terms of demands, threats, and the severity of sanctions. It usually takes quick, decisive action to prevent escalation and the talent for this kind of action is rare.

The Call for Allies

The cost of sanctions goes up, the tempo of the action increases, and the specific issues begin to escalate toward attacks on the decision system. Then there is a spreading effect as the conflict draws in other groups. The students call for faculty help, the Commerce faculty pressures the AAUP, and the administration appeals to faculty mediators. Other groups that have a stake in the outcome of the conflict and vested interests in the shape of power and authority quickly enter into the fray. Another axiom could be proposed: in an extended conflict the issue will expand until all groups with a major stake in the distribution of authority are included. Moreover, as the controversy escalates, officials at ever higher levels become involved. In California, for example, the increased intensity of campus conflict has drawn in not only the chancellor of the local campus but even the president of the state system, the board of regents, the state legislature, and the governor. Thus there is a spreading effect as partisans form coalitions and authorities appeal for help to higher and higher levels.

Mediation and Conciliation

As the conflict rages mediators begin to emerge. As a rule these are people who were not at first a part of the conflict but were drawn into it as it expanded. In every major student revolt the original conflict was between the administration and the students, but the faculty was caught up in it almost immediately. Many faculty members join sides, but a large segment usually tries to play the mediator role. This was true at Berkeley, Columbia, San Francisco State, and Stanford as well as at New York University. The effectiveness of the mediation attempts depends on many factors, among them being the severity of the sanctions already in effect, the rigidity of the conflicting groups, the degree of involvement of outside groups, and the mediation talents of given individuals. In the conflict between the Commerce faculty and the central administration the deans played a mediating role; in many faculty strikes the AAUP, state investigating committees, and accrediting agencies have played leading mediator roles. At this stage compromises are forged, and the men who loudly announce that they will never "make deals" turn out to be the very ones in the smoke-filled rooms.

The Bureaucratization of Conflict

Every revolution has a period in which things return to relative calm. In an organization this almost always assumes the form of "bureaucratization of conflict." The compromises and deals that were hammered out in the mediation are now converted into bureaucratic action. Committees are appointed, commissions report, and interest dies down. The McKay and Griffiths committees, for example, were institutionalized leftovers of the student revolt. This is not to say, however, that no real change has occurred, for most major revolutions do leave their mark—although seldom as dramatic as the partisans had hoped or the authorities had feared.

An interesting feature of this stage in the conflict is the changeover in leadership that usually occurs in the partisan group. The idealists and revolutionaries find that they cannot lower themselves to "compromise with the Establishment" and they drift off to other activities. It was noted earlier that the more radical leaders of the Ad Hoc Committee refused to participate on the McKay Committee or to run for student-body offices with the VOICE Party. By life-style and political ideology the revolutionary is unsuited to the role of bureaucrat. Nevertheless the bureaucratization of conflict goes on apace. All of Chapter IX is devoted to expanding on the legislative phase in which this bureaucratization occurs. Figure 8-9 illustrates the cycle of conflict.

Figure 8-9. The Cycle of Conflict

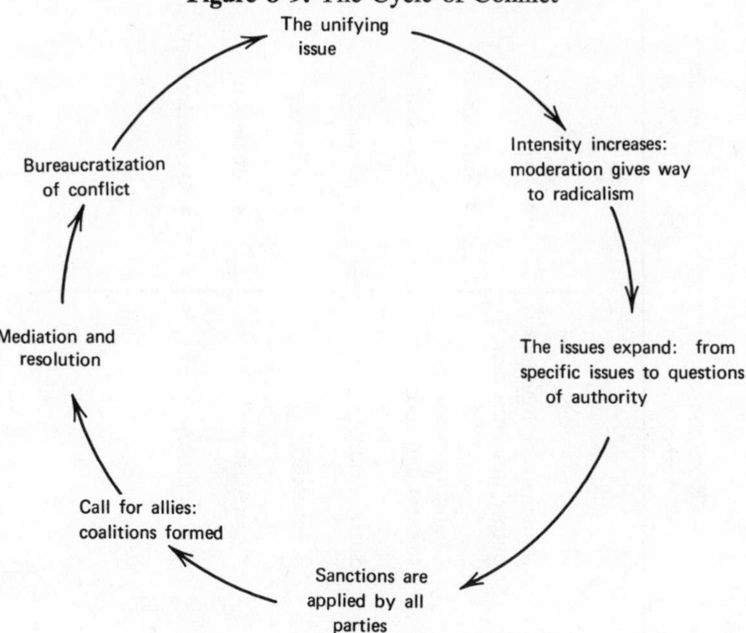

SUMMARY

The discussion of the cycle of conflict brings the chapter's analysis of the interest articulation process to a close. This is obviously a complex issue, for it deals with the many ways in which partisan groups pressure authorities during organizational conflicts. First, the *development and organization of partisan groups* were explored, beginning with unorganized quasi groups and moving on to the four active interest groups: anomic groups, partisan-dominated cliques, authority-dominated cliques, and associations. Second, the partisan's degree of *trust* was noted as a critical dimension in the conflict, for variations on the confidence/alienation continuum will greatly influence the goals a group will select and the tactics it will use. Next, a *hierarchy of issues*, varying from the specific issue to the decision structure itself, was suggested. Groups with more alienation try to escalate to more severe demands and more far-reaching goals. Fourth, the *resources* of groups were analyzed in four separate sections: bureaucratic, professional, coercive, and personal. Next, the *responses of authorities* to partisan pressure were examined. Finally, a *cycle of conflict* was proposed in which all these ideas could be unified as part of the action. Taken together, these points outline the major considerations of the interest articulation process, as shown in Figure 8-10.

Figure 8-10. A Graphic Summary of the "Interest Articulation" Process

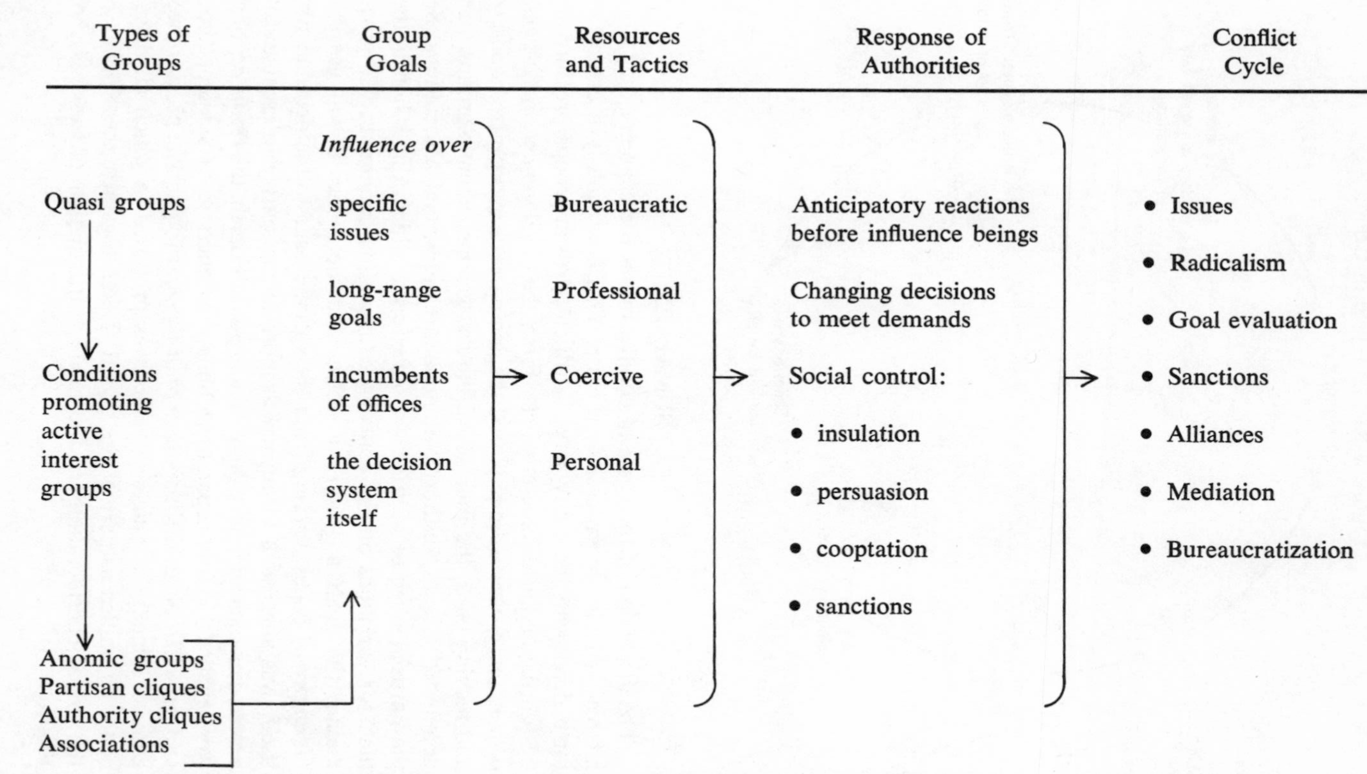

Chapter IX

THE LEGISLATIVE PROCESS

WHO DECIDES WHAT, AND HOW?

So far the discussion of university governance has moved through two stages. The first was an examination of the university's social structure, both internal and external. The second was an analysis of the interest articulation processes by which partisan groups apply pressure on policy decisions. Now we turn to the last step in the policy-formulation process, the "legislative" phase in which authorities translate partisan demands into viable policy for the organization. Figure 9-1 shows how this chapter fits into the whole political model.

Political scientists have been studying the legislative processes of the larger society for a long time. Their studies have been facilitated by the existence of the governmental legislature, a clearly defined body that meets regularly and holds public sessions. Studying the legislative processes in a university, however, is complicated because there is no single legislative body; the legislative processes occur all up and down the multiple levels in the formal structure. Moreover, in contrast to state or federal governments the "executive" and "legislative" functions often overlap. The university has a more *diffuse* legislative structure than the state or national

Figure 9-1. Chapter Nine Focuses on the "Legislative" Stage: The Transformation of Influence into Policy

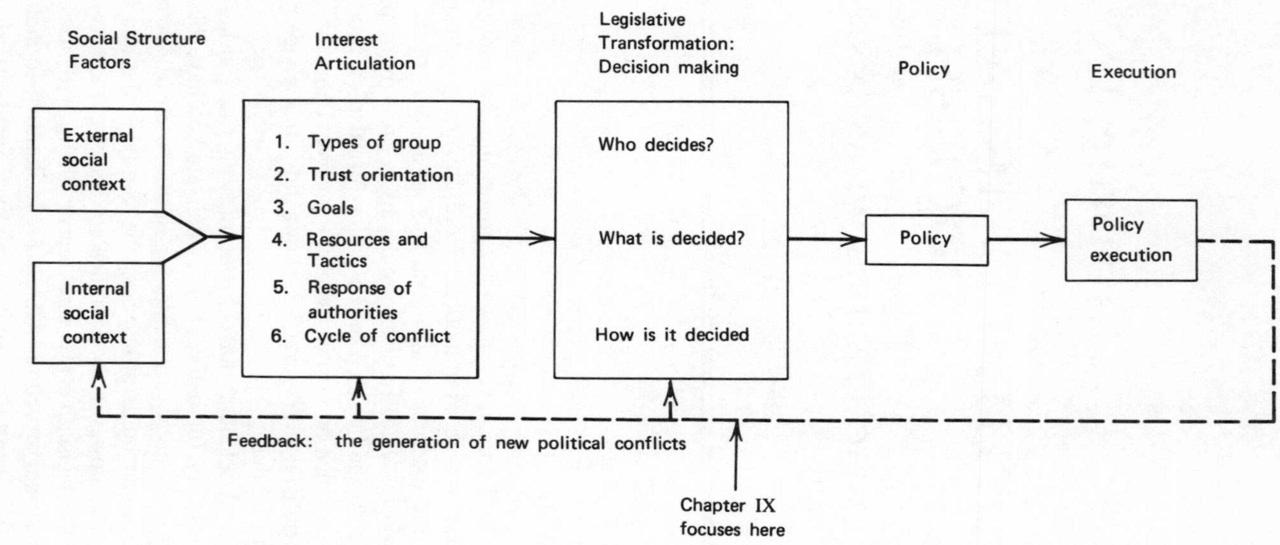

governments, or, to put it another way, the decision structures of the university are *less differentiated* than those of the government.

All this adds up to a vague, diffuse legislative process that must be examined at many points in the organization. Indeed, the decision process in the university is such a complicated phenomenon that it is impossible to chart every important aspect. We can, however, suggest a few important features of the process by asking the basic questions: *Who* decides *what* and *how?* The chapter is organized around these questions. First, the "who" question is examined: Is there a "power elite" and who participates in the decision processes? Second, the "what" question is explored: What are the spheres of influence of various groups in the university? Finally, the "how" question is considered: What are the dynamics that frame the decision process?

WHO MAKES BINDING DECISIONS?

We have already suggested that it is the "authorities" who make "binding decisions" which commit the university to specific policies. However, this becomes complicated because there are many different groups of "authorities" in a large organization. In fact, most members of the university community can claim some participation in the decision-making process at some level. Administrators, faculty, students, and trustees all participate to varying degrees. The degree of participation and the "openness" of the decision system are a matter of major debate.

Who Makes Decisions: The "Power Elite" Debate

Sociologists and political scientists have always been fascinated by the question who makes decisions in a social system. One of the most persistent debates in political theory concerns the existence of a "power elite" or "ruling oligarchy." Robert Michels long ago advanced the "iron law of oligarchy" which insists that all organizations develop ruling elites while the masses are inactive. Michels' study of European socialist parties showed that oligarchial elites inevitably arose even in those supposedly model democratic organizations. Michels concludes:

> "The appearance of oligarchical phenomena in the very bosom of the revolutionary parties is a conclusive proof of the existence of imminent

oligarchical tendencies in every kind of human organization which strives for the attainment of definite ends."[1]

James Bryce put it in even more sweeping terms:

> In all assemblies and groups and organized bodies of men, from a nation down to the committee of a club, direction and decisions rest in the hands of a small percentage, less and less in proportion to the larger and larger size of the body, till in a great population it becomes an infinitesimally small proportion of the whole number. This is and always has been true of all forms of government, though in different degrees.[2]

Although they may not have read the literature, the current generation of radicals are essentially rephrasing Michels and Bryce when they complain about an "Establishment" that controls the major decisions and excludes the "people." Student and faculty revolutionaries, of course, are charging that the university is a tightly closed system in which most members of the organization have little influence over its decisions. The basic premise of such a charge is that the university's decision system is a political enterprise and that all members of the community should have a voice in its governance.

Has the university a "tendency toward oligarcy" and an "establishment" power elite, or is its decision system relatively open to influence from its members in a "democratic" fashion? In many ways these questions are extremely difficult to answer. By comparison with other complex organizations (such as government bureaucracies, business firms, or prisons) the university is more democratic and has more channels of influence for its members. By comparison with the democratic ideals of the revolutionaries or the democratic practices of a New England town meeting, however, the university exhibits a rather rigid structure in which the trustees and officials have the most influence over policies, the faculty, a moderate influence, and the students, very little. Thus the university is certainly more democratic than most other organizations but certainly less democratic than many people think would be ideal.

[1]Robert Michels, *Political Parties: A Sociological Study of the Oligarchial Tendencies of Modern Democracy*, translated by Eden and Cedar Paul. London: Jarrold & Sons, 1915, p. 14. Republished by Free Press, Glencoe, Illinois, in 1949.

[2]James Bryce, *Modern Democracies*. New York: Macmillan, 1921, Vol. II, p. 542. In the literature on power in city governments this debate recently raged between Floyd Hunter, who claims to have discovered a power elite in Atlanta, and Robert Dahl and his associates who claim to have destroyed the power-elite theory with their work on New Haven. See Floyd Hunter, *Community Power Structure*. Chapter Hill: University of North Carolina Press, 1953; Robert Dahl, *Who Governs?* New Haven: Yale University Press, 1961. For a review of the debate see Nelson Polsby, *Community Power and Political Theory*. New Haven: Yale University Press, 1963.

In many respects the either/or question (democracy or oligarchy) is misleading. It is more profitable to ask: *How* are various groups involved in the decision process and *to what extent* is the university more or less democratic? To answer these questions it is necessary to begin with the flat assertion that most people simply are *not* involved in decision making to any significant degree. Robert Dahl put it quite frankly while talking about the involvement of voters in the politics of the city:

> It would clear the air of a good deal of cant if instead of assuming that politics is a normal and natural concern of human beings, one were to make the contrary assumption that whatever lip service citizens may pay to platitudes, politics is a remote, alien, and unrewarding activity.[3]

The same must be said about university politics, for the vast majority of students, faculty, and outsiders in the university community are much too concerned about their private affairs to care about the university's governance, regardless of whether it is "democratic" or "oligarchical."

The "Scale of Participation"

However, definite scales of activity range from the most intensely active officials down to the most inactive student or professor. David B. Truman noted the same type of "activity scale" in his study of political interest groups:

> Participation of the membership of a group, moreover, is a matter of degree, scaling down from continuous activity in a few cases to what can be called apathy in a large number. Individuals may move up and down this scale of participation as circumstances inside and outside the group change. Leadership of the group is a rate and type of participation, a relationship with others on the scale.[4]

It is possible to construct a four-step scale of participation in the university.[5] First, there are the *officials* who are committed by career, life-style, and ideology to the task of running the organization. They constitute by far the most politically active segment of the university community and have the most influence over organizational decisions. At the second level of participation are the *activists,* a relatively small body of people intensely involved in the university's politics even though they do not hold full-time

[3] Robert Dahl, *Who Governs?* New Haven: Yale Press, 1961, p. 279.

[4] David B. Truman, *The Governmental Process.* New York: Knopf, 1951, p. 155.

[5] This scale refers to administrators and faculty members. There was no data available on student participation, but a similar pyramid of activity probably exists for them.

administrative posts. On the one hand these activists serve as part-time authorities by working in the official committee system and in the complex network of advisory councils. On the other they are the partisans who work outside the formal system by joining partisan cliques or associations. Surprisingly enough, the activists seem to be able to switch roles rather easily, at one moment sitting on an official committee and the next moment sitting with their partisan cliques planning strategies that will influence the officials. The activists are usually faculty members who lead dual lives as professors and amateur organization men.

At the third step down the activity scale is the attentive public—the sideline watchers interested in the activities of the formal system. They regularly attend and vote at faculty meetings but usually are not on committees or study groups. Their rate of participation is situationally oriented. When a "hot issue" comes along, they jump into the conflict; otherwise they are basically just active onlookers. They are potentially a powerful bloc when aroused and therefore they have a great deal of indirect control over the authorities. The *attentives* have less influence than the activists—but are by no means powerless.

Finally, at the lowest level of participation are the *apathetics*—those who almost never serve on committees, rarely show up for faculty meetings, and in general could not care less about the politics of the university. The apathetics come in many stripes, from the star professor who is simply "too busy to mess with this kind of nonsense" to the teaching assistant who is politically disfranchised in spite of his teaching service. The 1968 NYU Survey included only full-time personnel and thus the vast majority (79.4%) reported official activity on some level. However, the part-time faculty, the teaching assistants, the lecturers, and other "quasi faculties" constitutes a huge group of apathetics which does not show up in a survey of full-time faculty; more than half of NYU's faculty falls into this group. The apathetics probably are a large majority in spite of the contrary statistics found in a survey of full-time faculty members.

Scale of Activity by Levels in the University

The number of people at each step of the activity scale varies considerably by levels in the university. The 1968 NYU Survey tried to determine the degree of participation in the departments, the colleges, and at the university level. Figure 9-2 shows that there is a high degree of integration of the full-time faculty into the departments' decision-making structure, but as we move up the scale to college and all-university politics the percentage of activists decreases sharply.[6] In effect, then, many people are active in department decision making, but only a small minority participates in college or all-university decision councils.

Figure 9-2. The "Activity Pyramid" at Different Levels

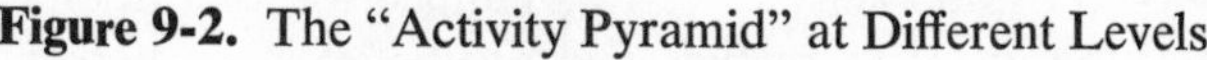

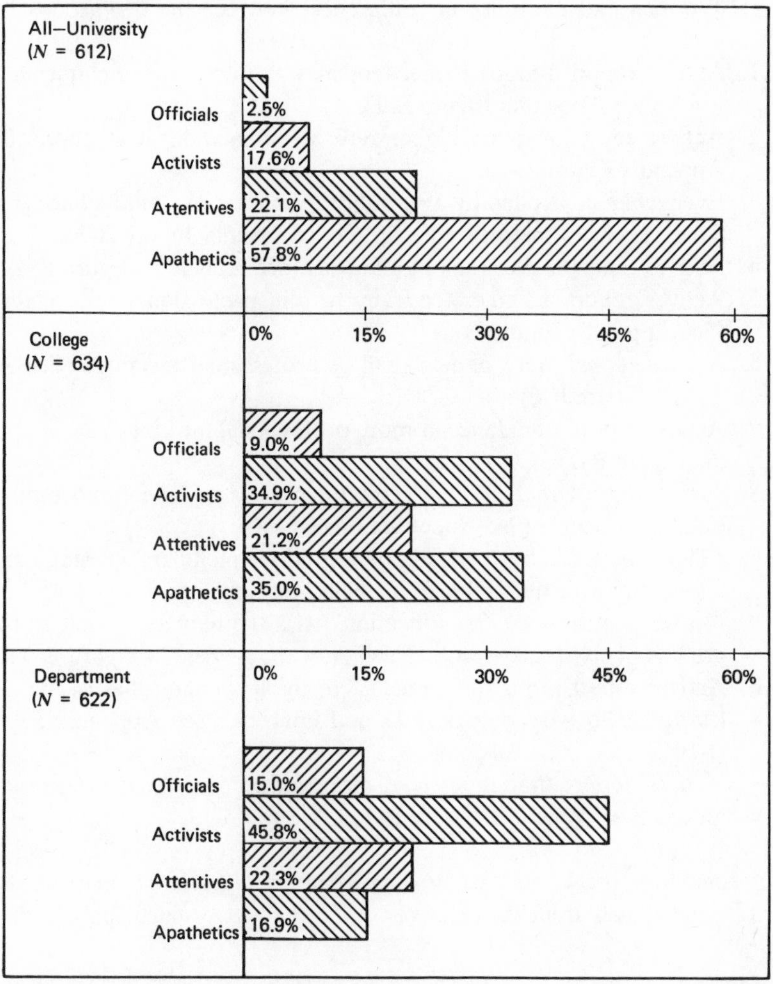

[6]Using Section VI in the questionnaire (see Appendix A) *apathetics* were defined as those who reported nothing more than informal, personal contacts; *attentives* were defined as those who reported nothing more than attendance at faculty meetings (except at the university level where there are no general faculty meetings; here informal personal contact was taken as evidence of concern). *Activists* were defined as those who reported, in addition to the above, membership in a committee or an advisory group; *officials* were defined as those who held official offices.

Characteristics of "Actives" Versus "Inactives"

It is interesting to note that people located at different points on the activity scale display a whole series of critical differences. In order to simplify matters the officials and activists can be lumped together in one group (the actives), and the attentive publics and apathetics into another (the inactives). We then find the following differences between the two groups:[7]

1. Actives report a much higher tendency to join partisan cliques at all levels (See Appendix Figure B-1).
2. Actives report a much higher rate of publication at all levels (See Appendix Figure B-2).
3. Even when controlled by age, publication rates are still higher for actives, except in the oldest group (See Appendix Figure B-3).
4. Actives report higher rank at all levels (See Appendix Figure B-4).
5. Actives report a higher tendency to join professional organizations (See Appendix Figure B-5).
6. Actives report more papers read at professional meetings (See Appendix Figure B-6).
7. Actives report attendance at more professional meetings (See Appendix Figure B-7).
8. Actives report that they perceive themselves as having more power than other people (See Appendix Figure B-8).
   (Thus the "objective" criteria of committee membership, etc., correlate highly with the "subjective" belief that one has power.)
9. Actives report more "identification" with the university; that is, they are less likely to take a job elsewhere (See Appendix Figure B-9).
10. Actives report more "attachment" to the university; that is, they are less likely to have outside jobs and interests (See Appendix Figure B-10).
11. Actives report that they have more influence on outside pressure groups (See Appendix Figure B-11).

In summary, there seem to be three distinct clusters of behavior that separate the actives from the inactives. First, the actives participate in many

[7] The supporting data for these statements are given in a series of detailed tables in Appendix B. In these tables further refinements are made among the actives, taking into account the different levels within the university (department, college, and all-university). The major differences, however, were between the actives and the inactives, and the detailed analysis by levels would not be of general interest. However, they are included in Appendix B for anyone who wants to make a detailed study of the characteristics of actives at different levels in the university.

more activities that give them influence on policy. By definition they serve on many committees and hold many official offices, but in addition they have higher rank, join more partisan cliques, and report more personal feelings of influence over policy. Moreover, they report that their high internal influence is matched by a high degree of contact with outside influence groups such as government agencies, foundations, and accrediting agencies.

The second cluster of activities concerns disciplinary associations and scholarly achievement. This analysis seems to contradict the common campus myth that actives are usually mediocre scholars who forfeit disciplinary achievement in order to gain local influence. In fact, these data show just the opposite, for the actives have significantly higher professional achievement than the inactives, including more publications, more professional memberships, more attendance at professional meetings, and more disciplinary papers read at meetings. The campus myth about actives being mediocre scholars may have to be re-examined in light of these data.

The third set of differences is the tendency of actives to report more loyalty and involvement with the university. Actives indicated that they were less willing to leave the university for other jobs and that they had fewer outside interests than the inactives. Thus it seems that the actives have a whole set of intense involvements with the university, of which political activism is only one.

Is the University Becoming More Democratic?

The foregoing discussion suggests some answers to the question of who is involved in decision making. A further question, however, concerns the changes that are taking place in the university. All over the world students and other groups are demanding that the university's decision systems be made more democratic and that previously excluded groups be allowed to take part in the decision processes. To use a phrase consistent with our political interpretation, they are demanding that the "polity" and the "electorate" be expanded to cover groups that were previously disfranchised. Regardless of the merits or problems associated with any specific proposals, it is clear that these demands are having an effect on university legislative processes. There are definite signs that universities are paying more attention to demands made by students, faculty, and community groups.

There were two obvious examples in the NYU research. First, the students were able to wring several major concessions from the University Senate in the aftermath of the student revolt. The most important result was that students gained the right to sit on a wide variety of decision-making committees throughout the university. The students managed to open the door to the decision councils and were now seen as legitimate participants in the legislative process. The second example of the democratizing movement was the Taggart Commission report which recommended a series of changes in the composition of the University Senate. The report called for a restructuring of the Senate's membership to include more faculty members and fewer administrators. It also argued that the restructured Senate should have more authority over more issues, thus expanding considerably the faculty's role in the legislative process.

Both examples suggest that the national movement for a more "democratic" university was having some limited success at NYU. Of course, only time will tell if the changes represent major readjustments or merely minor moves that will not really affect the legislative processes. However, the examples fit a national pattern that seems to be running in the direction of more influence for student, faculty, and community groups previously excluded from the decision networks.

Who Makes Decisions: Conclusion

This section has focused on the question: "*Who* decides?" First, the "power elite" debate was discussed, and we noted several tendencies which press toward a more "democratic" university in spite of some obviously oligarchial factors. The next step was to propose four participation levels, from the "officials" to the "apathetics." There was a pyramid of activity with high integration of the faculty into departmental activities but decreasing participation at higher levels. In effect, many people make decisions but have widely different amounts of influence. Finally, some of the differences between actives and inactives were suggested. Those who participate in the decision system seem to be different in many ways from those who do not.

The discussion certainly does not settle the "power elite" question, but it does give some clues. First, the officials do constitute something of a power elite, for they certainly have more influence than most people. This oligarchial tendency, however, is limited by the high degree of participation found in the faculty, most of whose full-time members are involved to some extent in the decision networks. Moreover, many democratizing currents seem to be at work that may well change the entire scene in the next few years, especially as students are included in the decision process.

In conclusion, the answer to our question of "*who* decides" is that many, many people are involved to a greater or lesser degree in the decision processes. They are sometimes intensely involved and at other times apathetic; they are full-time officials or only part-time activists; they are involved only in their own departments or perhaps at other levels. In short, the "who decides" question has a whole series of answers, depending on the level in the university and on the specific issue.

WHO DECIDES WHAT: "SPHERES OF INFLUENCE"

Questions about *who* makes decisions naturally lead to the issue of *what* decisions are made. Several times earlier we noted that influence patterns in the university had to be specified by levels, for there are different dynamics in the departments, in the colleges, and at the university level. However, there is an additional complication, for influence and authority are not only related to *levels* they are also tied to specific *issues*.

In other words, groups in the university generally carve out "spheres of influence" for themselves and thus avoid conflicting directly with other groups. Almost every writer on university governance notes that the faculty claims some areas, such as curriculum and degree requirements, whereas the administration claims others, such as budgets and building programs. There has been little systematic work to chart the areas of responsibility, and for that reason the 1968 NYU Survey tried to determine how members of the university community viewed the division of responsibilities among levels and among issues.

Mapping the Spheres of Influence

The questionnaire asked the respondents to give their impression of what groups controlled the issues (Appendix A, Section VIII). Six groups were listed: the trustees, the central administration, the deans, the college faculty, the departmental faculty, and the individual faculty members. The respondents were then asked to rank the influence of the various groups on 10 specific issues. Their answers, shown in Figure 9-3 illustrate the patterns of influence that the respondents *believed* existed, though there is, of course, no guarantee that this is "actually" the way influence is distributed. For convenience the same data are reported in two different ways. Figure 9-4 lists the *areas* of responsibility one at a time and shows the controlling groups. Figure 9-4 also lists the *groups* one at a time and shows their areas of responsibility. Thus both figures report the same data broken down from two different viewpoints.

The charts suggest that instead of one dominant power elite there seems to be a fragmented system of influence, for different groups are strong in different spheres of influence and no single group dominates everything. The trustees are strong on budgetary planning, physical plant maintenance,

Figure 9-3. Who Has Influence on Various Areas? (% of Each Group Reported with *High* Influence in that Area)*

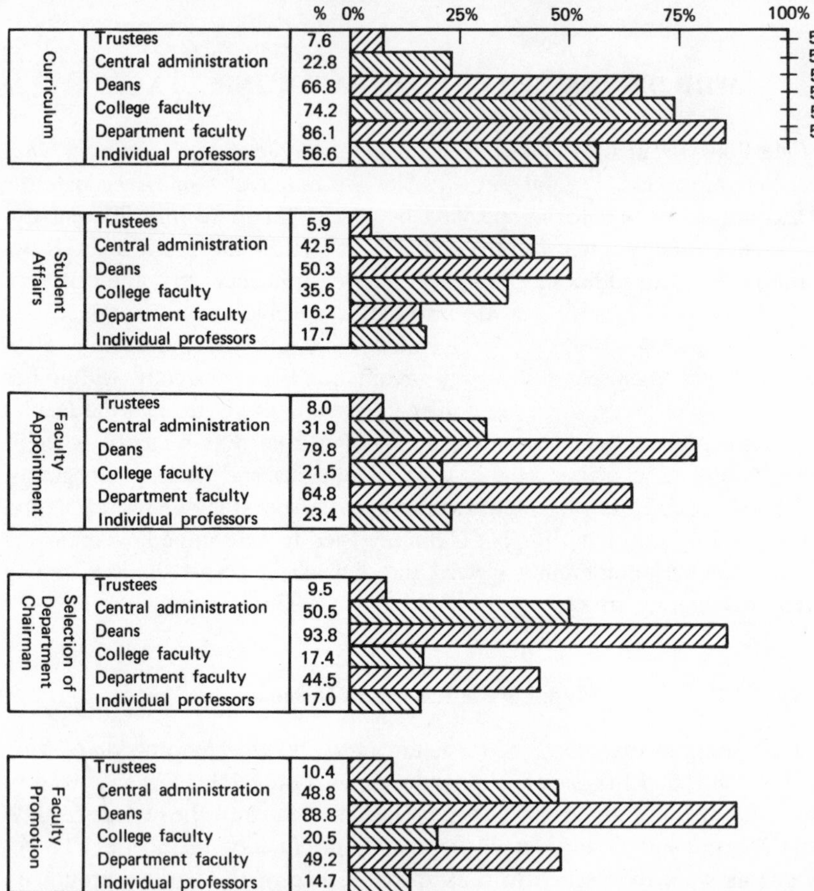

*Taking the first line at the top as an example, this chart should be read as follows: Of e504 respondents (the N listed on the right) who answered the question, 7.6% felt that trustees have high influence over curriculum. Of the 532 respondents who answered the question, 22.8% felt that the Central Administration has high influence over curriculum. (Etc.) N's are same for every chart; refer back to first one.

long-range planning, and public relations. The central administration's influence is strongest in personnel appointment, budgetary control, planning, and public relations. The deans have very broad power, indeed, with considerable influence in all areas. By contrast, the college faculty and the individual professor seem to have the narrowest range of influence, mostly concerned with curriculum. Finally, the departmental faculty has fairly

Figure 9-3. (*Continued*)

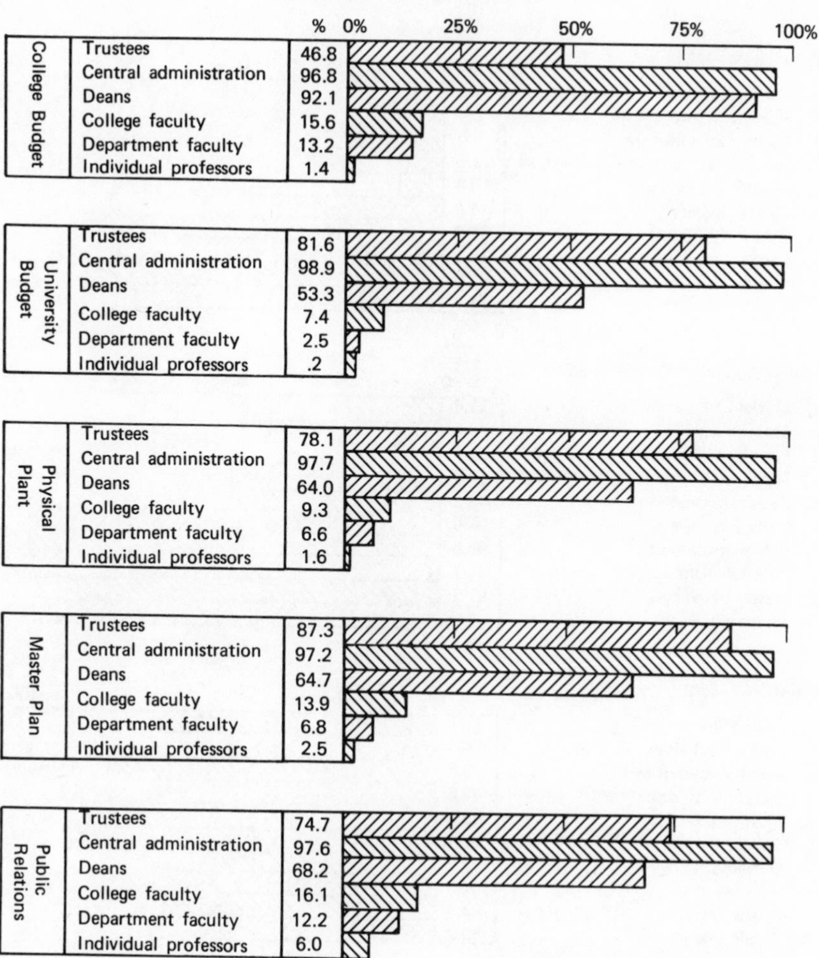

broad influence on curriculum, faculty appointment and promotion, and selection of the department chairman. All in all, the distribution of influence appears to be diffuse and specifically attached to definite issues.

Conflict Over Spheres of Influence

There are several problems in discussing the spheres of influence. First, a survey such as this is able to describe how people think influence *is* distributed but not how it *ought* to be distributed. Merely mapping the spheres

Figure 9-4. Influence Exerted by Groups on Given Issues (% Reporting *High* Influence)*

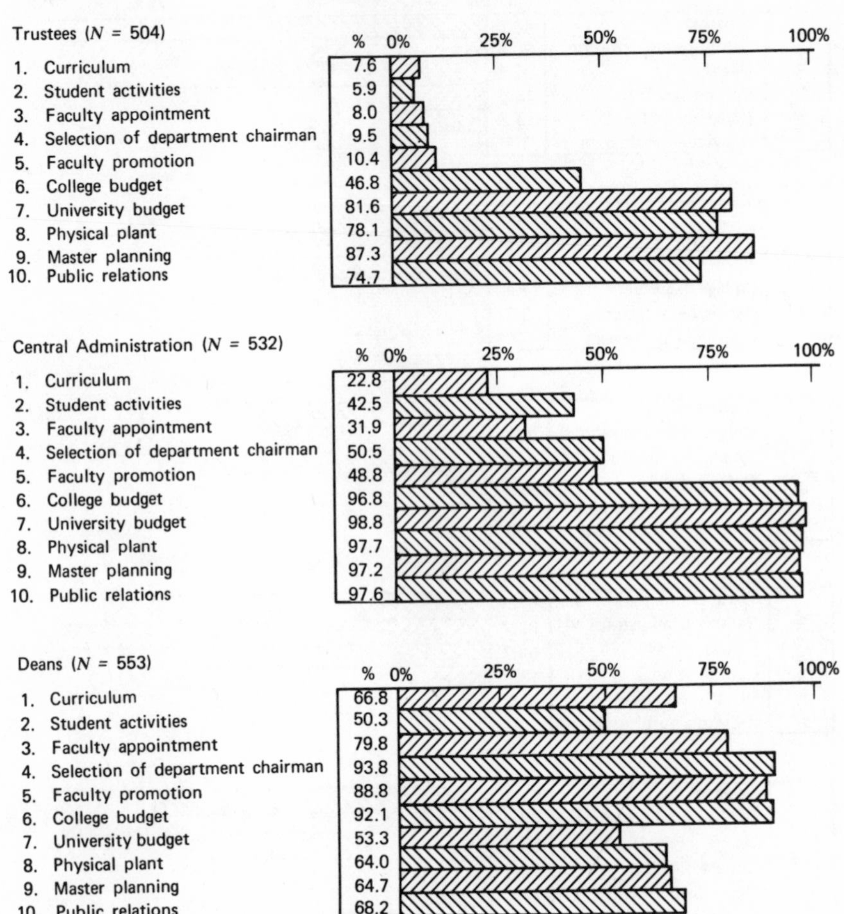

*Taking the top line as an example, this chart should be read as follows: of the 504 respondents who rated the trustees, 7.6% felt the trustees had high influence on Student Activities, etc.

at one point in time does not necessarily mean that this is the optimally efficient or the politically most just arrangement, nor that the distribution is static and unchangeable. One young radical professor who saw the questionnaire results suggested that they should not be published[8]:

[8]Interview No. 71, p. 1.

Figure 9-4. (*Continued*)

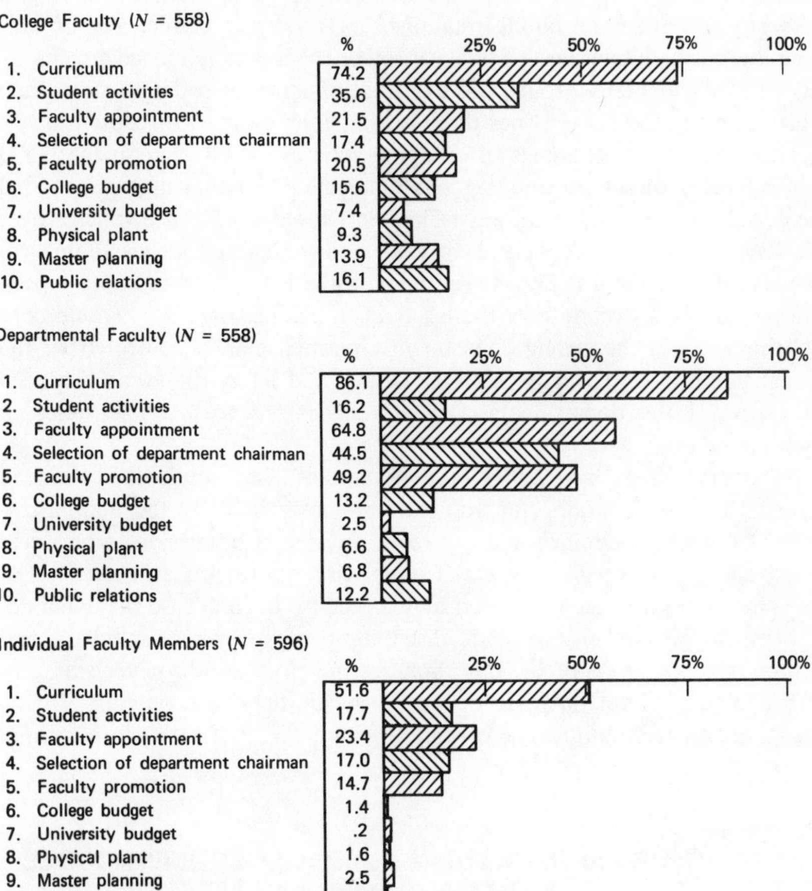

> You shouldn't publish those figures. Just as sure as you say "this is how it *is*" people will start saying "this is how it *ought* to be." Listen, I don't like the way it is, and hopefully we can carve up that cake differently in the future!

Of course, there is no necessity for viewing the spheres of influence issue in static terms, for certainly the areas of influence do change. Earlier, in Chapter VII, we discussed the "domain" that an organization carves out in its relation to other organizations. Essentially the spheres of influence issue is a discussion of *internal* domains. In the earlier chapter we noted the constant tension between "domain consensus" and "domain conflict." The same kind of tension exists internally, for there are varying degrees of consensus about the internal spheres of influence. Some spheres, such as the control over physical plant or public relations, are relatively stable, and on this issue there is high consensus. However, other spheres of influence are changing rapidly and many groups are exerting influence in order to strengthen their positions. On these issues there is high conflict and low consensus.

There are many examples of changing spheres of influence in the NYU research. One of the outstanding was the cycle of conflict that surrounded the departmental reorganizations (Chapter VI). The influence spheres over admissions and budgets were clearly located with the college administrations before the 1950's. The consensus on these issues, however, was upset, and for nearly a decade now there has been conflict over who would control them. First, the strong department chairmen gained control from the deans; then the shift was back to the deans; and lately the swing has been back toward the departments. Low consensus led to a whole series of conflicts.

Of course, there are many other examples. The students demanded control of student affairs and tuition, previously held by the administration. The central administration wrested control of admissions from local colleges and schools. The Taggart Commission argued for an expansion of the spheres of influence controlled by the faculty. In each case the dynamics of conflict had shaken the static distribution of spheres of influence and change was the order of the day. Spheres of influence are never static, as simple charts would have us believe; instead, they are dynamic, living, changing arenas of political activity in which conflict and change are normal.

HOW ARE DECISIONS MADE: A POLITICAL PROCESS MODEL OF DECISION MAKING

So far the discussion has focused on *who* makes *what* decisions. Now the final question must be raised: *How* are decisions made? In spite of decades of research, social scientists still know very little about the process of making decisions. Generally it has been understood in a very formalistic fashion, but this research suggests some qualifications that must be made to take account of the political nature of the legislative process. First, let us examine the more traditional, formalistic approach to decision making and then suggest some reinterpretations that emerge from the New York University study.

Formal Decision Theory

Most traditional decision theory starts with a basic assumption: Mr. X (the dean, the president, or whoever it may be) is faced with the problem of making a decision and from conflicting advice must somehow form a judgment. The formalists suggest that there is a definite, rational approach that will lead to an optimal decision. Edward Litchfield's outline may be taken as representative of this approach, although he is only one writer among literally hundreds who deal with this topic. Litchfield says that the decision process can be analyzed in five steps:

1. Recognition of need.
2. Analysis of the existing situation.
3. Identification of alternative courses of action.
4. Assessment of the probable consequences of each alternative.
5. Choice among alternatives.[9]

Many writers have offered some version of this step-by-step approach to rational problem solving. Of course, each step is extensively analyzed and much advice is given about how the stages can be effectively executed. Recently linear programming has been coupled with "systems analysis" in computerized decision systems that supposedly help the executive make the best choice.[10]

Contributions of the Political Model to Decision Making

We need not reject the formal types of decision theory, but nevertheless it seems that they stop far short of explaining the decision dynamics of most complex organizations. A political interpretation suggests that several new questions must be asked about the decision process if decision theory is to be more than a formalist, impractical scheme.

[9]Edward Litchfield, "Notes on a General Theory of Administration," *Administrative Science Quarterly*, Vol. 1, 3–29 (1956). For reviews of the decision-making literature, see Donald W. Taylor, "Decision Making and Problem Solving," *Handbook of Organization*, 48–86 (1965); W. Edwards, "Theory of Decision-Making," *The Psychological Bulletin*, Vol. 51, 380–417 (1954); and W. Gore and R. Silander, "A Bibliographical Essay on Decision-Making," *Administrative Science Quarterly*, Vol. 4, 97–121 (1959).

[10]For a critique of the formal approach to decision making see Charles Lindblom, "The Science of Muddling Through," *Public Administration Review*, Vol. 19, 78–88 (1959).

The first new question posed by the political model is *why* a given decision is made at all. The formalists have already indicated that "recognition of the problem" is one element in the process, but it seems that entirely too little attention has been paid to the activities that bring a particular issue to the forefront. Why is *this* decision being considered at *this* particular time? The political model insists that interest groups, powerful individuals, and bureaucratic processes are critical in drawing attention to some decisions rather than to others. A study of "attention cues" by which issues are called to the community's attention is a vital part of any analysis.

Second, a question must be raised about the right of any person or group to make the decisions. Previously the *who* question was seldom raised, chiefly because the decision literature was developed for hierarchical organizations in which the focus of authority could be easily defined. In a more loosely coordinated system however, we must ask a prior question: Why was the legitimacy to make the decision vested in a particular person or group? Why is Dean Smith making the decision instead of Dean Jones or why is the University Senate dealing with the problem instead of the central administration? Establishing the right of authority over a decision is a political question, subject to conflict, power manipulation, and struggles between interest groups. Thus the political model always asks tough questions: Who has the right to make the decision? What are the conflict-ridden processes by which the decision was located at this point rather than at another? The crucial point is that often the issue of *who* makes the decision has already limited, structured, and pre-formed *how* it will be made.

The third new issue raised by a political interpretation concerns the development of complex *decision networks*. As a result of the fragmentation of the university, decision making is rarely located in one official; instead it is dependent on the advice and authority of numerous people. Again the importance of the committee system is evident. It is necessary to understand that the committee network is the legitimate reflection of the need for professional influence to intermingle with bureaucratic influence. The decision process, then, is taken out of the hands of individuals (although there are still many who are powerful) and placed into a network that allows a *comulative buildup* of expertise and advice. When the very life of the organization clusters around expertise, *decision making is likely to be diffuse, segmentalized, and decentralized*. A complex network of committees, councils, and advisory bodies grows up to handle the task of assembling the expertise necessary for reasonable decisions. Decision making by the individual bureaucrat is replaced with decision making by committee, council, and cabinet. Centralized decision making is replaced with diffuse decision making. The process becomes a far-flung network for gathering expertise from every corner of the organization and translating it into policy.

The Political Decision Model

These comments may be summed up by proposing a "political-process" model of decision making. The political model suggests the following things. First, powerful political forces—interest groups, bureaucratic officials, influential individuals, organizational subunits—cause a given issue to emerge from the limbo of on-going problems and certain "attention cues" force the political community to consider the problem. Second, there is a struggle over locating the decision with a particular person or group, for the location of the right to make the decision often determines the outcome. Third, decisions are usually "pre-formed" to a great extent by the time one person or group is given the legitimacy to make the decision; not all options are open and the choices have been severely limited by the previous conflicts. Fourth, such political struggles are more likely to occur in reference to "critical" decisions than to "routine" decisions. Fifth, a complex decision network is developed to gather the necessary information and supply the critical expertise. Sixth, during the process of making the decision political controversy is likely to continue and compromises, deals, and plain head cracking are often necessary to get any kind of decision made. Finally, the controversy is not likely to end easily. In fact, it is difficult even to know when a decision *is* made, for the political processes have a habit of unmaking, confusing, and muddling whatever agreements are hammered out.

This may be a better way of grappling with the complexity that surrounds decision processes within a loosely coordinated, fragmented political system. The formal decision models seem to have been asking very limited questions about the decision process and more insight can be gained by asking a new set of political questions. One interview from NYU offers a classic illustration. When asked about decision processes this official said:

> Most of the decisions I make are really already made; I just give a nod to what has already happened. There is usually a long build-up period, with concern about this issue arising at some point down the line. There is often a period of debate, in-fighting, and revision long before I've even heard about the problem. By the time I know about it there isn't much I can do, without bringing the roof down on my head, except approve whatever compromises have already evolved.
>
> Oh, of course, it's not always like that, and there is that rare occasion when I actually get to make a choice among alternatives, but this is indeed unusual. Only once in a blue moon do I have time to sit down and study the problem, gather lots of data, and make a rational choice. This is rare—the usual situation is that the issue is largely settled by debate and "politicing" between people on various sides of the issue. You might say I "finalize" the procedure, sort of a "capping process."[11]

[11]Interview No. 46, p. 2.

Thus the decision model that emerges from an investigation of the university's political dynamics is more open, more dependent on conflict and political action. It is not so systematic or formalistic as most decision theory, but it is probably closer to the truth in many respects. Decision making, then, is not seen as an isolated technique but as another of the critical processes that must be integrated into a larger political image of the university.

SUMMARY

The legislative process transforms partisan pressures into viable organizational policy. The authorities try to reach workable decisions by balancing the many pressures against each other and against the needs of the organization. In the university this is a particularly complex process, for the legislative dynamics are diffuse and decentralized. In this chapter a fundamental question about that legislative process was raised: *Who* decides *what* and *how*?

The *who decides* question is quite difficult to answer, for there are many "authorities" located throughout the organization and many members serve as decision makers in some capacity. There is a definite scale of activity, from most active to least active: officials, activists, attentives, and apathetics. The university is moderately democratic in comparison with most other complex organizations, and it seems to be getting even more democratic in some respects. There are definite oligarchical tendencies, however, for full-time officials certainly have the most influence and many junior faculty and students have very little.

The *what is decided* question raises the issue of "spheres of influence." By and large there are agreed-on areas of influence for the major groups, and conflict is often avoided because each group controls its particular area. Of course, the degree of consensus on who controls what varies over time, and often there is conflict as one group tries to redefine its domain at the expense of another.

Finally, the *how are decisions made* question deserves more than the formalistic answers that are usually given. A political interpretation insists that a whole new set of issues must be examined. The role of attention cues, the struggle over granting jurisdiction to an authority, and the role of partisan-interest group pressures are all new topics that must be analyzed if the "how" question is to be answered.

In conclusion, the legislative process in the university tends to be complex and highly diffuse. Figure 9-5 summarizes this chapter's discussion. No single legislative body makes binding policy decisions, but instead a fragmented, segmentalized process occurs throughout the organization.

Figure 9-5. A Summary Chart: The Legislative Stage: *Who* Decides *What*, and *How*?

Who Decides?	*What* Are the Areas of Influence?	*How* Are Decisions Made?
1. "Authorities" make binding decisions But . . . —there are many different authorities at different levels. —Many different people are authorities to some extent through committees, etc.	On most issues there are "spheres of influence" with different authorities having influence over different issues.	1. "Rational" decision schemes give some insight but are generally quite limited.
2. There is a "scale of participation" in decision making: —officials, —activists, —attentives, —apathetics. 3. The university is moderately "democratic" and the decision process is *diffuse*.	The consensus on domains may go down and conflict over spheres may result. This is a major cause of changes in the university.	2. A "political" decision model suggests that the following should be considered: —"Attention cues" that call attention to a problem. —The struggle over who is authorized to make the decision. —The political pressure brought to bear on authorities by partisans. —The continuing political process after the policy is set.

PART FOUR
Conclusions

Chapter X

CONCLUSIONS

The task of this final section is to review the book and to draw some conclusions about general organizational processes. Each of the book's three parts had a different task. The goal of Part One was to review several previous interpretations of academic governance and to offer some suggestions for a new political image. First, the "bureaucratic" and "collegial" models were evaluated in terms of their strengths and weaknesses. Second, several bodies of theory were suggested as the foundation for a new approach: conflict, interest group, and community power. Third, by building on these three bodies of theory the bare skeleton of a political model was outlined.

Part Two reported on the field research at New York University. Three events were selected for intensive study: a change in the university's educational philosophy, a student revolt, and a departmental reorganization. These events gave concrete points of reference as we moved on to the theoretical analysis.

Part Three returned to the skeleton of the political model that was offered in the beginning and elaborated each part, filling in the theoretical discussion with concrete data from the NYU events. First, the "social structure" of the university was analyzed, with its complex formal system and its fragmented array of value stances. Second, the "interest articulation" processes were explored to show how partisan interest groups—developing out of the complex social structure—put pressure on policy decisions. Finally, the "legislative" process was reviewed to explain how partisan pressures are transformed into official policy in the decision-making councils of the university. In each case the theoretical analysis of Part Three referred back to the empirical events of Part Two. In this chapter we sum up with a few concluding observations about politics in the university.

REVIEWING THE NYU EVENTS IN LIGHT OF THE POLITICAL MODEL

Up to this point the analysis has generally focused on the political model. Empirical events have been inserted as illustrations of theoretical points. Now we reverse that process and review each of the events at NYU by imposing the theoretical ideas on the empirical situations.

Changes in NYU's Educational Philosophy

Chapter IV surveyed a series of changes that shook NYU during the 1960's. A number of *social structural* features were critical. Internally the university was split into many factions, some wanting to continue the "school of opportunity" philosophy and some wanting to upgrade standards and combine the liberal arts programs. Externally the public universities were offering such severe competition for students that NYU faced major readjustments in its educational role. Thus NYU's internal and external social contexts offered many impetuses for change but also many forces for the status quo.

In the *interest articulation* process the central administration took the lead in developing a series of changes designed to cope with the problems. Many groups, including most liberal arts professors, members of the central administration, and members of the Graduate School of Business, pressured for the changes. However, many groups resisted what they believed to be intrusions on their domains. The Schools of Education and Commerce were leaders in fighting increased admissions standards, and the Heights campus joined with them to fight the Coordinated Liberal Studies Program that would unite all the departments. At this stage each group used whatever resources it had to fight for its programs.

In the *legislative* phase decisions were reached and compromises forged. The central administration was able to redefine the spheres of influence so that admissions policies, traditionally the domain of the individual schools, were centralized and consequently raised. In the Coordinated Liberal Studies a compromise was forged, for although the program was started it involved only freshmen and sophomores. In addition, severe adjustments were made in the School of Commerce and to a lesser degree in the School of Education.

The Student Revolt

Chapter V reported on student activism from 1966 through 1968. The student *social structure* was changing rapidly. Apathetic "vocational" subcultures were being supplemented by activist subcultures composed of "academics" and "nonconformists." In addition, the resident student body was growing and a more diversified group of students was being recruited. Moreover, sweeping events on the national scene were impinging on the local campus, including hostility toward the Vietnam war, concern over the inadequacies of the civil rights movement, and involvement in national student radicalism.

In the *interest articulation* stage the students formed a number of partisan groups to fight the authorities on a tuition increase. The conflict escalated considerably and the demands shifted from the tuition question to the larger issue of student participation in decision making. Both the partisans and the authorities made threats, carried out sanctions, and eventually compromised.

In the *legislative* phase the conflict on the streets was channeled into decision-making councils of the university. The students demanded that channels be opened so that they could have continuing, legitimate influence on the decision process. The University Senate appointed the McKay Commission and the Griffith Committee, both of which reported back with a series of reforms on student issues. The partisan pressure so skillfully articulated by the students resulted in major policy revisions.

The Departmental Reorganization

Chapter VI examined a series of departmental reorganizations. This time the major *social structure* factors dealt with the formal bureaucratic arrangements of the university. The university had previously had a fragmented formal structure, in which most decisions were decentralized to the level of schools or colleges. Throughout the late 1950's and the 1960's, however, the formal system was restructured a number of times, and control fluctuated from the schools to the departments to the central administration, and then back again in a complex cycle. The structure of the formal system itself was generating all sorts of tensions and conflicts.

In the *interest articulation* processes the various groups struggled to have the policies formulated in their favor. The deans and department heads clashed over budgetary control and the central administration pushed for maximum coordination of the liberal arts units. The Heights campus struggled for autonomy and in the process its provost resigned. Each group used its resources against the others to marshal support for its perspective.

The *legislative* process transformed these conflicts into policy, but that policy was reformulated and redirected many times as the tensions pulled first one way and then the other. This issue provided the clearest example of how policies grow and change in response to on-going processes and tensions.

POLICY FORMULATION, CONFLICT, AND CHANGE

In the first chapter we listed policy formulation, campus conflict, and organizational change as the three critical emphases of the research. Throughout the analysis these three issues have been the center of attention. Crucial to this approach is the assumption that the governance of the university is essentially a political process, not merely a bureaucratic one. Within this political process policy formulation emerges from a complex set of political schemes. It then follows that conflict is to be expected and is the natural result when competing groups struggle to influence policy.

Comments on the "Communication Fallacy"

In emphasizing the importance of conflict it is necessary to reject one of the most commonly held myths about organizational strife. This is the "communications fallacy," which in effect argues that conflict and strife in an organization are due primarily to misunderstandings and communications breakdowns. Over and over this issue was raised in the interviews, especially in reference to the student upheavals. People constantly argued that all the issues could be solved if only the two sides would sit down and "reason together." In fact, there is a whole school in organization theory that emphasizes the importance of communications blocks in promoting conflict. Many of the so-called "human relations" theorists are convinced that free-flowing communication and "psychological open-ness" would break down the communications barriers and eliminate most conflict.

Amitai Etzioni offered an amusing little critique of this approach in *Modern Organizations.*[1] If we substitute the administration and students for management and workers and a tuition increase as the issue instead of new machines, this little story would clearly apply to NYU's student strike.

[1]For a discussion and critique of the human relations school of organization theory see Amitai Etzioni, *Modern Organization*. Englewood Cliffs, New Jersey: Prentice-Hall, 1964, pp. 32–49.

In a typical Human Relations training movie we see a happy factory in which the wheels hum steadily and the workers rhythmically serve the machines with smiles on their faces. A truck arrives and unloads large crates containing new machines. A dark type with long sideburns who sweeps the floors in the factory spreads a rumor that mass firing is imminent since the new machines will take over the work of many workers. The wheels turn slower, and the workers are sad. In the evening they carry their gloom to their suburban homes. The next morning the reassuring voice of their boss comes over the inter-com. He tells them that the rumor is absolutely false; the machines are to be set up in a new wing and more workers will be hired since the factory is expanding its production. Everybody sighs in relief, smiles return, the machines hum speedily and steadily again. Only the dark floor sweeper is sad. Nobody will listen to his rumors anymore. The moral is clear: had management been careful to communicate its development plans to its workers, the crisis would have been averted. Once it occurred, increase in communication eliminated it like magic.

The Structuralist [another branch of organization theory that opposes the Human Relations approach] would not question the validity of this training movie. Problems initially created by false communication (the floor sweeper rumor) and by lack of authentic communication can be eliminated or at least largely reduced through increase in authentic communication. The question the Structuralist is compelled to raise is what would management have done if the rumor were correct, if it were forced to reduce its labor force, let us say, because of automation? Even here communication might have somewhat eased the situation by clarifying the extent of the expected firings and the procedure to be followed, but surely it could not have eliminated or even significantly reduced the alienation of those to be fired, and of many of their friends whose turn might come next. Differences in economic interests and power positions cannot be communicated away.

This illustration from a factory setting certainly applies to the university. Interestingly enough the prevalence of the "academic community" imagery seems to be a prime force that keeps the communications fallacy alive on the campus, for it would appear that in a close-knit scholarly community agreement surely could be reached by open and frank discussion. Once again we see that our models of reality are not innocent, for the prevalence of the academic community imagery hides the fact that there are real conflicts of interest that cannot be talked away. This does not mean that communications never help, for this would certainly be swinging the pendulum too far in the other direction. Many problems of university governance are indeed related to poor communication and many knotty problems could be alleviated by increased communication and consultation. However, there are many examples of real conflict that cannot be communicated away. The students protesting the tuition raise were not fools; they knew that all the talk and clarity in the world would not ease the burden of extra tuition costs. The professors in the School of Commerce were not blind; the loss of their jobs could not be "communicated" away, regardless of the understanding that communication might bring. All too often the problem is *not* that the two sides do not understand each other and that this misunderstanding generates conflict. No, often the two sides *do* clearly understand each other, and the recognition of the other's possible gain at their expense causes the strife. As one rather cynical student activist put it, "It's not a lack of communication that's causing the problem. In fact, if we knew more about what they were doing it would probably make us *more* militant rather than less!" Communications may help, but it is usually not enough to resolve genuine conflicts of interest. The "communications fallacy" must be avoided if we are to understand the political dynamics of conflict. No strategy for effectively dealing with conflict is likely to emerge from a naive view that denies the conflict even exists.

The Nature of "Strategic Conflict"

Although a political interpretation is based on conflict theory, it does not mean that the university is torn apart by ceaseless conflict. Conflict can be and often is quite healthy, for it may revitalize an otherwise stagnant system. If Marx taught us anything it was that conflict is often necessary and beneficial, for it constantly provokes the social system into self-examination and change. Of course, there is always the danger that conflict may tear the organization apart. It is sometimes difficult to determine the fine line that separates a revitalizing reformation from a self-destructive revolt. This is the dilemma that faces many of our universities today, for upheavals shaking the campus contain both the seeds of reform and the seeds of destruction.

It is helpful to examine some ideas from Thomas Schelling's provocative book *The Strategy of Conflict.*[2] Schelling argues that conflict is best understood as a complex interaction that is middle-ground between complete conflict and complete cooperation; that is, Schelling believes that all-out conflict, the do-or-die type of strife in which annihilation of the enemy is the goal, is not a realistic interpretation of most social conflict. This is the famous *zero-sum* theory of power: my gain is always your loss and vice versa. On the other hand, Schelling suggests that *pure cooperation* is also rarely found in human relations, since every man is usually looking out for his own interests. The most realistic interpretation of conflict, Schelling believes, must

[2]Thomas Schelling, *The Strategy of Conflict.* Cambridge: Harvard University Press, 1960. This discussion is taken mainly from pages 84 to 91.

be in the middle ground, for it includes elements of both conflict and co-operation, a relation that he calls *strategic* conflict. The typical relationship between disputers, for example, is that of exchange: I will trade you an advantage if you will give me one. Only as a last resort will all-out conflict result, for this is expensive and dangerous. The typical form of conflict, then, is strategy and negotiation in which each party trades favors in order to gain advantages. Schelling's discussion might look like this in graphic form (Figure 10-1).

Figure 10-1. Schelling's Model: Comparison of Three Images of Conflict

Complete Conflict	"Strategic Conflict"	Complete Cooperation
Zero-sum concept	Negotiation	Cooperation
1. Your loss is my gain and vice versa.	1. Exchange and bargaining for advantage.	1. Identical interests.
	2. Mixed motive: both cooperation and conflict.	2. Our action is for our mutual benefit.
Game theory equivalent	Game theory equivalent	Game theory equivalent
1. Pursuit or chess.	1. Mock labor negotiations.	1. Rendezvous or charades.
2. One person's loss is the other's gain.	2. Each side wins some and loses some.	2. No one wins unless both do.

Conflict in the university is essentially strategic, for interest groups in the academic community are struggling with one another and at the same time cooperating. Complete antagonism is not the normal kind of conflict in the academic setting. Even in the most violent student demonstrations both the administration and the students have as many common interests as they have conflicting interests. The essence of their conflict is negotiation and the exchange of advantages and favors. In spite of the rhetorical excesses of a fringe group most students have no real interest in bringing the university down; instead their objective is to wring concessions and advantages from a reluctant power structure.

The political model, then, is premised on a conflict orientation to university politics but it is a strategic kind of conflict in which both parties have at the same time common interests and points of conflict. Probably the most helpful imagery is labor/management negotiations in which each side has a mutual need and interest in the other but each is also seeking to gain as many advantages as it can without totally destroying the other.

THE PRACTICAL IMPLICATIONS OF AN IMAGE

Many people who read organization theories are pragmatic administrators who want to know the practical payoffs of such research and who hope to find information that will help them run their own organizations more successfully. For that reason it is sometimes difficult to argue that a theoretical approach has "practical" consequences unless it can be immediately cashed in for money, better coordination, or more efficient operational techniques.

In the face of such a pragmatic stance this book argues that the theoretical perspective of a political analysis is in itself the most important practical consequence of the research. In other words "theory" and "practice" are not divorced; if the political model gives a more adequate conceptualization of the university's dynamics, this in itself will have significant practical consequences. Thus the most important practical implication of the research is the ability to see the university's governance process in a different light, to understand it from a different perspective. Man's social world is bounded by the models and images he creates. The introduction of a new model, a new social definition of reality, will naturally lead to practical consequences. If the bureaucratic mentality is partly replaced by a political mentality, it will be impossible to stop the consequences that will develop. Men may begin to act in light of that new definition of reality and the image itself may generate untold amounts of practical results. People may look at the university's world through a different pair of glasses and consequently will *act* differently.

NEW STYLES OF LEADERSHIP

The campus leader today is a mediator, a negotiator, and a man who jockeys between power blocs, trying to carve out viable futures for his institution. Unlike the autocratic president who ruled with an iron hand, the contemporary academic president finds that he must play the political role by pulling together coalitions to fight for desired changes. The academic monarch of yesteryear has almost vanished and in his place has come not the academic "bureaucrat," as many suggest, but the academic "statesman." Robert Dahl paints an amusing picture of the political maneuvers of Mayor

Richard Lee of New Haven and the same description applies to the new academic political leaders:

> The mayor was not at the peak of a pyramid but rather at the center of intersecting circles. He rarely commanded. He negotiated, cajoled, exhorted, beguiled, charmed, pressed, appealed, reasoned, promised, insisted, demanded, even threatened, but he most needed support and acquiescence from other leaders who simply could not be commanded. Because the mayor could not command, he had to bargain.[3]

The political interpretation of leadership can be pressed even further, for the governance of the university more and more comes to look like a "cabinet" form of administration. The key figure today is not simply the president, the solitary giant, but the political leader surrounded by his staff, the prime minister who looks to them for information and expertise that is used for constructing more realistic policy. It is the "staff," the network of key administrators, that makes most of the critical decisions. The university has become much too complicated for any one man, regardless of his stature. Cadres of vice presidents, research men, budget officials, public relations men, and experts of various stripes surround the president, sit on the cabinet, and help reach collective decisions. Expertise becomes ever more critical and leadership becomes ever more the ability to assemble, lead, and facilitate the activities of men who have expert knowledge.

The cabinet is not only a formal system, like the executive group at NYU, but also an informal network of advisors, faculty politicians, and behind-the-scenes influentials. Testimony to that informal network came in an interesting comment that one administrator made about his neighbor in Vanderbilt Hall. When asked about that man's rather ambiguous title, the administrator answered:

> Well, you see, that title has very little to do with his actual role. Sure, he holds the post of ______________, but in fact he is the "resident sage," the wise man who sits in on everything, offering his accumulated wisdom. We really couldn't run the place without him; he's sort of a floating idea man.[4]

As the cabinet form of administration emerges, the hero is replaced by the prime minister; the giant is replaced by the manager of an expert staff. This is not to say, however, that the president has little personal influence, that he becomes merely a technical bureaucrat. On the contrary, since he is at the center of this network of expertise he comes to enjoy a new type of power, a power based on the control of information and the manipulation of expertise rather than on the force of personality alone.

[3]Robert Dahl, *Who Governs?*, New Haven: Yale Press, 1961, p. 204.
[4]Interview No. 43, p. 2.

It is for this reason that the president must be seen as a "statesman" rather than a "bureaucrat." The bureaucratic image might be appropriate for the man who merely assembles data in a routine manner and churns out routine decisions with the help of a computer. In fact, this image may be quite appropriate for many of the middle echelon officials in the university. The statesman's image is much more accurate for the top administration, for here the influx of data and information gives real power and real possibilities to creative action. The statesman is the creative actor who uses information, expertise, and the combined wisdom of the cabinet to plan for the institution's future; the bureaucrat is merely a number manipulator, a routine user of routine information for routine ends. The use of the cabinet, the assembly of expertise, and the exercise of political judgment in the service of institutional goals—all this is part of the new image of the statesman president which must supplant both the hero president and the bureaucrat president.

MAINTAINING THE "DECISION NETWORK"

One of the most important practical implications emerging from this study is the importance of maintaining the "decision network." Several lines of thought intersect here. First, the professional/bureaucratic dualism has been mentioned time and time again. If this dualism is so critical to the operation of the university, it is extremely important to maintain the channels of communication and the exchange of influence between them. Second, the role of expertise has been a dominant theme and it becomes ever more critical to assemble and use the expert advice of men located throughout the political system. Third, the diffuseness of influence and power in the university makes it all the more necessary to work diligently at the task of collecting and integrating information from all parts of the fragmented system.

At least three pieces of advice flow from the "decision network" discussion. First, we are in a sense back to the old human relations argument about the importance of "communications." We have never denied the value of communications and in fact strongly affirm it as a necessary enterprise in a loosely coordinated organization. However, communications are not the panacea for all ills nor the magic cure for all conflict. Nevertheless, the need for expertise, the demand for influence sharing, and the problems of coordination all require the development and maintenance of communications and advice systems at all levels.

Second, one of the most critical goals of every administrator must be the development of a large back-up staff of experts. The decline of the hero leader brings new responsibilities for providing expert leadership from a cabinet, a staff of experts. No responsibility of a president or dean is any more pressing than the assembly of an excellent supporting staff that can provide information and collective wisdom. Only the most arrogant leaders will still insist on personally making all the critical decisions in an organization that lives off specialized knowledge.

Third, the maintenance of the decision network means that all significant interest groups and structural divisions must have a voice in policy that affects them. The cabinet of administrative experts is not enough, for these men come to represent the administrative and bureaucratic ethos and are not always in touch with the needs and desires of divergent groups throughout the institution. *Access* to the decision councils for all groups—faculty, students, and administrators—is an absolute minimum. Moreover, this must be structurally built into the system, for informal consultation is not enough even when it is based on sincere motives. Academic councils, as they are presently constructed, are unnecessarily oligarchical and tend to represent only the most conservative elements in the community. Almost all universities have committees, councils, and advisory boards that supposedly represent different segments, but in fact many significant groups are politically disfranchised. Moreover, boards of trustees should be restructured so that all segments of the community, students included, have a real voice in policy making. Much of the present turmoil on the campus comes from efforts by various segments of the political community to gain access and influence in the decisions that affect them. There is reason to believe that the political franchise in the university will follow the same democratizing trend that it has followed in the larger society. To embrace and constructively plan for this trend seems to be the better part of political wisdom.

APPENDICES

A. RESEARCH METHODS

Item One: Interview Guide
Item Two: Types of Document Used
Item Three: Questionnaires

B. SUPPORTING DATA FOR CHAPTER IX

The Problem of Indices: The Levels of Activity

Appendix A

RESEARCH METHODS

Item One: INTERVIEW GUIDE

1. What are some of the critical changes in NYU you have observed over the last few years?
   A. Why do you feel they were critical?
   B. Who promoted the changes?
   C. Were there external factors promoting change?
   D. Who resisted change? Groups? Individuals?
2. Can you think of any major conflicts over policy that recently occurred at your college or at the university? Please describe the nature of the conflict, the participants, and the outcome.
3. What are the critical administrative problems that you see in your department? In your college? At the university?
4. Does the concept of "pressure group" have any meaning to you? Are such groups functioning at the university?
5. Who are some of the most powerful and influential people in your college and at the university? Why do you think these people are influential? Over what areas do they have influence?
6. Do you feel that the faculty has enough control over policies in your department? College? University? How would you improve the faculty's voice?

7. How do you feel about student influence at this university? Is it growing? If so, how? Are there faculty pressures for change that parallel the student action?

8. Over what policies would you say the following groups have control?
   A. Individual professors
   B. Departmental faculty
   C. Department head
   D. Deans
   E. Central administration
   F. Trustees

9. Information on respondent:
   A. Field
   B. Rank or position
   C. Length of time at NYU
   D. Organizations to which he belongs
   E. Committees, etc.

The interviewing took about 10 months, beginning in August 1967 and running through May 1968. In all, 93 interviews were conducted. The following chart gives a breakdown of the statuses of the persons who were interviewed.

Figure A-1. Status of Persons Interviewed

Members of the central administration	18
Deans and other college administrators	13
Department heads or chairmen	19
Faculty:	
Professors	61
Associate professors	8
Assistant professors	2
Committee chairmen	13
Members of University Senate	18
Students	14
Total interviews	93[a]

[a] Total is excluding duplication; for example, Senate members are also listed as faculty or administrators; administrators usually hold faculty appointments; several people were interviewed twice or more.

Item Two: TYPES OF DOCUMENT USED

Minutes of faculty meetings
Minutes of administrative meetings
University Senate reports
Long-range planning reports, such as the report to the Ford Foundation
Histories of the university[1]
The University "Self-Study"[2]
Official enrollment statistics
Official factulty statistics
Reports on the budget
Presidential reports to the trustees
Faculty handbooks
Catalogs of the various schools and colleges
Bylaws of the university
Organizational charts

[1]T. F. Jones, *New York University, 1832-1932* (New York: New York University Press, 1933).

[2]New York University, *The New York University Self Study* (New York: New York University Press, 1956).

Item Three: QUESTIONNAIRES

On April 3rd, 1968, questionnaires were mailed to all full-time members of the faculty, excluding those of the medical and dental schools. In addition, questionnaires were sent to all the university administrators defined in the Official Directory as "general officers" and to any persons listed in the Directory who had "dean" listed in their titles. This made a total of 65 administrators (not including departmental officers, who were included as faculty members).

Among the 1748 questionnaires sent out, 693 were finally returned and useable. This is a return of 40%, a rate in line with general expectations for this kind of survey. Figure A-2 lists some of the characteristics of the respondents, comparing them with known facts about the entire university faculty. It is obvious from the comparisons that the sample is quite representative of the entire faculty. The only exceptions appear to be that the Graduate School of Arts and Sciences is slightly over-represented and the School of Continuing Education, under-represented. Otherwise the comparisons are similar.[3] Following the figure the entire questionnaire is given.

[3]In 1959 a similar study was conducted by the University Senate. From time to time data from that survey is used for comparative purposes. To avoid confusion the two surveys will be referred to as the 1968 NYU Survey, and the 1959 Faculty Senate Survey.

Figure A-2. Characteristics of the Questionnaire Respondents Compared With Known Characteristics of University Faculty

By School or College	Entire Faculty %	Respondents %
School of the Arts	0.4	1.3
School of Commerce/Graduate Business	8.8	11.5
School of Education	18.0	19.3
School of Engineering/Courant Institute	11.8	10.9
Graduate School of Arts and Sciences	8.8	13.6
Public Administration/Social Work	2.9	2.7
School of Law	4.0	4.8
University College	14.8	11.0
Washington Square College	22.2	21.1
School of Continuing Education	6.5	3.8
	100.0	100.0
By Academic Rank		
Professor	35.5	33.2
Associate professor	23.8	23.7
Assistant professor	19.7	20.6
Other	21.0	22.4
	100.0	100.0
	$N = 1748$	$N = 693$

NEW YORK UNIVERSITY

Project on University Governance

This questionnaire is part of a research project which has been under way at NYU for nearly a year. The main goal of the research is the development of a theory of administration which can be applied to universities. Already there have been interviews with scores of people throughout the university, but it seems necessary to get the opinion of the entire faculty and staff on some critical issues.

The questionnaire has been reviewed by the Faculty Council and by the Chancellor's office. Both have given their approval to it. Fortunately, we can compare many of these results with a similar project which the Faculty Senate carried out in 1959. After a decade of rapid change it will be interesting to chart the changes in faculty and staff opinions.

All responses will be *strictly confidential*, and no individual's responses will be released. The questionnaire is organized for quick answering, so it will take no more than 20 minutes to finish. If you have already talked to me in a personal interview, please complete it anyway, since it now contains much new information. Summary results of the questionnaire will be reported back to the university community over the coming months.

When you have finished return it by campus mail. Use the same envelope, cross out your name, and address the next box to

Victor Baldridge
Department of Sociology
19 University Place, 3rd Floor
Washington Square

Thank you for your cooperation!

Victor Baldridge
The Department of Sociology
Yale University

NEW YORK UNIVERSITY GOVERNANCE RESEARCH

Confidential Questionnaire

SECTION I: BACKGROUND INFORMATION

1a. Your present academic rank:

Professor . . . . ______1
Associate professor . . . . ______2
Assistant professor . . . . ______3
Instructor . . . . ______4
Lecturer . . . . ______5
Teaching fellow, graduate or research assistant . . ______6
Any other factulty appointment . . . . ______7
Member of staff without faculty appointment . . . ______0

1b. Administration

I do not hold an administrative position . . . . ______1
I hold a full-time post in the central administration.
Please specify ______________________ . ______2
I hold a full-time post in a college or school administration.
Please specify ______________________ . ______3
I hold a post in a department (chairman, head)
Please specify ______________________ . ______4

1c. College or school affiliation

(If more than one, list *prime* appointment)
I am not associated with any college or school . . . ______0
Graduate School of Arts and Sciences . . . . . ______1
University College . . . . ______2
Washington Square College . . . . ______3
School of Commerce (or) Graduate School of Business ______4
School of Arts . . . . ______5
School of Education . . . . ______6
School of Engineering & Science (or) Courant Institute ______7
Graduate School of Public Administration
(or) Social Work . . . . ______8
School of Law . . . . ______9
Division of General Education . . . . ______10

1d. Are you a member of the AAUP chapter? Yes . . ______1
No . . ______2

1e. How many years has it been since you received your highest degree? . . . . (write in) ______

1f. Where did you obtain your highest degree? (write in) ______

1g. Are you a member of the Graduate School of Arts and Science faculty? . . . . Yes ______1
No ______2

1h. Is your school or college organized by departments?
No (or you don't belong to a school or college) . . ______1
Yes . . . . ______2
If "Yes", please specify your department ______________

1i. How long have you been on the NYU staff?
1-3 years . . . . ______1
4-8 years . . . . ______2
9-15 years . . . . ______3
More than 15 years . . . . . ______4

1j. Employment status:
Full-time, tenured . . . . . ______1
Full-time, nontenured . . . . ______2
Part-time . . . . ______3

1l. Sex:
Male . . . . ______1
Female . . . . ______2

1m. What is your age?
Under 30 . . . . ______1
30–40 . . . . ______2
41–50 . . . . ______3
51–60 . . . . ______4
Over 60 . . . . ______5

1n. Highest degree earned:
Bachelors or less . . . . . . ______1
Masters . . . . ______2
Professional, other than
masters (e.g., M.D., LLB. . . ______3
Ph.D., Ed.D., or equivalent) . . ______4

SECTION II: PROFESSIONAL ACTIVITIES

(Check one in each row across)

2a. Number of books, monographs and articles published under your authorship in the last five years (include joint).

None	1–2	3–4	5–7	8–10	11–19	20+

2b. Of the above publications, how many were full books?

None	1	2	3	4	5	6+

2c. Number of state, regional, national, or international professional organizations to which you belong.

None	1–2	3–4	5–7	8–10	11–19	20+

2d. Number of professional meetings attended in past 12 months.

None	1	2	3	4	5–6	7+

2e. Number of papers presented during the last two years at professional meetings.

None	1	2	3	4–5	6+	

2f. About what percentage of your working time do you spend in nonteaching activities (research, consulting, etc.).

0–10%	11–26%	26–50%	51–75%	76–100		

SECTION III

(Check one in each row across)

	Very Little	Moderate Amount	Very Much	Question doesn't apply to me
3a. Compared with other members of your department, how much influence do you believe *you* have on policy in your *department?*	1____	2____	3____	0____

3b. Compared with other members of your college or school staff, what influence do *you* have on *college or school* policy?	1____	2____	3____	0____
3c. Compared with other members of the university staff, have *you* much influence on *university-wide* policy?	1____	2____	3____	0____
3d. Taking your departmental faculty as a group, how much influence do they have on your *department's* policy?	1____	2____	3____	0____
3e. Taking your college or school faculty as a group, how much influence do they have on your *school or college* policy?	1____	2____	3____	0____
3f. Taking the university faculty as a group, how much influence do they have on *university-wide* policy?	1____	2____	3____	0____

SECTION IV

4a. There are frequent debates about whether there should be *university-wide* standards on such matters as admissions, salary schedules, and degree requirements or whether each individual *school and college* should set its own policies. Concerning this issue, which of the following statements most accurately describe your opinion?

—We already have too many university-wide standards and regulations. We ought to turn more of these matters over to the colleges and schools so that they can have the autonomy to plan their own programs without interference from the rest of the university . . . . ______1

—The number and types of university-wide regulations are about right. There is a fairly good balance between the needs of the individual colleges and schools and the needs of the whole university . . . . ______2

—There aren't enough university-wide standards. The university needs more centralized guidance to achieve unity and to maintain uniformly high quality . . . . . . ______3

—I have no opinion on this matter . . . . . . ______0

4b. Which of the following statements most accurately represents your understanding of the relative places of liberal arts and occupational training in the undergraduate curriculum?

—Liberal arts is by far the most important element of the undergraduate curriculum . . . . ______1

—Liberal arts and occupational or professional preparation are both desirable, but the liberal arts element is more important than the others . . . . ______2

—Liberal arts and occupational or professional preparation are both desirable, and it is impossible to say one is more important than the other . . . . ______3

—Liberal arts and occupational preparation are both desirable, but the occupational or professional element is more important than the liberal arts . . . . ______4

—Occupational and professional constitute by far the most important elements in the curriculum . . . . . . ______5

4c. Your identification with the university, as related to employment possibilities elsewhere.

—My identification with this university is *very strong*. I probably would not leave except under very unusual circumstances . . . . ______1

—My identification with this university is *moderate*. I probably would leave for a better job . . . . ______2

—My identification with this university is fairly *weak*. I probably would leave for a better job and perhaps even for a less desirable job . . . . ______3

4d. People have differing degrees of attachment to the university. Which of the following statements best characterizes your relations to NYU?

—My university position is one of the most important aspects of my life. It is my prime job and consumes most of my nonfamily time . . . . ______1

—Although my university relation is important, it is only one of several important activities. Other activities, such as practicing a profession or consulting, are of similar importance ______2

—My relation to the university is fairly modest. I have other activities which are more important, such as finishing a degree, practicing a profession, or working in business . . ______3

SECTION V: INFORMAL ACTIVITIES

5a. There are many campus organizations which try to influence university policies. Examples include the AAUP, AFCT, and the Faculty Committee on War and Peace. List below any policy-influencing organizations in which you participate. Include campus groups which have indirect influence even though this may not be their prime goal. However, do not include professional organizations unless you feel that they have considerable influence on NYU's policy.

List here:	(How much influence does this group have?) Very Little	Moderate Amount	Very Much
____________________	1._____	2._____	3._____
____________________	1._____	2._____	3._____
____________________	1._____	2._____	3._____
____________________	1._____	2._____	3._____
____________________	1._____	2._____	3._____

5b. In general, how much overall effect would you say such organizations have on university policies?

Very much . . . . ______1
Moderate . . . . ______2
Very little . . . . ______3

5c. In addition to campus organizations, there are also many strictly informal groups. Sometimes these groups have nicknames, such as the "Young Turks," or the "Old Guard." More often, of course, they are simply groups of friends who discuss policy issues over lunch or plot strategy before a meeting. Make a rough guess and *write in the number* of these informal groups you belong to which try to influence policy:

At the departmental level . . . ______
At college or school level . . . ______
At the university level . . . . ______

5d. In general, how much overall effect would you say such informal groups have on policies?

Very much . . . . ______1
Moderate amount . . . . . . ______2
Very little . . . . ______3

5e. While you have been on the staff of NYU have you ever participated in a demonstration, picket line, or sit-in which tried to influence university policies?

Yes . . . . ______1
No . . . . ______2

5f. In general, how much overall effect would you say such activities have on policies?

Very much . . . . ______1
Moderate amount . . . . . ______2
Very little . . . . . . ______3

5g. Have you actively worked with student groups who were trying to influence university policies?

Yes . . . . ______1
No . . . . ______2

5h. Have you ever attempted to influence internal university policies by appealing to *outside* groups? Check any of the following and add others you have done. Include only those activities that were specifically intended to influence some policy, whether you intended to *support* that policy or *oppose* it. Do not include any contact that was not directly addressed to policy. (Example: If you appeared on TV to announce a new scientific discovery, *don't* include that. However, if you appeared on TV to suggest that NYU must raise salaries or lose its faculty, then *do* include that.)

Letters to newspapers . . . . ______
Magazine or newspaper articles addressed to policy . . ______
TV or radio reports addressed to policy . . . . . ______
Appeals to influential alumni or benefactors . . . ______
Appeals to accrediting agencies . . . . ______
Attempts to influence foundations . . . . ______
Appeals to influential governmental officials . . . ______
Testimony about the university before government committee ______
Appeals to professional associations . . . . . . ______

Specify other: ____________________ . . ______
Specify other: ____________________ . . ______
Specify other: ____________________ . . ______

SECTION VI

Directions: Please check the number beside each activity in which you regularly participate. *Check as many as applicable*; more than one may be checked under each question.

6a. Departmental Activities

—Informal, person-to-person contact which might influence departmental policy and decisions . . . . . . ______1
—Departmental meetings . . . . ______2
—Departmental committees . . . . ______3
—Departmental executive committee or advisory group . ______4
—Hold official position in department (head, chair) . ______5

6b. College or School Activities

—Informal, person-to-person contact which might influence college or school policy and decisions . . . . . . ______1
—College or school general meetings . . . . . . ______2
—College or school committees . . . . ______3
—College or school executive or advisory committee . ______4
—Hold official position in the college or school (such as dean or other full-time position) . . . . ______5

6c. All-University Activities

—Informal, person-to-person contacts which might influence all-university policy or decisions . . . . ______1
—University committees . . . . ______2
—University Senate, major university commissions (such as graduate studies, student life) . . . . ______3
—The university executive group . . . . . . ______4
—Hold an official position on the central administration of the university . . . . ______5

SECTION VII: GENERAL EVALUATION OF THE UNIVERSITY

Directions: Please evaluate the following aspects of the university by circling the number beside each question which most nearly expresses your evaluation.

1—Very Poor
2—Poor
3—Average

4—Good
5—Very Good
NO—No opinion, or question doesn't apply to your situation

IBM Codes	Poor ⟷ Good	
(76)	1 2 3 4 5 NO	7a. Your office facilities at the university.
(77)	1 2 3 4 5 NO	7b. Your present annual salary.
(78)	1 2 3 4 5 NO	7c. Extent of faculty participation in the determination of academic policies and procedures.
(79)	1 2 3 4 5 NO	7d. Extent of faculty participation in the development of budgets at the school & college level.
(80)	1 2 3 4 5 NO	7e. Extent of faculty participation in the development of university-wide budgets.
(8)	1 2 3 4 5 NO	7f. Extent of faculty participation in the development of the university building program.
(9)	1 2 3 4 5 NO	7g. Ease and readiness of communication between faculty in your school or college.
(10)	1 2 3 4 5 NO	7h. Ease and readiness of communication between faculty and central university administration.
(11)	1 2 3 4 5 NO	7i. Your general confidence in the leadership of the university.
(12)	1 2 3 4 5 NO	7j. The general competence of your colleagues on the faculty.
(13)	1 2 3 4 5 NO	7k. The general promise of the students you know in this university.
(14)	1 2 3 4 5 NO	7l. The general quality of the undergraduate program of this university.
(15)	1 2 3 4 5 NO	7m. The general quality of the graduate program of this university.
(16)	1 2 3 4 5 NO	7n. The general quality of the student extracurricular life.
(17)	1 2 3 4 5 NO	7o. The value of the University Senate as an avenue for faculty influence on university policy.
(18)	1 2 3 4 5 NO	7p. The value of your college or school's faculty meetings as an avenue for faculty influence.
(19)	1 2 3 4 5 NO	7q. The value of committees as an avenue for faculty influence on policy.

SECTION VIII: SPHERES OF INFLUENCE

This section deals with your perception of the influence that groups within the university have over certain issues. The issues are listed down the side and the groups are listed across the top. Start with the "Individual Professor" in the first column, and go *down* the issues. Beside each issue put the amount of influence the group has over that issue.

1 = *Little* or *no* influence
2 = *Some* influence
3 = *Moderate* amount of influence
4 = *Very much* influence

	INDIV. FACULTY	DEPT. FACULTY	COLLEGE FACULTY	DEANS	CENTRAL ADMIN.	TRUSTEES
1. Curriculum . . .	20	30	40	50	60	70
2. Student extra-curricular . . .	21	31	41	51	61	71
3. Faculty appointments . . .	22	32	42	52	62	72
4. Selection of dept. heads . . .	23	33	43	53	63	73
5. Promotion and tenure	24	34	44	54	64	74
6. College/school budget	25	35	45	55	65	75
7. University budget	26	36	46	56	66	76
8. Physical plant	27	37	47	57	67	77
9. Long-range university plans . .	28	38	48	58	68	78
10. External or public relations	29	39	49	59	69	79

Appendix B

SUPPORTING DATA FOR CHAPTER NINE

Figure B-1. The Higher the Participation, the Higher the Clique Membership (% Reporting *High* Clique Membership)

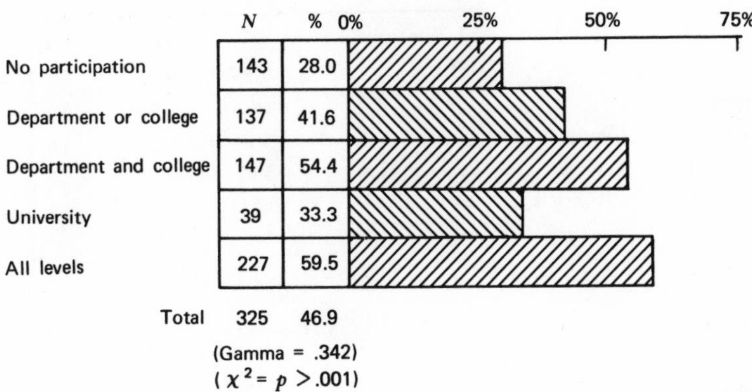

Figure B-2. The Higher the Participation, the Higher the Publications (% Reporting *High* Publication—3 or More)

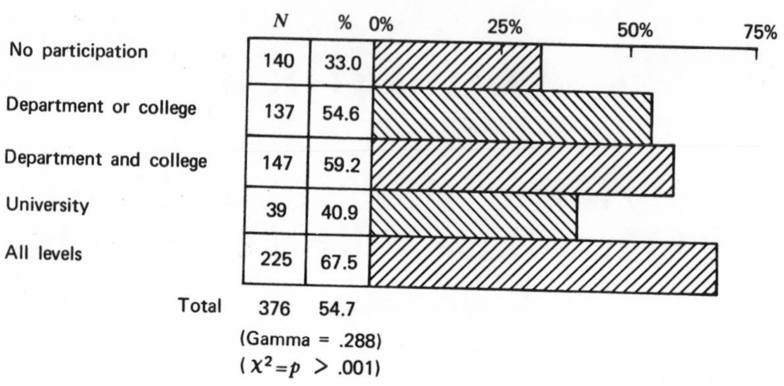

Figure B-3. The Relationship Between Participation and Publication, Controlling for Professional Age[a]

(% reporting *high* publication by age groups)

	Professional Age					
	1–5 years		6–15 years		Over 15	
	(*N*)	(%)	(*N*)	(%)	(*N*)	(%)
No participation	14	16.3	15	45.5	17	70.8
Department *or* college	23	41.1	36	69.2	16	57.1
Department *and* college	24	41.4	38	71.7	25	69.4
University	4	25.0	5	71.4	7	46.7
All levels	28	51.9	51	75.9	73	69.5
Total	93	34.4	145	68.1	138	66.3
	(Gamma = .368		(Gamma = .265)		(Gamma = .069)	
	(χ^2 P > .001)		(χ^2 P > .01)		(χ^2 not sign.)	

[a] Publication is definitely related to "professional age," that is, the number of years since highest degree. Therefore it seemed important to control for this factor. The high relationship between participation and publication still holds, except for the oldest group.

Figure B-4. Higher Ranks Have Higher Participation Rates[a]

1. Where do the different ranks have high participation? (Read *down*.)

	Professor	Associate	Assistant	Other
No participation	6.2%	11.7%	22.0%	48.5%
Department *or* college	15.5	24.5	25.5	16.0
Department *and* college	19.9	23.3	28.4	14.7
University only	5.8	3.1	2.8	10.4
All levels	52.7	37.4	21.3	10.4
	100.0%	100.0%	100.0%	100.0%
	$N = 226$	$N = 163$	$N = 141$	$N = 163$
				Total $N = 693$

2. Of those with high participation rates, what are their ranks? (Read *across*.)

	Professor	Associate	Assistant	Other	Total	*N*
No participation	9.8%	13.3	21.7	55.2	100.0	143
Department or college	25.5	29.2	26.3	19.0	100.0	137
Department and college	30.6	25.9	27.2	16.3	100.0	147
University only	33.3	12.8	10.3	43.6	100.0	39
All levels	52.4	26.9	13.2	7.5	100.0	227
						693

[a] This is the same table; only percentages have been reported first in one direction and then in the other.
(Gamma = .453)
(χ^2 $P >.001$)

Figure B-5. High Participators Report More Memberships in Professional Associations (Those Reporting *High* Membership—3 or More)

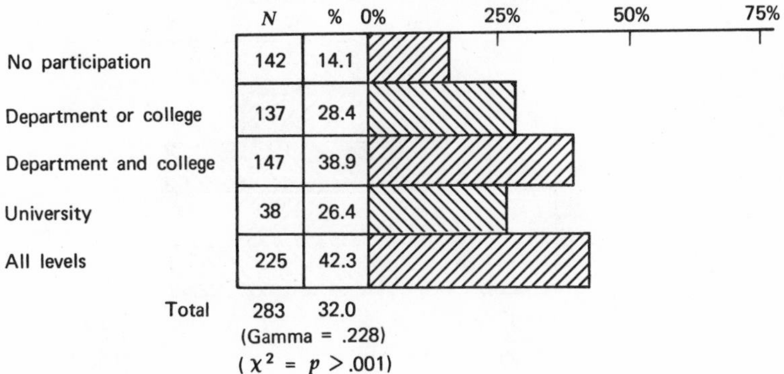

Figure B-6. High Participators, Report More Papers Read at Professional Meetings (% Reporting *High* Number of Papers—2 or More)

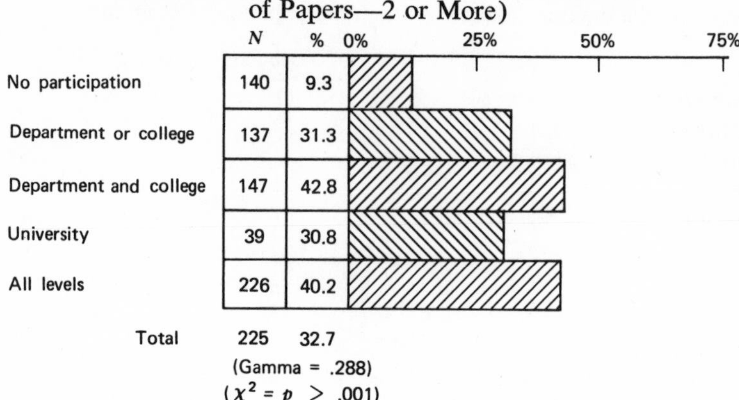

Figure B-7. High Participators Report More Professional Meetings Attended (% Reporting *High* Number of Meetings—3 or More)

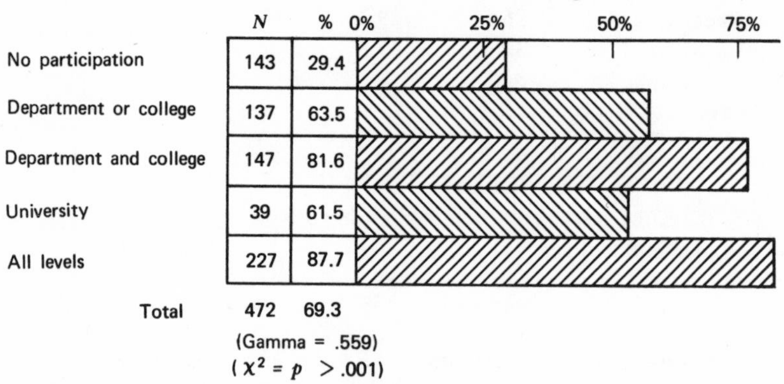

Figure B-8. High Participators Report More Perceived Influence (% Reporting *High* Perceived Influence)

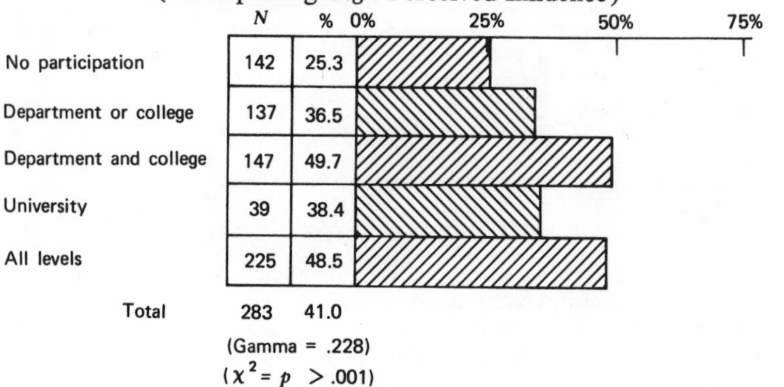

Figure B-9. High Participators Report More Identification with the University (% Reporting *High* Identification)

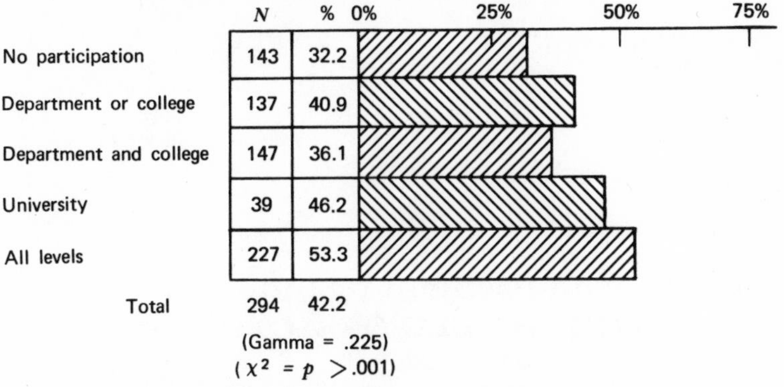

Figure B-10. High Participators Report More Attachment to the University (% Reporting *High* Attachment)[1]

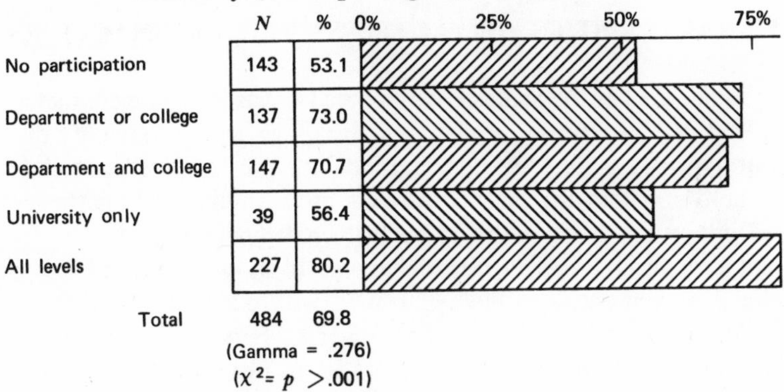

Figure B-11. High Participators Report More Influence with Outside Groups (% Reporting *High* Influence)

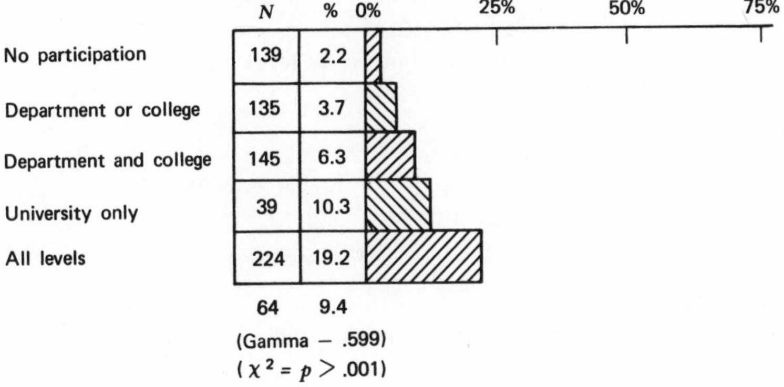

The Problem of Indexes: THE LEVELS OF ACTIVITY

CHARACTERISTICS OF "ACTIVES" VERSUS "INACTIVES"

One major goal of the analysis in Chapter IX was to isolate characteristics of the "actives" as opposed to the "inactives." In order to simplify the task the four types of activity were collapsed into the "actives" (officials and formal activists) and the "inactives" (attentive publics and apathetics). It seemed important, however, to make a finer distinction to account for the different structural levels in the university. It would make little sense to combine a person active in his department with one who was active in his department, in his school, and in the University Senate. For this reason the analysis was finally broken down into five steps, from the totally inactive up to those who were active on every level.

1. Inactives (at all levels).
2. Active in department *or* college.
3. Active in department *and* college.
4. Active at the university level only.
5. Active at all levels.

The process of building the combinations of activities was as follows: first, the activities on each of the three levels (department, college, and university) were dichotomized into high and low by actually dividing the entire sample at the median in each case. Thus any individual could have high or low on each of the three levels.

Second, eight possible combinations emerged:

	Department	College	University	
1.	Low	Low	Low	(inactives)
2.	High	Low	Low	(department or college)
3.	Low	High	Low	
4.	High	High	Low	(department and college)
5.	Low	Low	High	(university only)
6.	Low	High	High	
7.	High	Low	High	(all levels)
8.	High	High	High	

Third, several of the categories were almost empty and were combined with others. Thus 2 and 3 were combined and 6, 7, and 8 were combined.

Finally, every individual could be placed empirically into one group. It was completely empirical, for the classification was actually derived from the empirical distributions of the respondents, not from some arbitrary scheme set up in advance.

INDEX